FLORIDA GULF
TRAVEL✦SMART

SUNSET VIEWING NEAR NAPLES PIER

Lee Island Coast Convention and Visitors Bureau

FLORIDA GULF COAST
TRAVEL ✦ SMART®

Second Edition

Carol J. Perry

John Muir Publications
Santa Fe, New Mexico

Acknowledgments
The author wishes to express her appreciation to the many Florida freelance writer friends who shared their own very favorite places for the readers of this book. Special thanks to Marti Martindale, John O. Burke, Sherry O'Connor, Suzanne Norman, Julie Root, and Jeff Corydon.

John Muir Publications, P.O. Box 613, Santa Fe, New Mexico 87504

Copyright © 2000 by John Muir Publications
Cover © 2000 by John Muir Publications
Maps © 2000, 1997 by John Muir Publications
All rights reserved.

Printed in the United States of America.
Second edition. First printing January 2000.

ISSN 1525-156X
ISBN 1-56261-441-X

Editors: Ellen Cavalli, Bonnie Norris, Sarah Baldwin, Ginjer Clarke
Graphics Editor: Ann Silvia
Production: Janine Lehmann
Design: Marie J.T. Vigil
Cover design: Janine Lehmann
Typesetting: Cynthia Carter
Map style development: American Custom Maps–Jemez Springs, NM
Map illustration: Julie Felton, Kathleen Sparkes
Printing: Publishers Press
Front cover photos: small—© Photo Network/Jeff Greenberg (Stouffer Vinoy Resort, St. Petersburg)
                     large—© Photo Network/Jeff Greenberg (Naples)
Back cover photo: Lee Island Convention & Visitors Bureau (Sanibel Island)

Distributed to the book trade by
Publishers Group West
Berkeley, California

While every effort has been made to provide accurate, up-to-date information, the author and publisher accept no responsibility for loss, injury, or inconvenience sustained by any person using this book.

FLORIDA GULF COAST TRAVEL•SMART: A GUIDE THAT GUIDES

Most guidebooks are primarily directories, providing information but very little help in making choices—you have to guess how to make the most of your time and money. *Florida Gulf Coast Travel•Smart* is different: By highlighting the very best of the region and offering various planning features, it acts like a personal tour guide rather than a directory.

TAKE THE STRESS OUT OF TRAVEL
Sometimes traveling causes more stress than it relieves. Sorting through information, figuring out the best routes, determining what to see and where to eat and stay, scheduling each day—all of this can make a vacation feel daunting rather than fun. Relax. We've done a lot of the legwork for you. This book will help you plan a trip that suits *you*—whatever your time frame, budget, and interests.

SEE THE BEST OF THE REGION
Author Carol J. Perry has lived on the Florida Gulf Coast for 20 years. She has hand-picked every listing in this book, and she gives you an insider's perspective on what makes each one worthwhile. So while you will find many of the big tourist attractions listed here, you'll also find lots of smaller, lesser known treasures, such as Bradley's Country Store in Tallahassee or the backstage tour of the Asolo theater in Sarasota. And each sight is described so you'll know what's most—and sometimes least—interesting about it.

In selecting the restaurants and accommodations for this book, the author sought out unusual spots with local flavor. While in some areas of the region chains are unavoidable, wherever possible the author directs you to one-of-a-kind places. We also know that you want a range of options: one day you may crave red snapper Pontchartrain and Caesar salad, while the next day you would be just as happy (as would your wallet) with fried catfish and hush puppies. Most of the restaurants and accommodations listed here are moderately priced, but the author also includes budget and splurge options, depending on the destination.

CREATE THE TRIP YOU WANT
We all have different travel styles. Some people like spontaneous weekend jaunts, while others plan longer, more leisurely trips. You may want to cover as much ground as possible, no matter how much time you have. Or maybe you

prefer to focus your trip on one part of the state or on some special interest, such as history, nature, or art. We've taken these differences into account.

Though the individual chapters stand on their own, they are organized in a geographically logical sequence, so that you could conceivably fly into Pensacola, drive chapter by chapter to each destination in the book, and end up close to another major airport. Of course, you don't have to follow that sequence, but it's there if you want a complete picture of the region.

Each destination chapter offers ways of prioritizing when time is limited: in the Perfect Day section, the author suggests what to do if you have only one day to spend in the area. Also, every Sightseeing Highlight is rated, from one to four stars: ★★★★—must see—sights first, followed by ★★★ sights, then ★★ sights, and finally ★—or "see if you have time" sights. At the end of each sight listing is a time recommendation in parentheses. User-friendly maps help you locate the sights, restaurants, and lodging of your choice.

And if you're in it for the ride, so to speak, you'll want to check out the Scenic Routes described at the end of several chapters. They take you through some of the most scenic parts of the Florida Gulf Coast.

In addition to these special features, the appendix has other useful travel tools:

- The Planning Map and Mileage Chart help you determine your own route and calculate travel time.
- The Special Interest Tours show you how to design your trip around any of six favorite interests.
- The Calendar of Events provides an at-a-glance view of when and where major events occur throughout the state.
- The Resource Guide tells you where to go for more information about national and state parks, individual cities and counties, local bed-and-breakfasts, and more.

HAPPY TRAVELS

With this book in hand, you have many reliable recommendations and travel tools at your fingertips. Use it to make the most of your trip. And have a great time!

WHY VISIT THE FLORIDA GULF COAST?

If you think Florida's Gulf Coast is one long undulating beach, with the vast Gulf of Mexico gently splashing along the shoreline, think again. Oh, there are plenty of beaches here all right—lovely wave-scrubbed, quartz-white, sandy ones. Half a dozen of the area's beaches are ranked among America's top 20, along with Florida's "Best Walking Beach" (Crescent Beach at Sarasota) and Florida's "Most Romantic Beach" (Captiva Island off Fort Myers). "Dr. Beach," Stephen Leatherman of the University of Maryland, hailed Grayton Beach at South Walton as the "Best Beach in the Continental United States" in 1994. But this gently curving coast is so much more than just sand and seashells.

The Florida Gulf Coast's unique geography and semitropical climate have bred a rich natural environment. Estuaries abound in Florida, supporting a fascinating diversity of ecosystems. Cypress stands, mangrove swamps, and marshes provide prime nursery conditions for a complex cycle of animals, grasses, and sea creatures. In addition to these natural attractions, bustling cities boast mirrored skyscrapers and big-league sports teams, while small towns still hold Fourth-of-July parades and county fairs.

Geography and climate have blessed Florida's Gulf Coast, beckoning visitors from all over the globe. But perhaps the most fascinating attributes of the coastal towns and cities are the people who have come here to stay. Almost from its beginning, Florida has been a haven for refugees. Through the years different immigrant groups have distinctly influenced the development of the state. Though not "immigrants" in the true sense of word, the Seminole Indians were among the first settlers of Florida's west coast. The Seminole Indians of today are descendants of a few hundred "unconquerables" who resisted nineteenth-century United States government officials and refused to move westward to reservations. These native people's fierce commitment to their heritage and resistance to invading forces earned them the name "Seminole" (pronounced sem-in-NO-lee by the Indians), which means "wild, nondomesticated" in the Mikasuki and Muskogee languages, both of which remain part of Seminole culture. The Seminoles are the only Indians east of the Mississippi River who have been able to preserve their culture, languages, and traditions. The Miccosukee branch of the Seminoles still lives close to its roots along the Tamiami Trail (old Route 41), where many own large herds of cattle.

African Americans have long played an important part in Florida's history. In 1559 about 100 blacks, most of them slaves, arrived in Florida with Don Tristan de Luna and his contingent of Spaniards, and helped establish a settlement on what is now Pensacola Beach. Others gained freedom from slavery by escaping to Florida—many of them joining the elusive Seminoles in the Everglades area. Later, because the former slaves spoke the Indian languages as well as English, they became valuable interpreters during treaty negotiations. Today's African Floridians have won acclaim in the space program, the armed forces, arts and entertainment, education, and politics.

In 1959 Fidel Castro's takeover of Cuba sparked a steady exodus of Cubans. Many of them headed for the west coast of Florida, where Cubans almost a century before had followed Vincente Martinez Ybor to make cigars—and stayed to cheer rebel leader Jose Marti. Nicaraguans, Guatemalans, and Hondurans, and other Spanish-speaking people who have faced turmoil in their countries of origin, have also emigrated to the Gulf Coast. Immigrants from the West Indies, Bahamas, Jamaica, and Haiti likewise populate Florida's west coast.

Refugees of another sort—retirees from all over America—have chosen to make the Florida Gulf Coast home, so you'll hear voices from every state while you're here. In the midst of all this diversity are the descendants of early European settlers and cowboys. These "Florida Crackers" earned their name from long whips they cracked while rounding up cattle back in pioneer days. Today's Crackers are still very much a part of the scene here. You'll meet many of them up in the Panhandle area.

Visitors to Florida's Gulf Coast have the opportunity to enjoy a wonderful variety of multicultural experiences. And you'll come away with wonderful vacation memories and a deep appreciation for the remarkable diversity within this unique and sun-blessed coastline.

LAY OF THE LAND

Most of the Sunshine State is flat, with the coastal area at sea level. Because of the state's elongated shape, no matter where you go, you won't be more than 60 miles away from the ocean. Look closely at a map of the Florida and you'll see some long skinny strips of land here and there along the Gulf Coast shoreline. These are the coastal barrier islands, the vital defenders of the coast during storms. Most of these islands are connected to the mainland by causeways, and when the weather is fine these narrow stretches of sandy shore are among the coast's nicest places to visit.

Geologists tell us that hundreds of millions of years ago, Florida was actually an arc of volcanic mountains. The advance and retreat of ancient salt seas produced a tremendously thick bed of extremely porous limestone, and eventually the aged mountains sank beneath thousands of feet of limestone sediment. Today Florida continues to re-form itself as rain, wind, and seawater act upon the land. In some areas the soft limestone sediment is dissolving and forming underground caves. When the limestone underpinning wears away, the soil on the surface gradually sinks, making a round depression in the ground—what Floridians call "sinkholes." Once, in Winter Park, a sinkhole swallowed up a house, six automobiles, a swimming pool, and a big chunk of a city street. But don't worry, most sinkholes are so small nobody even notices them.

Another result of the state's unusual underground aquifer is the production of a remarkable amount of spring water. Because Florida rests on such a porous foundation, water for hundreds of thousands of years has seeped, flowed, and trickled through it. The aquifer now holds billions of gallons of water. (Some geologists think that water from as far away as the Great Lakes eventually finds its way to the state.) Florida has 320 known springs, and 27 of them are "first-magnitude" springs—the kind that produce more than 65 million gallons of water every day. Seventeen of these amazing first-magnitude springs are situated along the Gulf Coast.

Once long ago Florida was almost all forest, but intensive lumbering activity over the years has changed that. Even so, nearly half of Florida's land area is heavily timbered today. The Apalachicola National Forest alone covers 557,000 acres. Sometimes visitors to the state's west coast are surprised by that fact; campers, hikers, hunters, and wildlife enthusiasts are, of course, happy about it.

FLORA AND FAUNA

Postcards from Florida invariably picture palm trees. While we do have lots of palms—more varieties than in any other state—you'll notice plenty of other kinds of trees, too. The state has more pine trees, for example, than palms, and they come in several varieties: sand pine, shortleaf pine, slash pine, longleaf pine, loblolly pine. These trees are good looking and commercially valuable as well. The large spreading branches of the Florida live oak can be found just about everywhere in our state, and our laurel oak makes a nice shade tree. And the weeping banyan, with its enormous, visible, strangling roots, is one of Florida's most prevalent oddities.

You may be surprised to learn that we have trees that change color with the seasons. Though the display is perhaps not as spectacular as you would see during a New Hampshire autumn, the colors of Florida trees are bolder and more lasting. Our southern sugar maples turn lovely shades of red and yellow, and the royal poinciana turns a brilliant, showy scarlet. In spring the handsome Chickasaw plum tree blossoms with dazzling white flowers, while the bigleaf magnolia produces huge white blooms nearly a foot across in diameter. The jacaranda greets spring with its unique vibrant purple flowers, and the red bottlebrush briefly yields elongated flower that resemble their namesake. The golden-rain tree produces cheery yellow blossoms to bid the summer good-bye, and then ushers in the fall with puffy pink seedpods that blanket the ground where they fall. Of course, our ever-present citrus trees delight with fragrant blossoms in backyards and groves everywhere.

BEACH DUNES WITH SEA OATS

Visit Florida

As you visit the Gulf Coast beaches, note the clumps of graceful, reedy golden-colored sea oats. Look, but don't touch. They are essential to holding the sand in place, protecting the shores from erosion. State law prohibits picking them. You may also encounter the prickly sandspur, so be advised to wear sandals when walking on the beach.

Although seemingly abundant, plant life in Florida is engaged in an uphill battle against urban sprawl. Florida's flora, among the most diverse in North America, continues to lose ground to shopping malls, subdivisions, office buildings, citrus groves, and cattle herds. Some experts believe that some of our gourds, vines, and plants will become extinct within a decade. Yet concerned citizens and organizations have established public and private gardens to harbor as many endangered plant species as possible, and plan to reintroduce the flora into a safe habitat in the future.

Another favorite Florida postcard subject is the alligator. Yep, we have 'em. Some experts say that there's at least one alligator in every body of fresh water in the state. These animals are neither cute nor friendly. Don't ever feed one—it's against the law and it's dangerous. They are interesting creatures, though, and you can view them safely at various zoos and aquariums around the state, and in local lakes as long as you keep your distance. These ancient animals have been around these parts for a long time. Fossil hunters have found remains of alligators, as well as birds, rodents, big cats, dogs, even camels and a strange mammoth, along the coastline. And not all of the fossils are buried; you can sometimes find sharks' teeth and pieces of fossilized marine mammal skeletons lying right out in plain sight.

Occasionally you'll spot a yellow road sign with a silhouette of a bear on it. Does this mean "bear crossing"? Sure does. Be especially watchful while driving along the coast during early spring evenings, when the black bears are just beginning to move about after winter hibernation. Perhaps you'll be lucky enough to spot a mother with cubs.

Gulf Coast beaches are important nesting sites for several varieties of threatened sea turtles. Loggerheads, green turtles, snapping turtles, and occasionally even the rare Kemp's ridley come ashore on early summer nights to scoop out shallow nests and deposit their eggs. You may hear about a "turtle walk" sponsored by one of the government environmental agencies. If you get chance, go along on one of these walks to witness the fascinating egg-laying events—the giant turtles don't seem to mind a bit. And try to see at least one West Indian manatee while you're here. These large, slow-moving, rather goofy-looking mammals can be found in spring-fed rivers, grazing on vegetation. Floridians love their manatees. That's why the whole state is a manatee sanctuary.

Bird-watchers, too, will enjoy a visit to our coastline. Brown pelicans are great fun to watch as they dive and swoop above the Gulf waters. Keep a lookout for sandhill cranes—not as numerous as they once were but still here—and for another long-legged handsome bird, the great blue heron. Another Florida native bird whose numbers have been declining for some time is the osprey, a hawklike fish eater who builds big bulky nests of twigs and sticks in the oddest places—look for them on top of utility poles as you drive around.

We have some pesky critters here, of course. "Love bugs" are sticky little pests that show up along our coast every May and September. They got their name because they tend to fly around in mating posture. They don't bite or sting, but if they get smashed against your automobile, wash off the mess right away, or they may damage the paint. It's a good idea to carry insect repellent if you intend to investigate woodlands or marshes. Biting, stinging things tend to hang out in those places.

Remarkably, considering the wealth of natural wonders with which this state was blessed, only recently has Florida really become "environmentally aware." Once the railroads arrived and the real estate magnates discovered Florida's amazing salability, the state went wild with development. Bulldozer madness and "condo-mania" went unchecked right up through the 1970s. It's surprising that so many scenic wonders escaped the wrecker's ball. It's surprising, too, that so many creatures and plants once threatened with extinction have made comebacks.

Our alligators are no longer considered endangered. In fact, they appear legally on some adventurous restaurant menus. Manatee populations, although still threatened, are slowly climbing. Great white egrets and roseate spoonbills, hunted to near-extinction for their plumes, once again glide above clean waterways. The red-cockaded woodpecker makes slow, but encouraging, population gains. Yet the picture isn't entirely a happy one. The handsome Florida panther's numbers continue to decline. Far too many of our black bears are run over by automobiles every year. The Kemp's ridley nests are fewer every year. Despite these unfortunate instances, generally speaking, Florida is trying hard to preserve its remaining natural beauty and diverse wildlife treasures.

HISTORY

When Columbus arrived in the New World, the thatched-roofed communities of the Timucuan Indians already dotted the west coast of Florida. Historians aren't sure which European explorer was the first to land on Florida's Gulf Coast, but one of the earliest, Amerigo Vespucci, was probably here in 1498.

Juan Ponce de León stopped near the Manatee River on his famous quest for the Fountain of Youth in 1513, and in 1528 Pánfilo de Narváez sailed into Tampa Bay on his futile search for El Dorado—the City of Gold. In 1539 west coast Indians watched in amazement as 10 ships bearing Hernando de Soto's army of 630 men arrived near Fort Myers, searching for gold and glory.

Sadly, diseases to which Europeans had built up resistance were soon spread among the Indians, who had no immunities to these illnesses. Measles and even the common cold devastated Florida's native people. Most heavily hit were the Tocobaga Indians of Tampa Bay, the Timucuan tribes in the forest, and the Apalachee of the Panhandle. By the time the French built Fort Caroline in 1562 and the Spanish established St. Augustine in 1565, the Native Americans had lost at least 25 percent of their population. Throughout the seventeenth century, Spanish priests at the many mission churches made notes about the numerous "pestilences" that felled mission Indians.

By 1710 most of the North Florida Indians had either died or moved westward out of Florida, while the more southerly Indians, the Tocobaga, the Calusa, and the Tequesta, slowly declined in numbers. However, the Creek Indians from Georgia and Alabama made their way south to North Florida, where they established communities and gained control of the area. The Spanish mostly settled in Pensacola to the west and St. Augustine to the east. Because the Floridian Creeks had left their villages in Georgia and Alabama, the Spanish sometimes referred to them as *cimarrones*, meaning "wild ones" or "runaways." Eventually the word found its way into both the English and Indian languages as "Seminoles."

By the end of the seventeenth century, Spain had built forts at Pensacola and St. Augustine, but in 1719 the French captured Pensacola only to return it to Spain in 1722. During the Seven Years War from 1756 to 1763 (also called the French and Indian War), the Creek Indians sided with the Spanish against the English. Spain lost, and the Treaty of Paris awarded Spanish Florida to Britain.

By 1783 Spain had it back again. In 1821 General Andrew Jackson convinced the Spanish to sell the undeveloped and increasingly bothersome colony to the United States, and the Stars and Stripes became the fourth national flag to fly over Florida.

When Jackson became president, he promised to "rid Florida of Indians" and attempted to move all of the Seminole Indians to Oklahoma. Seminoles angrily rejected the plan as Seminole leader Osceola stepped forward and "signed" the hated treaty with his quivering knife blade. The U.S. Army and the Seminoles fought from 1835 to 1842 and, technically, the tribe remains at war with the United States to this day.

Florida became a state in 1845 but seceded from the Union in 1861 at the start of the Civil War. During the war, daring west coast sea captains kept the Confederacy supplied with beef, leather, produce, salt, and sugar. After the war Florida was readmitted to the Union, and during Reconstruction new settlers arrived as cattle ranches, citrus groves, and small farms prospered. Railroads reached the Gulf Coast during the 1880s, providing a fast way to ship produce and beef to northern markets. But perhaps the biggest change railroads brought to the state was the ease with which people could come here as visitors, speculators, or settlers. The influx of new people and ideas sparked the growth of the area's cities.

When the 1920s rolled around, thousands more tourists, driving the recently invented automobile, arrived to enjoy Florida's beaches, springs, hotels, and health resorts. But by 1930 Florida, along with the rest of the country, was in the depths of the Great Depression. Tourism took a temporary but significant dive. However, the economic decline opened the way for the Civilian Conservation Corps (CCC), which began operations in 1933, initiating the fine state parks system Florida enjoys today.

World War II began a new era of growth and renewal as thousands of armed forces personnel came to Florida—many with their families. After the war the Sunshine State quickly adjusted to peacetime pursuits and continued to grow, not only in population, but also in industry, agriculture, and, of course, tourism.

CULTURES

The west coast of Florida offers a surprising diversity of cultures. We retain numerous place-names given us by the various local Native Americans. Many come from the Seminole tongue. *Chassahowitzka* means "hanging pumpkins," *Okaloocoochee* means "little bad water," *Panasoffkee* means "deep ravine," *Wacasassa* means "some cows there," and *Thonotosassa* means "place of flints." The mark of those early Spanish, English, and French explorers is still evident today in terra cotta tile roofs, Spanish mission–style churches and homes, ornate wrought-iron balconies, Tudor facades, and brick-paved streets.

The original Florida Crackers created thriving lumber, farming, and ranching businesses from the semitropical jungle. Their descendants still work on the same agricultural enterprises handed down by their forefathers. The Greek sponge divers who settled in Tarpon Springs have contributed to the cross-cultural feel of Florida. So did the Cubans who rolled fine cigars in Tampa and created one of the area's tastiest sandwiches, the "Cuban." Even the infamous pirates who plied their trade along the coastline lent a certain ribald mystique to the area.

Floridians celebrate many of these cultures with traditional festivals and feasts, and visitors are cordially invited to join right in, party hearty, and experience the various ethnic foods, music, art, history, religion, and folklore of our state. See the next chapter (Planning Your Trip) and the Calendar of Events in the appendix for more information about these festivals and events.

In addition to the groups mentioned above, the west coast of Florida has had several other notable influences. Thanks to the Gulf of Mexico, fishermen of all nationalities have passed through here and shared their knowledge of the sea and its gifts. Seafood festivals are year-round events, with each fishing community sharing its own specialty. The military, too, has long been a presence in Florida, with a U.S. Naval base in Pensacola and an Air Force base in Tampa. Often, military people retire here. So do circus people. After all, the winter quarters of the great Ringling Brothers Barnum and Bailey Circus was in Sarasota for many years, and many "show people," as they prefer to be called, have learned to call this coast home.

THE ARTS

As recently as 20 years ago one hardly dared to utter "Florida" and "the arts" in the same sentence for fear the words would be greeted with a snooty sniff or mumbles about a "cultural wasteland." No more. Major museums with jaw-dropping world-class exhibits dot the coastline. The music of first-rate symphony orchestras makes life sweeter. Ballet companies, Broadway shows, playhouses, dinner theaters, motion picture studios, writers' conferences, mega art exhibits, trendy galleries, jazz festivals—Florida has it all, and then some.

Sarasota is sometimes called the Cultural Coast, and no wonder. Art is everywhere, from side-street storefront galleries to the amazing Ringling complex, where the European and American fine art on display spans the fifteenth through twentieth centuries (including the world's most important collection of Rubens's work). The ornate eighteenth-century Asolo Theater is nationally renowned; seeing a performance in this stunning opera house makes for an enchanted evening.

In St. Petersburg, too, the art and culture scene sparkles. The Salvador Dalí Museum has the world's largest collection of the surrealist's work, the Museum of Fine Arts features wonderful displays of European and American fine art, and the Florida International Museum offers world-class traveling exhibits every year. The American Stage Company performs Shakespeare in the Park every spring for delighted audiences. And Tallahassee has a Shakespeare festival every year, as well as its springtime Jazz and Blues Festival with nonstop jazz, blues, and gospel.

Indeed, during the winter months (Florida's high season), arts and craft shows and music festivals happen weekly. Some are huge affairs, while others are smaller, more intimate events. Watch the local paper for a weekend-events section. Take in a concert, kick back at a bluegrass festival, enjoy a Broadway musical, check out a museum exhibit, or just get out of the hot sun and wander through a few cool art galleries. You'll be surprised and impressed.

CUISINE

Even without the beaches, attractions, shopping, and climate, Florida would be worth visiting just for the food. Author and editor Jeanne Voltz—who's written about the cuisines of the United States—credits Florida with "a cuisine of more ethnic diversity than any in America, and possibly in the world." She's probably right. Perhaps the secret of the charm of West Florida is the same as the secret of its cooking—a multitude of fresh ingredients and the diverse influences of a cosmopolitan population.

European foods began to influence Florida's Native American eating customs way back when Ponce de León showed up with cows and pigs. Early Franciscan friars introduced rice, spices, and egg custards. Oranges and grapefruit arrived from the Caribbean, and Cuban immigrants made dishes golden with saffron and sparked with red peppers. Homesteaders came with a taste for biscuits and gravy, and good ol' Cracker boys liked their fried chicken and grits. Blacks brought along eggplants, yams, and okra, while Creole gumbos and jambalaya made their way across from Louisiana. Greek sponge fishermen added honey, olive oil, capers, and lemon sauces to grilled fish. Recently, Chinese, Mexican, Indonesian, Cambodian, and Vietnamese immigrants have added their own special flavors to this already complex mix.

You'll find recommended restaurants in each destination chapter, but the truth is there are so many restaurants—and the competition is so stiff—that it's unusual to find a bad one. With our proximity to the Gulf, it's natural that there are plenty of seafood places. Red snapper, grouper, flounder, and mahi-mahi appear as "catch-of-the day" on menus almost all the time. Kingfish, scamp, snook, cobia, wahoo, and amberjack are more seasonal. Shrimp and crabs abound in gulf waters, and if you happen to visit during stone crab season, lucky you. (Eat stone crab claws like lobster, hot or cold with drawn butter.) Oyster fanciers love the tender morsels harvested from the waters off Apalachicola, and dainty bay scallops are found all along the coastline. Even those who prefer an old-fashioned steak or prime rib have come to the right place. Visitors are often surprised to learn that Florida is the biggest cattle-producing state east of the Mississippi.

OUTDOOR ACTIVITIES

Combine year-round warm weather with a big sparkly body of water, and you know you're in a place where just about everyone likes to go outdoors and play. Of course, all of that water means that residents and visitors enjoy boating, fishing, swimming, scuba diving, canoeing, parasailing, and zipping around on personal watercraft almost every day. And quartz-white sandy beaches provide the perfect place for volleyball, surfcasting, shelling, sandcastle building, strolling, or just sunbathing.

The clear waters of the Gulf of Mexico and the many freshwater springs make Florida's Gulf Coast a favorite spot for divers. You can find dive shops in most coastal locations that provide up-to-date information on the best sites, along with equipment rentals and dive-boat arrangements. Sport fishing, too, is a big deal here; boats are available for charter at both private and municipal marinas for half- and full-day trips. Larger "party boats" or "head boats" carry more passengers, are less expensive, and provide a good day's adventure for the whole family.

Walkers, hikers, joggers, bikers, and skaters find the many county, state, and national parks and forests perfect places to exercise, have fun, and get back to nature. There are even 36 canoe trails—publicly owned streams totaling 950 miles and offering a lovely way to explore the unique and diverse environment. If you prefer sidewalks to trails, many of the Gulf Coast cities offer walking tours of historic districts; some are guided, some self-guided—all are interesting and offer good exercise.

If you drive a little bit inland, you can find some great mom-and-pop places serving fried freshwater catfish, hush puppies, and maybe even real key lime pie (the filling should be yellow, never green).

Golf courses, both public and private, dot the landscape like big green oases. Some are famous fancy ones while others are relatively unknown. You'll find some of each described in the destination chapters, and you may discover others on your own. Recreation departments in various cities and towns offer a variety of outdoor sports and activities for people of all ages. Many recreation departments maintain tennis courts and some have swimming pools, soccer fields, and even archery or rifle ranges. In-line roller-skating and skateboarding enjoy growing popularity here, and "skateparks" are beginning to spring up.

PLANNING YOUR TRIP

Before you set out on your trip, you'll need to do some planning. Use this chapter in conjunction with the tools in the appendix to answer some basic questions. First of all, when are you going? You may already have specific dates in mind; if not, various factors will probably influence your timing. Either way you'll want to know about local events, the weather, and other seasonal considerations. This chapter discusses all of that, while the Calendar of Events in the appendix provides a month-by-month view of major area events.

How much should you expect to spend on your trip? This chapter addresses various regional factors you'll want to consider in estimating your travel expenses. How will you get around? Check out the section on local transportation. If you decide to travel by car, the Planning Map and Mileage Chart in the appendix can help you figure out exact routes and driving times, while the Special Interest Tours provide several focused itineraries. The chapter concludes with some reading recommendations, both fiction and nonfiction, to give you various perspectives on the area. If you want specific information about individual cities or counties, see the Resources section in the appendix.

WHEN TO GO
Every season in the Sunshine State has something to offer, and, indeed, people visit the Gulf Coast throughout the year. Most of the coastal area's tourism

13

has traditionally been packed into the winter season—Thanksgiving to Easter—and that's still the most popular time to visit along most of the coast. While much of the country is enduring freezing temperatures, Floridians are picking a breakfast grapefruit from a backyard tree, going swimming on New Year's Eve, or strolling barefoot along the beach in February. But Florida attracts plenty of summertime tourists, too. Every year from Memorial Day to Labor Day, visitors flock to the beaches along the Panhandle—the cooling Gulf breezes keep the coastline pleasant despite the high humidity and temperatures that may hover in the 90s for days on end.

That said, Florida has the highest year-round average temperature in the United States mainland: summertime is hot, especially during July, August, and September. No doubt about that. But everything is air conditioned, and our proximity to the Gulf means that we generally stay about 10 degrees cooler than inland locations. Slather on the sunblock and go to the beach in the early morning or late afternoon. The season offers plenty of baseball, fishing, and bargains in lodgings, restaurants, and attractions. Be aware that the state has some horrendous summer thunderstorms, and Florida claims to be the lightning capital of the United States. While these natural light shows are fascinating and exciting, it's best to watch them from a safe indoor vantage point.

Fall can be lovely, with warm soft-scented air. But it's also hurricane season, which can be scary. (Always take hurricane warnings seriously, by the way. If officials tell you to leave an area, do it.) Perhaps the best weather of all is from October to November and April to early May, when temperatures are ideal and humidity is low. Beaches are less crowded, water is still warm, and highways are not quite so busy. If you're planning a mid-winter visit, remember that you may have to contend with the occasional cold spell. If you happen into one—and sometimes it can be cold, gray, and miserable for a whole vacation week—just bundle up in a nice souvenir sweatshirt and spend the rest of the day visiting the area's myriad indoor amusements and attractions.

Folks have figured out that Florida is more than a great big theme park. Interest continues to grow in historic sites and in Florida's unique natural beauty. These season-spanning "learning vacations" draw visitors year-round from all over the world. The area's cultural diversity makes for yet another draw: Florida is admittedly festival happy, and most of the big fairs, festivals, fiestas, feasts, and flings are held during the peak tourist season—January, February, and March—a grand time for all concerned. Floats and bands trundle through the streets, midways explode with sound and color, fireworks reflect on the Gulf waters, and there's great food everywhere. In short, Florida definitely knows how to throw a party. Some of these events are described here; for a more comprehensive list, see the Calendar of Events in the appendix.

On Guavaween, a Halloween event peculiar to the Tampa Hispanic community, the mythical Mama Guava heads the Guava Stumble, a parade of sorts that rocks, rolls, and reggaes around historic Ybor City (pronounced EE-bore). Every December down at the edge of the Everglades, the Miccosukees host an Indians-only art festival featuring works from tribal artists throughout the hemisphere, while the Seminoles hold rodeos and pow-wows several times each winter. In January on the Greek holiday of Epiphany, young men descended from Greek sponge divers vie for the honor of retrieving a gold cross that is tossed into the chilly winter waters near Tarpon Springs. If you're visiting in February, check out Tampa's Gasparilla, a week-long celebration of the legendary pirate Jose Gaspar, or visit Fort Myers, where inventor Thomas Edison's birthday is celebrated with a Pageant of Light. During March in Dunedin, Scottish clans gather for the annual Highland Games; visitors cheer the pipers, the dancers, and the military tattoos. Every June Pensacola hosts the Fiesta of Five Flags in honor of its multicultural history.

HOW MUCH WILL IT COST?

One of the best things about Florida as a vacation destination is that visitors can spend pretty much whatever they care to. For instance, in Tampa you could take a family of four to see exotic animals from four continents in reconstructed habitats at Busch Gardens, and spend around $175 for admission and parking. Or you could take the same family to see exotic animals from four continents in reconstructed habitats at the Lowry Park Zoo, and spend about $30 for admissions and parking. If you'd like to go deep-sea fishing, for around $400 you could charter a private boat to take the family out into the Gulf for half a day. Or for about $150 you could take the family on a larger boat with other fishermen for half a day.

A surprising amount of the fun in Florida doesn't cost anything at all. Beaches are always free, although some have metered parking lots. People fish for free from bridges just about everywhere. Watch the weekend section of the local paper for listings of current free outdoor events, such as art shows or concerts. Look for discount coupons in brochures, newspapers, and "shoppers" (free tabloid-size newspapers). These coupons offer buy-one-get-one-free, or buy-one-get-one-half-price, or some other special bargain rate on meals, attractions, and places to stay. If you see a pile of those little papers on the counter or in a rack outside a restaurant or motel, take a minute before you order or check in—there's probably a money-saver inside.

Accommodations come in all shapes, sizes, and costs. Prices vary with the seasons, of course, but some generalities apply all year long: the closer you get to the Gulf, the more expensive the lodging is going to be. If your hotel or motel is on the beach side of the street, it will be more expensive than similar accommodations on the other side. If your room faces the water, it will be more expensive than a similar room facing the pool or the parking lot. If you don't mind side-street lodging and traveling a block or two to the waterfront, your savings will be even greater.

You'll typically pay between $45 and $89 a night for average accommodations in off-beach locations. On or close to the beach or in the center of major cities, rooms average between $90 and $130. First-class, prime-location, luxury places charge between $200 and $400 a night. At the other extreme, camping is an option everywhere along the coast, and a pretty nice option at that. Park your RV or motorhome or pitch your tent at a site with a water view or one with a wooded vista. While some sites are within public parks and others are within privately owned properties, all have the expected amenities— showers, laundry facilities, and pools. Many have "camping cabins" available, too, in case you don't have a camping vehicle or tent but enjoy the ambiance of a campsite.

Watch for coupons offering "buy-one-get-one-at-half-price" in local papers. These discount offers can help you make smart restaurant decisions. If you don't mind having dinner a bit early, you can save money on "early-bird specials." These are the same items that appear on the evening menu, but usually are offered between 4 and 6 p.m. at considerable savings.

To find accommodations to suit your budget and style, refer to the lodging listings in each destination chapter and write to or visit tourist welcome centers, chambers of commerce, and convention and visitor bureaus. These organizations generally provide lists of accommodations, including condominiums or luxury apartments for rent if your stay is for a month or more (see the Resources section in the appendix).

Florida restaurants come and go with baffling rapidity, and sometimes yesterday's chi-chi gourmet palace reopens tomorrow as a take-out hamburger joint! So please don't drive long distances with your mouth watering for *Coquilles Saint Jacques* only to find that the restaurant has a new name and the special of the day is chili dogs. Call ahead first.

The restaurant business here is so competitive that prices tend to be quite reasonable. Most of the moderately priced places mentioned in this book offer some tasty entrées in the $10 to $12 range. (In Florida, an entrée usually includes salad; vegetable; meat, fish, or poultry; bread and butter; and, often, coffee. If you order shrimp cocktail before and key lime pie after, your bill will rise accordingly.) Some of the more casual beachfront eateries will feed you a satisfying meal for around $5 to $8.

ORIENTATION AND TRANSPORTATION

Every year more than 40 million travelers visit Florida, and the state is pretty adept at moving people around—whether by road, rail, or air. Air travelers usually fly into one of the major airports, such as Orlando International or Tampa International, but plenty of smaller airports dot the Gulf Coast, including Pensacola Regional, Tallahassee Regional, St. Petersburg/Clearwater International, Panama City International, and Southwest Florida International in Fort Myers. Consider flying into Pensacola and working your way south along the coast. Amtrak passenger trains bring people here from all around the country, making Gulf Coast stops at Tallahassee, Tampa, and St. Petersburg. Greyhound and Trailways bus stops are located in most major cities, too. Within the cities themselves, public transportation is okay where it exists, although sometimes it takes a lot of transferring from bus to bus to get from here to there.

Without a doubt the best way to see Florida's coastal communities is on wheels—your own or rented ones. Car rentals are available everywhere and are pretty competitive (check around for the best rates). You can even rent RVs in many places. The state highway system is a fairly efficient one, even if it's not particularly scenic. The main north-south routes are I-75 (on the west

RULES OF THE ROAD

- Seat-belt laws are enforced here, and child-safety restraints are absolutely necessary, carrying a hefty fine if you don't comply.
- When visibility is less than perfect due to weather conditions, drive with headlamps on.
- Never throw anything out of the car. Litter laws are strictly enforced, and if caught, you may be fined.
- It's okay to make a right turn after you stop for a red light, unless a sign tells you otherwise. You're supposed to stop on an amber light as well as a red one.

coast) and I-95 (on the east coast). The main east-west arteries across the top of the state are I-10 and U.S. 90. The Tamiami Trail, or U.S. 41, links Miami to Fort Myers and continues north to Tampa. (Tamiami sounds like an Indian name, doesn't it? But it just stands for Tampa and Miami.) The highway system provides plenty of public rest areas that are generally well maintained, well lighted, and security patrolled. You can get some good road maps at no charge by writing to the Florida Department of Commerce, Collins Building, Tallahassee, FL 32303.

RECOMMENDED READING

Evidentally there's something about Florida that sparks the literary muse, as many writers have set their mysteries, romances, and adventures here. A good many authors live here, too. One terrific resource for literary types is *The Book Lover's Guide to Florida*, edited by Kevin M. McCarthy, which describes famous and lesser known Florida writers, points out literary landmarks, and provides a fine list of Florida bookstores. Published in 1992 by Pineapple Press, it is widely available throughout the state.

History enthusiasts will enjoy Marjory Stoneman Douglas's *Florida: The Long Frontier*, which tells the story of Florida from its geological formation to the present. Published way back in 1967 by Harper & Row, it's still stocked by many bookstores. (Douglas is revered in Florida for her earlier work, *The Everglades: River of Grass*.) Anne Morrow Lindbergh also wrote some wonderful books; perhaps her most famous is *Gift from the Sea* (Pantheon, 1955), a collection of meditations about shelling on Captiva. It's been reprinted many times and makes a fine souvenir of a Gulf Coast vacation. Marion Coe's *Legacy* (Southlore Press, 1993) evokes the Florida Gulf Coast on the verge of post–World War II changes. Set in John's Pass, just off the St. Petersburg coast, it gives readers a graphic picture of a not-so-long-ago Florida.

Jeff Klinkenberg writes excellent nature pieces for the *St. Petersburg Times.* Read his delightful book, *The Real Florida: Key Lime Pies, Warm Fiddlers, A Man Called Frog and Other Endangered Species* (Down Home Press, 1993). I. Mac Perry's carefully researched *Indian Mounds You Can Visit* (Great Outdoors Publishing Company, 1993) describes 165 aboriginal sites of West Coast Florida. For a chronological compilation of wrecks along the Florida coasts from the 1500s to the present, check out *Shipwrecks of Florida: A Comprehensive Listing* (Pineapple Press, 1992)—a must-read for divers and researchers.

Mystery writers find Florida's Gulf Coast a good setting for intrigue. John MacDonald wrote many books, including *Condominium* (Lippincott, 1977), a nail-biter set on the Gulf Coast. Mickey Friedman writes fine suspense novels with a wonderful sense of place; *Riptide* (Harper, 1994) tells a finely tuned tale set in the Florida Panhandle.

You should also check out local author and photographer Winston Williams's affordably priced *Florida's Fabulous* series. These thin, easy-to-pack books on native trees, birds, flowers, reptiles and amphibians, and seashells are chock full of beautiful pictures and useful information to make you a more aware traveler. Self-published with World Publications, P.O. Box 24339, Tampa, FL 33623, the books are available at area bookstores.

1
PENSACOLA

Pensacola has an almost tangible sense of history—and a long and turbulent history it's been. This seaside city was actually the first European settlement in America, established when Spanish conquistador Don Tristan de Luna landed here in 1559. Along with him came 1,000 settlers who were just getting adjusted to their new home when a devastating hurricane pummeled the coast, forcing them all to flee. (That is why Pensacola, though founded six years before St. Augustine, had to defer the title of oldest permanent existing European settlement in North America to St. Augustine.)

The flags of five different nations have flown over Pensacola, including those of the Confederacy and the United States, and it's changed hands more than a dozen times over the years as different conquerors took over. The result is a hardy community of folks, many of mixed English, Scottish, French, and Spanish descent.

Street names, district distinctions, even restaurant menus offer an interesting combination of many cultures. History buffs will love strolling Seville Square Historic District within Pensacola Historic Village, where nineteenth-century buildings have been skillfully restored and now house art galleries, antique and curio shops, museums, and restaurants. Beach-goers, too, love this place and would be hard pressed to find a prettier 40 miles of beach anywhere. Pensacolans love a good festival, so be on the lookout for one or more big celebrations while you're here.

DOWNTOWN PENSACOLA

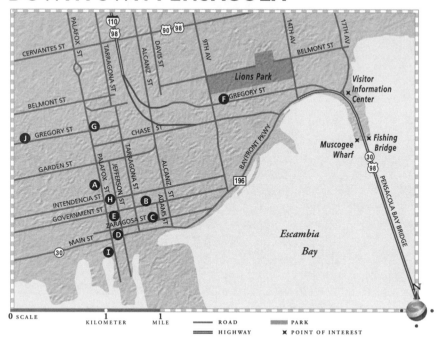

SIGHTS
- **A** Civil War Soldiers Museum
- **B** Pensacola Historic Village
- **C** Pensacola Historical Museum
- **D** Pensacola Museum of Art
- **E** T. T. Wentworth Jr. Florida State Museum

FOOD
- **F** McGuire's Irish Pub
- **G** Picadilly Deli
- **H** The Screaming Coyote

LODGING
- **I** New World Inn
- **J** Pensacola Grand Hotel

A PERFECT DAY IN PENSACOLA

Maybe there's no such thing as a free lunch, but in Pensacola there are plenty of other free delights—all yours to sample. Start your day with the complimentary breakfast at your hotel, then head for Seville Square Historic District. Here is Pensacola's "crown jewel" of historic preservation. It's a 37-square-block area of wonderfully restored homes, specialty shops, and old-time taverns and eating places. Pause to read the many historic markers as you walk, pointing out significant sights along the way. Stop at the Pensacola Museum of Art. Don't let the barred windows scare you away; this used to be the city jail. The old cells provide an oddly attractive, rough-hewn background for exhibits of contemporary paintings and sculpture. Exhibits change about every other month, but you're sure to see something interesting. (There's no charge here, but it's nice to leave a donation.) Continuing your no-cost adventure, head across town to the National Museum of Naval Aviation. You'll see dozens of displays tracing the history of flight from wooden planes to the *Skylab* Command Module. The big-screen theater shows a film so realistic you'll feel like you're actually in the cockpit.

Well, that's enough culture for today. It's time to pack a lunch and head for the beach. Smear on some sunscreen and pick a spot for the towel on the miles of white sand, where rolling dunes are covered with sea oats and the Gulf is emerald green. Relax. Swim. Have fun.

You've saved so much money today, you can now go to the famous Boy on a Dolphin restaurant and splurge on a fancy seaside dinner!

ORIENTATION

Pensacola is in the heart of the Gulf Islands National Seashore—a stretch of unspoiled beaches, open spaces, and historic sites hopscotching along the coast from South Mississippi to West Florida. The city is flanked by a pair of barrier islands—Perdido Key to the west and Santa Rosa Island (better known as Pensacola Beach) to the east.

Palafox Street is the major north-south artery through town, and Garden Street (which becomes Navy Boulevard on the way to the naval station) runs east-west. To get to the Gulf Islands National Seashore park, you'll head east on Garden Street to Gregory Street to the Pensacola Bay Bridge, which goes straight to the beach.

Pensacola has the largest airport in Northwest Florida, Pensacola Regional Airport. The area also knows how to handle traffic. The major east-west routes are I-10 and U.S. 90 and U.S. 98. North-south highways are U.S. 29 and I-110.

SIGHTSEEING HIGHLIGHTS

★★★★ **NATIONAL MUSEUM OF NAVAL AVIATION**
Pensacola U.S. Naval Air Station, Naval Blvd., 800/327-5002 or 850/453-NAVY
This is one of world's largest museums dedicated entirely to air and space. Exhibits and displays take visitors from the wood-and-baling-wire beginnings of naval aviation right up to the high-tech present. See World War II fighters, the *Skylab* Command Module, and more than 100 important military aircraft. Kids of all ages will like climbing into the cockpits and sitting in the pilots' seats. There's a replica of a World War II aircraft-carrier flight deck with a working elevator. Ride the motion-based simulator on **Flight Adventure Deck** for a realistic thrill. An IMAX theater presents films on naval aviation every hour.
Details: Museum is about eight miles southwest of downtown. Daily 9–5; closed major holidays. Free. (1–2 hours)

★★★★ **PENSACOLA HISTORIC VILLAGE**
Bounded by Zaragosa, Tarragona, Alcaniz, and Intendencia Sts., 850/444-8905
A number of restored buildings within the historic district tell a compelling story about the lives of Gulf Coast Florida's nineteenth-century inhabitants. Costumed guides will escort you through some of the earliest homes. Tours of the **Charles Lavalle** house, the **Clara Barkley Dorr** house, and the **Julee Panton** cottage, within **Seville Square Historic District**, will give you a glimpse into the lives of the people who lived there long ago. Also within the bounds of the village is the **Colonial Archeological Trail**, highlighting an ongoing excavation program conducted by local archaeologists. Each June, this area hosts **Fiesta of the Five Flags**, complete with art shows, parades, contests, and reenactments of Pensacola's colorful history.
Details: Mon–Sat 10–4, closed holidays. $6 adults, $2.50 children, senior and military discounts. Tickets, available in several of the restored buildings, are valid for a week. For information on Fiesta of the Five Flags, call 850/434-1234. (3 hours)

★★★ **CIVIL WAR SOLDIERS MUSEUM**
108 S. Palafox St., 850/469-1900
This is a little gem of a museum that gives visitors a new insight into

the Civil War. Artifacts and memorabilia include touching letters written by soldiers to the folks at home. Dioramas, with life-sized figures, show both the tedium and horror of daily wartime life. It doesn't take long to see the exhibits, but the impact is remarkable.

Details: *Mon–Sat 10–4:30, closed major holidays. $4 adults, $2 children. (1 hour)*

★★★ THE ZOO
5701 Gulf Breeze Pkwy., 850/932-2229
Here's a real zoo combined with a botanical garden. The Safari Line Train lets everyone get a close-up look at some really neat animals. Photographers love getting pictures of the rare endangered animals amid natural-looking habitats. Behind-the-scenes action includes watching as the zookeepers prepare lunch for 700 hungry animals. You might even get to hand-feed a gentle giraffe. An attractive gift shop features environmentally conscious gifts. Take a spin on the carousel where each of the animals depicted on the seats is endangered.

Details: *Daily 9–5; winter hours 9–4. $9.75 adults, $5.75 children, $8.75 seniors 62 and over. (1–2 hours)*

★★ PENSACOLA MUSEUM OF ART
407 S. Jefferson St., 850/432-6247
Here's a good example of building recycling. The sturdy building with heavy doors and barred windows was once the city jail. Built in 1906, it has neat square cellblocks just the right size for hanging collections of contemporary art, along with traveling art exhibits. Exhibits include some international fine art, and they rotate items about every six weeks.

Details: *Mon–Sat 10–4:30. Donation requested. (1 hour)*

★ PENSACOLA HISTORICAL MUSEUM
405 Adams St., 850/444-8905
This fascinating old building, next to the Dorr House, was built in 1832. Originally the Christ Episcopal Church, during the Civil War it was used as a barracks, prison, hospital, and chapel by Union forces. Now a museum, it presents the history of the city of Pensacola. Here you'll see Indian artifacts, old glass bottles, silver, period clothing, and geological treasures.

Details: *Open Mon–Sat 9–4:30. $2 adults, $1 children. (1 hour)*

PENSACOLA AREA

Escambia Bay

SCENIC HWY
PERRY AV
BAYOU BLVD

Texar Bayou

PENSICOLA BAY BRIDGE
To Gulf Breeze

17TH AV

GREGORY ST
BAYFRONT PKWY

Pensacola

9TH AV
To H

CHASE ST

DAVIS ST

BARRACKS ST
JEFFERSON ST

ALCANIZ ST

110

PALAFOX PL

PALAFOX ST

SPRING ST

Pensacola Bay

29

YONGE ST
To F

Brownsville

CERVANTES ST

GREGORY ST

GARDEN ST

GOVERNMENT ST

ZARAGOSA ST

MAIN ST

292

PACE BLVD

To I

Bayou Chico

90

BARRANCAS AV

Warrington

JACKSON ST

NAVY BLVD

MOBILE HWY

295

NAVY BLVD

DUNCAN RD

RADFORD BLVD

LILLIAN HWY

West Pensacola

Myrtle Grove

727

GULF BEACH HWY

Bayou Grande

TAYLOR RD

US Naval
Air Station

A

298

98

FAIRFIELD DR

To I

BLUE ANGEL PKWY

173

To Perdido Key

HIGHWAY

ROAD

0 SCALE   2 KILOMETERS   2 MILES

★ T. T. WENTWORTH JR. FLORIDA STATE MUSEUM

330 S. Jefferson St., 850/444-8586

The building was the old Pensacola City Hall, built in 1907 and was recently restored to its original splendor reminiscent of the Italian Renaissance. (Although it technically isn't part of the Pensacola Historic Village, your village ticket will admit you here, too.) In addition to maps, artifacts, and old photos, which trace the city's history, the museum houses the hands-on Discovery Gallery for children and an impressive collection of Coca-Cola memorabilia.

Details: *Mon–Sat 10–4, Sun 1–4; shorter winter hours. Free with Pensacola Historic Village tickets; $5 otherwise. (1–2 hours).*

FITNESS AND RECREATION

Much of the recreation here is beach-centered, and why not? There are miles and miles of pure white, powdery sand—so pure each grain seems to sparkle in the sunlight, so fine it squeaks when you walk on it. The secret of this sand, apparently, is its quartz or silicon-dioxide base, polished and bleached and tumbled as it washed here all the way from the southern Appalachian Mountains. The Gulf Islands National Seashore encompasses upwards of 140,000 acres of Northwest Florida's barrier islands, including Perdido Key, where Pensacolans and their visitors enjoy swimming and playing on 14 miles of sugary shoreline just 15 miles southwest of the city off SR 292. There's another long stretch of beach at Fort Pickens, 850/934-2635, on Santa Rosa Island. Another old fort, Fort Barrancas, is located at the Naval Air Station, and they don't mind a bit if you bring the family over to use the picnic grounds and the nature trail. Blackwater River State Park, 850/623-2364, isn't actually in Pensacola but in nearby Milton, in Santa Rosa County, off U.S. 90. Here you'll find one of the purest sand-bottomed rivers in the world; you might want to take a day trip there for the nature trails,

SIGHTS	FOOD	LODGING
Ⓐ National Museum of Naval Aviation	Ⓑ Barnhill's Buffet	Ⓕ Ramada Inn North
	Ⓒ Hopkins Boarding House	Ⓖ The Seville Inn
	Ⓓ Skopelo's on the Bay Seafood and Steak House	Ⓗ Shoney's Inn
	Ⓔ Yamoto Oriental Cuisine	Ⓘ Sleep Inn

TREE-SHADED ROAD IN PENSACOLA

Visit Florida

canoeing, and good fishing. The Pensacola area has plenty of half- and full-day fishing boats available. Fishing from land is popular, too. Try wetting a line at the three-mile-long Pensacola Bay Bridge, which crosses the bay to Pensacola Beach and Gulf Breeze. Golfers can choose from several good courses. The Moors is a nice one, about five miles west of town off I-10 at Avalon Boulevard, 850/995-4653 or 800/727-1010.

FOOD

McGuire's Irish Pub, 600 E. Gregory St., 850/433-6789, is popular with local folks as well as visitors, and you might have to stand in line on Friday or Saturday night. Offering more than just pub grub, they serve seafood, steak, and pasta as well as burgers. **Picadilly Deli**, 102 Palafox Pl., 850/438-DELI, offers hefty deli-style sandwiches with cute names. Try the spanakopita (spinach pie). **The Screaming Coyote**, 196 Palafox St., 850/453-9002, specializes in Mexican foods. It's not all five-alarm hot stuff as the name might suggest—they have mild sauces, too. Everything is made fresh—great tacos, enormous burritos, and a really fine salsa bar. Enjoy a beautiful sunset over Santa Rosa Sound at **Boy on a Dolphin**, 400 Pensacola Beach Blvd., 850/932-7954. Lunch features pasta dishes and platters along with sandwiches and salads, while the dinner menu offers steak and seafood. They serve steak, seafood, wings, along with salads, burgers, sandwiches, and desserts. **The Great Brit Inn**, 49 Via de Luna Dr. on Pensacola Beach, 850/916-1288, offers traditional British fare. Sports fans will head for **Sidelines Sports Bar and Restaurant**, 2 Via de Luna Dr. on Pensacola Beach, 850/934-3660, with 17 TVs, three big screens, and three satellite dishes—even individual table speakers so you won't miss a play. Try bangers and mash or fish and chips—British ales are on draught. **Flounder's Chowder and Ale House**, 800 Quietwater Beach Rd., 850/932-2003, has long been a favorite hangout for locals of all ages, along with visitors who happen by. The food is standard beach fare, but the place is lots of fun, with a menu full of silly flounder jokes made up by "Fred Flounder, Founder."

Barnhill's Buffet, 8102 N. Davis Hwy., 850/477-5465, is one of those Florida favorites—the all-you-can-eat food bar. It offers Southern-style cooking (fried chicken, catfish, and the like) with very good homemade bread and desserts. The drink and food bar is always under $8, and kids eat even cheaper. If you like Japanese food, complete with flashing-knife preparation at tableside, check out **Yamoto Oriental Cuisine**, 131 New Warrington Rd., 850/453-3461, www.yamoto.pen.net. The chefs are certainly entertaining and the food is as fresh as it can possibly be. **Hopkins Boarding House**, 900 N. Spring St., 850/438-3979, is a little bit hard to find, so watch for the sign on Spring Street. It's a big old house with rocking chairs on the porch and lace curtains on the windows—the whole grandmother's-house experience. It's also a real boarding house, so you'll share a long table with whomever happens to be there. Heaping platters of good Southern food are offered at moderate prices. (Country breakfasts are very special here.) **Skopelo's on the Bay Seafood and Steak House**, 670 Scenic Hwy., 850/432-6565, overlooks Pensacola Bay and specializes in Greek cooking along with seafood and steaks. It's a pretty place with a nice view.

LODGING

New World Inn, 600 S. Palafox St., 850/432-4111, occupies a former factory building in downtown Pensacola. Vintage photographs are everywhere, and fans spin lazily from high ceilings. There's a lot of character here, and at reasonable prices, too. Its New World Restaurant is famous for desserts—the praline à la creme is divine. The **Pensacola Grand Hotel**, 200 E. Gregory St., 850/433-3336, houses guests in a contemporary 15-story tower that incorporates the old 1912 L&N Railroad depot. Wonderful old tile and marble baseboards decorate the structure, and a little library has chairs for your reading comfort. It's a tad expensive, but they often offer discounts.

GULF BREEZE

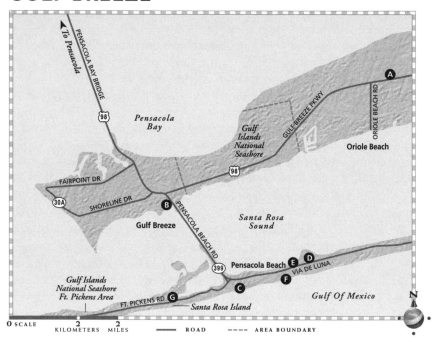

SIGHTS
🅐 The ZOO

FOOD
🅑 Boy on a Dolphin
🅒 Flounder's Chowder
and Ale House
🅓 The Great Brit Inn
🅔 Sidelines Sports Bar
and Restaurant

LODGING
🅕 Clarion Suites Resorts
and Conference
Center
🅖 Holiday Inn Express

The most expensive places are, of course, on the beach. **Clarion Suites Resorts and Conference Center**, 20 Via de Luna Dr., 850/932-4300, is a lovely one. The beach is at your doorstep in this big sprawling 86-suite Gulf-front facility with its "old Florida" look. There is no restaurant or lounge on the premises, but you have a kitchenette and you're within walking distance of several good restaurants. **Holiday Inn Express**, 165 Fort Pickens Rd., 850/932-5361, is newly renovated with 150 spic-and-span rooms. Décor is

Florida-tropical and each room has its own balcony—many overlooking the Gulf. They offer free continental breakfasts and four lighted tennis courts for your pleasure. **Ramada Inn North**, 6550 N. Pensacola Blvd., 850/477-0711, has more than 100 rooms and some of them have whirlpools and wet bars. There's a full-service restaurant and lounge. Come and go whenever you want. Everybody has an outside entrance. There's a free continental breakfast, too. The downtown location of **The Seville Inn**, 223 E. Garden St., 850/433-8331, makes it an attractive choice for sightseers. It's newly renovated and freshly decorated with a pastel Florida-tropical look. It's right next door to the Seville Dinner Theater for convenient dining/entertainment pleasure, and offers two pools and a continental breakfast. **Shoney's Inn**, 8080 N. Davis Hwy., 850/484-8070, is on the outskirts of town, just north of I-10. The five-story hotel is close to University Mall. You can bring your pet along if you want. There's a Shoney's restaurant right in front of the building, where the breakfast buffet alone makes it worthwhile to stay here. Economical lodgings can be had at **Sleep Inn**, 2591 Wilde Lake Blvd., 850/941-0908, with rooms under $50 and children stay free. (Kids like it because it's near McDonald's.)

CAMPING
Camping is popular in the Pensacola area largely because of the wonderful beaches. Big Lagoon State Recreation Area, on County Road 292A about 10 miles southwest of Pensacola, just across the Intracoastal Waterway from Gulf Islands National Seashore, 850/492-1595, has an observation tower for bird watching, and offers good swimming, fishing, and boating. Gulf Islands National Seashore, 1801 Gulf Breeze Pkwy., Gulf Breeze, 850/934-2600, encompasses nearly 74,000 acres in Florida and Mississippi. The seashore offers 169 campsites in various units near Pensacola. Picnic areas are located in Santa Rosa. All Star RV Campground, 13621 Perdido Key Dr., 850/492-0041 or 800/245-3602, is just off Gulf Beach Highway, directly on the beach. A fairly new place, it offers all the amenities. Navarre Beach Campground, 9201 Navarre Pkwy. (Hwy. 98), 850/939-2188, is two miles east of Navarre Bridge on Santa Rosa Sound. They have a pier and a pool as well as a fine beach.

NIGHTLIFE
Pensacola nightlife is on the quiet side. But, hey—you're only four hours away from New Orleans. McGuire's Irish Pub (see Food listings, above) is a bustling night spot that is open late. Stop by Tuesday through Saturday nights for live

Irish music—locals love to sing along with the jigs. Be prepared to wait in line. The Seville Dinner Theater, 241 E. Garden St., 850/469-1111, is perfect for those who want to sing for their supper; it offers Broadway musicals with dinner. There's a Hooter's on Pensacola Beach, 850/934-9464, and another one at 5052 Bayou Blvd., 850/447-3400.

2

THE EMERALD COAST— DESTIN/PANAMA CITY

Some call this sandy stretch of Florida's Panhandle "the Emerald Coast" be-cause the water lapping along the shore is an incredible shade of green. The beaches between Destin and Panama City include more than 20 individual beach communities. Naturally, all of this water and sand means that fun in the sun is an important part of life, but dining and shopping are practically art forms here. The peak season is summertime because it's at least 10 degrees cooler here than in southern Florida. It is also cooler in the winters, so, unlike most of Florida's beaches, the beaches here are uncrowded all winter. Visitors are often pleased and surprised to find themselves almost alone on a wide, white, perfectly wonderful beach. Fall and spring are especially lovely, with warm mild weather and quiet peaceful beaches.

A PERFECT DAY ON THE EMERALD COAST

Start your day at everybody's favorite breakfast spot, Donut Hole II, at Santa Rosa Beach, with a generous slab of Sadie's French toast made from home-made bread. Yum. Then head to nearby Grayton Beach State Recreation Area to walk the self-guided nature trail. Grayton Beach was once hailed as the "Best Beach in the Continental United States," by Dr. Stephen Leatherman (known as "Dr. Beach") of the University of Maryland's Laboratory for Coastal Research. It is the crown jewel of the county's beaches. Wander

PANAMA CITY BEACH

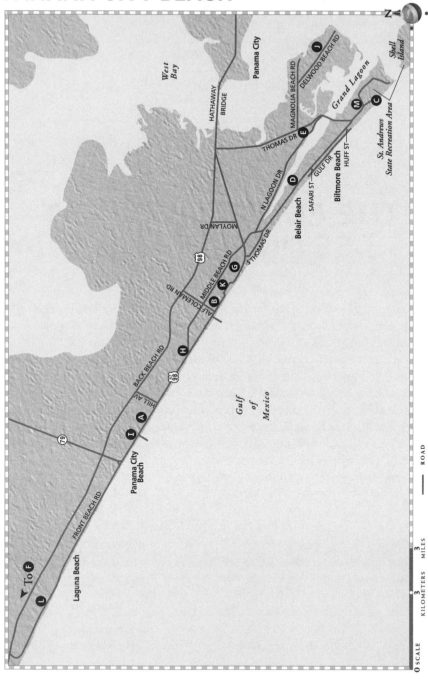

among the pristine coastal vegetation and the windswept dunes and marvel at the ecological diversity within this carefully protected gulf-side acreage. Then it's off to Destin's designer outlet center, Silver Sands Factory Stores—a shopper's dream come true with more than 100 top designer stores all in one place. Before you get shopping, have lunch at Morgan's—definitely not your typical food court. Buy something wonderful to wear to dinner at Criolla's, a five-star restaurant in Grayton Beach (start with the marvelous Kiss Yo' Mama Soup). After dinner go back to the beachfront hotel and fall asleep to the sound of gentle surf.

ORIENTATION

The Emerald Coast area spans some 40 miles of Gulf Coast shore from Destin to the west to Panama City to the east, with Santa Rosa Beach, Grayton Beach, and Seaside in between. From Pensacola, this region is easy to reach. U.S. 98 East takes you through many lovely beach communities, straight into downtown Panama City. If you're coming from the north or south on I-10, you can take SR 79 to the area west of Panama City or U.S. 231 directly to Panama City. Airline service is available to and from Panama City International Airport, 850/763-6751, and there's another airport at Fort Walton Beach, a few miles west of Destin, 850/651-7160.

Most of the motels, restaurants, and attractions are on U.S. 98-A, which is also called Scenic 98 because it runs along the beach. Parallel to Scenic 98 is Business 98, which goes through a small downtown area. Quite a few small highways connect Scenic 98 and Business 98; if you get the two mixed up, you can cut across. One such highway is Route 757, which will take you from the western end of Scenic 98 south to Captain Anderson's Pier and Marina. Be

SIGHTS
- Ⓐ Gulf World Marine Park
- Ⓑ Miracle Strip Amusement Park
- Ⓒ St. Andrews State Recreation Area

FOOD
- Ⓓ Boar's Head Restaurant
- Ⓔ Captain Anderson's Pier and Marina
- Ⓕ Rick's Crab Trap

LODGING
- Ⓖ Bikini Beach Resort Motel
- Ⓗ Chateau Motel
- Ⓘ Flamingo Motel/Flamingo Towers
- Ⓙ Marriott's Bay Point Resort
- Ⓚ Miracle Strip Beach Motel
- Ⓛ Sea Witch
- Ⓜ Treasure Island Motel

sure to check addresses carefully to be sure if they're on Scenic 98 or Scenic 98-A. (Also, note that the addresses on 98-A get higher as you go west.) And to make things sound more confusing than they really are, there's an old route also called 98. This is Old Scenic Highway 98, and it diverges from U.S. 98 near Miramar Beach from where it follows along the coast.

SIGHTSEEING HIGHLIGHTS

★★★★ GRAYTON BEACH STATE RECREATION AREA
357 Main Park Rd., Santa Rosa Beach, 850/231-4210
This sugary, dune-crested beach is consistently rated among the top 10 beaches in the United States by travel writers and beach experts alike. Wear your sunglasses here—the sand sparkles like new-fallen snow, and the perfectly clean and clear emerald green water will dazzle your eyes. The dunes look almost like abstract sculptures and the beach vegetation provides splotches of color here and there. If you visit during the fall, you may be lucky enough to observes thousands of migrating monarch butterflies as they flutter through the Panhandle area on their way to Mexico. Picnic tables are handy, and camping facilities are available with advance reservations. Call the number above for info.
Details: From Destin, drive east on U.S. 98 for 11 miles to Scenic Route 30-A. Head east on 30-A for nine miles. The recreation area is on the right. (3 hours–all day)

★★★★ GULF WORLD MARINE PARK
15412 Front Beach Rd., Panama City, 850/234-5271
This Panama City institution is one of Florida's nicest marine parks. Kids and grown-ups enjoy watching the spectacular acrobatic bottle-nosed dolphins and friendly performing sea lions, and most get a scary thrill from walking through the shark tank. It's show time all the time here—shows continue all day starting at 9 a.m. There are underwater shows and a colorful **Tropical Island** where parrots, flamingos, and peacocks do their thing amidst floral splendor. It's educational as well, with knowledgeable staff imparting information about the talented birds and beasts.
Details: Feb–Oct daily from 9 a.m.; rest of year Sat–Sun and holidays; hours vary seasonally, so call ahead. $17 adults, $10.50 children. (2 hours)

★★★★ ST. ANDREWS STATE RECREATION AREA
4607 State Park Ln., Panama City, 850/233-5140,
www.dep.state.fl.us/parks
This is a stunningly beautiful spot, with windswept dunes, white-quartz sand beaches, dense flatwoods, and well-planned nature trails. Visitors are delighted by some rare sightings of Florida's unique wildlife. Alligators, wading birds, deer, and raccoons are often spotted here, and the shoreline and jetties offer a fine place to observe marine wildlife. You can fish off the long pier, and snorkelers will be fascinated by the fish and plant life under the water. Birding is a real treat at this park. At the main gate you can get an extensive bird list. The recreation area offers picnic facilities complete with tables and grills.

Details: Open year-round. $4 per vehicle with up to eight passengers, $2 individual admission. (4–6 hours)

★★★ SILVER SANDS FACTORY STORES
U.S. 98 E., Destin, 800/510-6255 or 850/864-9780
Made to order for the shop-till-you-drop crowd, this is the third-largest designer factory outlet in America, with more than 100 big-name outlet stores such as Ann Taylor, Calvin Klein, Tommy Hilfiger, and Lenox. The food court at Silver Sands is an attraction in itself. **Morgan's** has a restaurant, pizza and pasta stand, bakery, deli, and more. Upstairs there's a whole entertainment complex with 160 futuristic video games and some virtual sports simulators. Keeps the kiddies busy while you shop.

Many Florida beaches use the "flag warning" system to help assure water safety. Here's how to read the flags:

Blue flag = Calm seas
Yellow flag = Use caution
Red flag = Stay out of the water!

Details: Silver Sands is about 11 miles west of the U.S. 98 and U.S. 331 junction; about one mile east of Sandestin resort. Open Mon–Sat 10–9, Sun 10–6. Call for Jan and Feb hours. Morgan's open daily 11–9. (4 hours)

★★ EDEN STATE GARDENS AND MANSION
Four miles east of U.S. 98 and U.S. 395 junction on County
Rd. 395, Point Washington, 850/231-4214

This was once the site of a busy, turn-of-the-last-century lumber mill. Today it's a tranquil park featuring elaborately manicured gardens abloom with many varieties of azaleas and camellias amid Spanish moss–draped oaks that are centuries old. The centerpiece of Eden is the **Wesley Mansion**, a handsome pillared Greek revival–style home. It's chock-a-block full of gorgeous antiques. In fact, there's a room here that contains the largest collection of Louis XVI Court furniture found in any one room in America.

Details: Guided tours of the mansion Thu–Mon 9–4 on the hour. Park admission $2 carload; tours $1.50 adults, 50 cents children. (1–2 hours)

★★ MIRACLE STRIP AMUSEMENT PARK
12000 Front Beach Rd., Panama City Beach, 850/234-5801, www.mspswi.com

If you're traveling with kids, they're not going to let you leave Panama City before they check out Miracle Strip's 2,000-foot-long roller coaster, the Starliner. There are other rides here, too, along with arcade games and miniature golf. They've also added a water park called **Shipwreck Island** (850/234-2282).

Details: Hours vary with the seasons—call ahead. Admission based on height: $16 for those over 33 inches to ride on all the rides, 33 inches and under free; $3 to walk around but not ride. (2–3 hours)

★ MONET MONET
100 E. Scenic Route 30-A, Grayton Beach, 850/231-5117

The building and grounds at this most unusual garden shop have been painstakingly designed to re-create the famous home of Claude Monet in Giverny, France. You'll see a reproduction of Monet's water lily pond and a Japanese footbridge, and on Wednesdays you can take a garden tour and hear a free lecture on "Claude Monet, the man, the artist, the gardener."

Details: Wed–Mon 10–5, closed Tue. Tour and lecture Wed 2–3. Free. (1–2 hours)

FITNESS AND RECREATION
This part of the Panhandle has been called a recreational paradise, and with good reason. Few places offer such a variety of activities. Whether your game is golf, tennis, boating, fishing, shopping, or enjoying a leisurely bike ride or hike

on one of the many nature trails or a brisk jog on the beach, you'll stay busy on the Emerald Coast.

Golfers usually gravitate to Sandestin, 9300 U.S. 98 W., Destin, 800/267-8135, the mega beach and golf resort that boasts three golf courses (63 holes). There are 13 tennis courts at Sandestin, too, including both grass and clay courts. The Grayton Beach State Recreation Area, off Scenic Route 30-A, lives up to its "Best Beach" reputation with a wonderful beach, amazingly complex vegetation, and even a lake. Follow the nature trail for an up-close look at "real Florida." Bring your camera. For another photo-op kind of excursion, take a ride on the Glass Bottom Boat (Boogie's Dock, foot of Destin Bridge), 850/654-7787, for a real dolphin encounter. Visitors view the playful mammals through 48 big underwater windows. Reef Runner Excursions, at Harborwalk Marina, Destin, 850/654-4655, will take you for a ride to where the snorkel adventures await. You get mask, fins, and snorkel to use. Shipwreck Island, 12000 Front Beach Rd., Panama City Beach, 850/234-2282, is a tropically themed water park. Float at a leisurely pace down the 1,600-foot Lazy River, or rush headlong down the 35-mph Speed Slide. There are all kinds of fishing opportunities. Folks fish from the shore, jetties, bridges, long piers, and boats. Call Captain Anderson's Pier and Marina, 5550 N. Lagoon Dr., Panama City Beach, 850/234-3435 or 800/874-2415, for a good selection of fishing options.

FOOD
Seafood is, of course, in evidence at virtually every restaurant and hole-in-the-wall along this bountiful coast. But most visitors are really surprised when they become aware of the great diversity of dining experiences available to them here. Eat your fill of seafood. It doesn't get much better than this. But also check out some of the many other foods Florida serves so well.

Criolla's, 170 E. Scenic Route 30-A, Santa Rosa Beach, 850/267-1267, offers dinner with a contemporary, tropical flair and a smiling, attractive staff. Try a Cuban Banana Bomba for dessert. Seafood reigns here and for a fresh seafood dinner, check out the menu at **Nick's on the Beach**, 2215 W. Scenic Route 30-A, Blue Mountain Beach, 850/267-2117. (They're closed December and January, but if you're here any other time, you can enjoy really fresh-off-the-boat local fish.) **Pompano Joe's**, 2378 Old Scenic Hwy. 98, Miramar Beach, 850/837-2224, has a fun family atmosphere, great big open-air windows offering the sights and sounds of the Gulf, and hearty servings of fresh seafood. **Seagar's**, at the Sandestin Beach Hilton, 4000 Sandestin Blvd. S., Destin, 850/622-1500, specializes in prime steak, live lobster, and fresh

EMERALD COAST

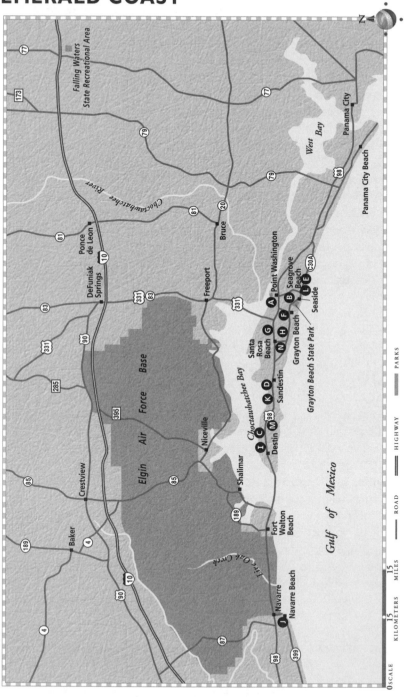

seafood. There's a walk-in cigar humidor and live entertainment. It's expensive but exquisite. Casual dining in a friendly, fragrant atmosphere makes the **Donut Hole II**, U.S. 98 E., Santa Rosa Beach, 850/267-3239, a local favorite. Enjoy big farmhouse breakfasts, hearty lunches, and dinners in homemade American style. There's a full bakery, too.

You may have read about **Boar's Head Restaurant**, 17290 Front Beach Rd., Panama City Beach, 850/234-6628. It's an award-winning restaurant overlooking a prize-winning beach. They're only open for dinner, but what a dinner. Check out the oyster bar—fabulous. Another famous waterfront place is **Captain Anderson's Pier and Marina**, 5551 N. Lagoon Dr., Panama City Beach, 850/234-2225. Voted by *Florida Trend Magazine* as "Florida's #1 Seafood Restaurant," the décor is nautical and the seafood is off-the-boat fresh.

At **Rick's Crab Trap**, 104 SW Miracle Strip Pkwy., Fort Walton Beach, 850/664-0110, the specialty is seafood—grilled, steamed, and fried—but they serve a good steak, too. Décor is nautical; servings are plentiful. There's a kids' menu and they have lunch specials.

If you're headed for the beach, stop for some good deli take-out food at **Cacoons**, 4101 E. Scenic Route 30-A, Seagrove Beach, 850/231-4544. They'll pack it up nicely for you and they're open at 7:30 every morning so you can get an early start on your day. **Morgan's**, U.S. 98 N., Silver Sands Factory Stores, Destin, 850/654-3320, is like no mall food court you've ever seen before. There are nine different food venues here, along with a market, a bakery, and an on-site brewery. There's sit-down service or you can serve yourself.

There are several cozy cafés along this coast that serve sandwiches, salads, homemade soups, and great desserts—just right when you want a light meal or a little pick-me-up at lunchtime. One place sure to please is the

SIGHTS
Ⓐ Eden State Gardens and Mansion
Ⓑ Grayton Beach State Recreation Area
Ⓑ Monet Monet
Ⓒ Silver Sands Factory Stores

FOOD
Ⓓ Beach Dream Cafe
Ⓔ Cacoon's
Ⓕ Criolla's
Ⓖ Donut Hole II
Ⓒ Morgan's
Ⓗ Nick's on the Beach
Ⓘ Pompano Joe's
Ⓙ Sailor's Grill
Ⓚ Seagar's
Ⓛ Studio 210
Ⓔ Sweet Dreams Café

LODGING
Ⓜ Frangista Beach Inn
Ⓝ Highlands House
Ⓞ Sugar Beach Inn Bed & Breakfast

Note: Items with the same letter are located in the same area.

SEASIDE

You've seen pictures of Seaside. *Magazine photographers often use this planned community in Florida's Panhandle as background for fashion layouts. It's been featured in all of the major architectural magazines, and if you've seen* The Truman Show, *you've seen Seaside in the movies. Just drive 60 miles east of Pensacola on U.S. 98 to U.S. 283 South to Scenic Route 30-A East and you're there.*

The town and the ideas behind it have won all kinds of awards and kudos. It started with the notion of reviving Northwest Florida's tradition of wood-frame cottages, beautifully adapted to Florida's climate. Deep roof overhangs sheltered porches from rainstorms, and, on pleasant evenings, people really sat on their porches. Award-winning builder Robert Davis used to come to such a cottage on summer vacations when he was a boy. His grandfather bought 80 acres bordering lovely Seagrove Beach, and he and young Robert used to walk around the tract. When he thought about making plans for the family property at Seagrove, he remembered those happy childhood days at the wooden beach cottage. He knew what kind of a community he wanted to build, but no one seemed to know just how to revive the tradition so long out of fashion.

Davis, along with architects and developers, began to travel around taking pictures, sketching, measuring, taking notes. It turned out that 80 acres was just the right size for a small town. He decided to call his little town "Seaside," and he built a couple of beach houses to test his ideas. Would an old-fashioned–looking wooden house near the beach be salable? He added

Beach Dream Cafe, 1688 Old Scenic Hwy. 98, just west of Sandestin, 850/837-4097, with its relaxing beach décor, big hefty sandwiches, and varied goodies for dessert. **Sweet Dreams Café**, 3723 E. Scenic Route 30-A, Seagrove Beach, 850/231-0011, serves breakfast and lunch complemented by gourmet coffees and homemade pastries. It's comfortable, attractive, and great smelling. If you're looking for something a little unusual, you might enjoy **Studio 210**, at the Ruskin Place Artists Colony, Seaside, 850/231-5202. It's a combination art gallery, coffee shop, and bed-and-breakfast. They serve breakfast, lunch, and dinner. Try their exceptional cappuccino and espresso, made from coffee beans imported from Italy. While you enjoy the food, look *another touch: a pavilion overlooking the Gulf—to serve both as a "gateway to the sea, and as a symbol of the neighborhood sharing of the beach." The houses sold. The master plan was drafted in 1982 and the building began in earnest.*

The cottages were built in the old way, with wood frames and overhanging roofs. Each one has a porch and a picket fence. And yet each house is quite different from its neighbor. They range in size from small and cozy to large and rambling. In the old days people used to name their summer cottages, and each of the Seaside houses has a name, too. Each street leads to the beach, and at the end of each street is a white wooden pavilion for chatting with neighbors, watching the children play, or admiring the sunset.

There are more than 300 cottages at Seaside now, and many are for rent to visitors, so you can enjoy the beautiful quaint pastel cottages, the picket fences and porches, the towers with tin roofs, the worn sandy footpaths leading to the beach, and the gardens filled with native plants. For shorter stays, hotels and guest houses are available. Some folks come here just for a day or even for a few hours. Visitors can rent bikes, eat in charming cafés and restaurants, and shop in the downtown area's more than 50 unique stores and galleries.

For more information about Seaside, write to Seaside Information, P.O. Box 4750, Seaside, FL 32459. For cottage rentals, call 800/277-8696 or 850/231-2222.

around. Creations by 21 different contemporary and traditional artists surround you. Sometimes there's even live entertainment.

Sailor's Grill, 1451 Navarre Beach Rd., Navarre Beach, 850/939-1092, specializes in "meal baskets" that include seafood, veggies, chicken, and steak. Look for the grass huts on your right. That's it.

LODGING
The area has such a variety of accommodations that you could happily stay in a different place every night for a month and not run out of delightful options.

Choose a national chain hotel, beachfront cottage, country inn, picturesque B&B, or whatever suits you at the moment. The **Frangista Beach Inn**, 1860 Old Scenic Hwy. 98, Destin, 800/382-2612, www.frangistaresort.com, is right on the beach overlooking the blue-green Gulf water; it has spacious apartments with 1950s clay-tile floors and color-washed furnishings. The Adirondack chairs on the porch give an old-time ambiance to this comfortable family hotel. **Sugar Beach Inn Bed & Breakfast**, Scenic Route 30-A, near Seaside, 850/231-1577, is probably what you imagine a gracious southern B&B should look like. Big broad verandahs overlook Gulf waters of an incredible shade of green. Antiques and wicker furnishings are cheery. There are even four fireplaces ready for chilly evenings. A **Highlands House**, 4193 W. Scenic Route 30-A, Santa Rosa Beach, 850/267-0110, www.bbonline.com/fl/highlands, is a gorgeous antebellum B&B directly on the Gulf. Wide porches overlook the dunes and water, and every room accesses the porch. Old South décor and a heavenly full breakfast start the day off happily.

Most of Florida runs on Eastern Standard Time, but the Panhandle, west of the Apalachicola River, is on Central Standard Time—an hour earlier. Make sure you set clocks and watches an hour ahead for Daylight Savings Time.

Marriott's Bay Point Resort, 100 Delwood Beach Rd., Panama City Beach, 800/874-7105, overlooks beautiful St. Andrews Bay and is a good choice for golfers—*Golf Illustrated* gives their 36 holes four stars. Even non-golfers will appreciate the 1,100-acre wildlife sanctuary in which the hotel is located. The **Sea Witch**, 21905 Front Beach Rd., Panama City Beach, 850/234-5722 or 800/322-4571, is designed as a family hotel. Away from the more populated beaches, this West Beach location offers adults and children alike an old-fashioned kind of vacation at the seashore.

Miracle Strip Beach Motel, 11827 Front Beach Rd., Panama City Beach, 850/234-3133, is a family-owned motel close to the amusement and water parks, so you know the kids will love it here. It's right smack on the beach and there's a Gulf-side pool, too. Efficiencies are available if you want to cook in, but you're within walking distance of restaurants both economical and elegant. **Treasure Island Motel**, 5005 W. Gulf Dr., Panama City Beach, 850/234-3552, is another older family-owned motel right on the beach. It's quiet and close to St. Andrews State Park. There are nice balconies for sunset watching and, if you feel like toasting that lovely event, just walk next door to Schooner's Beach Club. **Bikini Beach Resort Motel**, 11001 Front Beach Rd., Panama

City Beach, 850/234-3392, has been a popular spot for families for years. Waterfront rooms have spectacular views and there's a big pool facing the Gulf. A full game room keeps the kids entertained, and a casual beachfront bar provides poolside refreshments. Some call **Flamingo Motel/Flamingo Towers**, 15525 Front Beach Rd., Panama City Beach, 850/234-2232, quaint. It has a bit of a Key West ambiance with bright pretty rooms—lots of them big enough for six people. Part of the motel faces beachfront; part of it is across the street. The new Flamingo Towers is a modern, all-suite hotel with heated pool and spa. **Chateau Motel**, 12525 Front Beach Rd., Panama City Beach, 850/234-2174, is centrally located on gorgeous Front Beach, with parasailing, fishing, and snorkeling literally at the doorstep. From plain motel rooms to luxury suites, they offer six different room plans.

CAMPING

Development has been slow in coming to the Emerald Coast area, so for long stretches you can find beaches and vegetation just as nature designed them. It's a wonderful coast for campers. Grayton Beach State Recreation Area, 367 Main Park Rd., Santa Rosa Beach., 850/231-4210, has showers and electrical hookups; recreational activities include picnicking, hiking, swimming, saltwater fishing, and boating. Panama City Beach Campground & RV Resort, 11826 Front Beach Rd., 850/235-1643, is a very complete and accessible spot—especially for those with physical challenges—with the usual amenities. And it's okay to bring your pets along. You can camp within sight and sound of a spectacular waterfall at Falling Waters State Recreational Area, 50 miles north of Panama City on U.S. 231 or SR 77. 850/638-6130. RVs and tents are welcome. St. Andrews State Park Recreation Area, 4415 Thomas Dr., Panama City Beach, 850/233-5140, has complete camping facilities along with a store and a nice playground. Explorers and history buffs will enjoy the reconstructed "Cracker" turpentine still that was found within the park. There are lots of fishing opportunities, too.

NIGHTLIFE

There's a pretty good assortment of nightclubs and beach clubs along the beachfront. You can find out what's going on by picking up a copy of *Showcase—Emerald Coast's Entertainment Weekly, The Insider,* or *Time Out,* inserted in the Saturday edition of *The Destin Log/The Walton Log.*

Popular with locals is Purple Rooster Wine Bar, 1096 Old Scenic Hwy. 98, Destin, 850/650-8999. Watch for special dinners offered from time to time, featuring extraordinary wine and fabulous food tastings. Club La Vella, 8813 Thomas Dr., 850/234-3866, has five theme rooms; the club claims it's the biggest nightclub in America, and maybe it is—with 51 bars and 14 dance floors. The Curve, 4103 Thomas Dr., Panama City Beach, 850/234-1055, is an adult entertainment spot with disco, show bands, country music, and more for your dancing pleasure. Sharky's, 15201 Front Beach Rd., 850/235-2420, is a casual place with live entertainment, pool, electronic darts, Karaoke, and a fun tiki bar.

3
APALACHICOLA

A-pa-la-chih-CO-la. The name seems to just roll off the tongue. It's an Indian name purported to mean "Land Beyond." In some dialects it translates as "Friendly People." Apalachicola, or "Apalach" as many locals call it, is right in the heart of Florida's "Forgotten Coast." That name came about because in the early 1990s a major tourism promotion group published a map that "forgot" the entire section of Florida between Tallahassee and Panama City. But people who have visited here never forget this special place, with its slower pace, its handsome land and seascapes, and its strong sense of community. This is a working fishing port, so don't expect a lot of glitz and glitter. In fact, don't expect any. Instead, enjoy Apalach for what it genuinely is—a sportsperson's paradise with acres of untouched river and swamp land, a deep bay for incredible deep-water fishing, and a town that is an unpretentious treasure trove of historic buildings. Neighboring 26-mile-long St. George Island is easily accessible by causeways, and is justifiably famous for its vacation homes, water-related fun, restaurants, and clubs. To find Apalachicola from the Emerald Coast area, continue along U.S. 98 and enjoy the scenery until you've arrived.

A PERFECT DAY IN APALACHICOLA

Start with breakfast at the Gibson Inn and savor your coffee as you relax in a rocking chair on the broad verandah. You'll have a good view of the town

APALACHICOLA

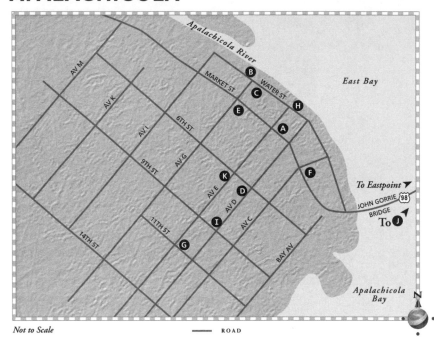

Not to Scale ——— ROAD

SIGHTS
A Apalachicola Historic District
B *Governor Stone* Gulf Coast Schooner
C Grady Market
D John Gorrie State Museum
E Market Street Emporium

FOOD
F Gibson Inn
G Magnolia Grill
H Rainbow Inn
I That Place in Apalach—The Owl Cafe

LODGING
J Best Western Apalach Inn
F Gibson Inn
K Historic 1905 Coombs House Inn

Note: Items with the same letter are located in the same area.

from here, so look around and decide which of those fascinating old buildings you'll visit today. Will you take a peek at the brick-fronted old Grady Market? It's been carefully renovated, and shelves that once stocked fish hooks and lanterns now hold upscale fashion items. Perhaps Apalachicola's most famous son was Dr. John Gorrie, a pioneer in the invention of the manufacture of ice and the development of air conditioning. Visit the John Gorrie State Museum—it has some strange and interesting things. Then head across the causeway bridge to St. George Island State Park. This is a real getaway place—you're 80 miles away from the nearest McDonald's, but if you just want to sit on the sand with a good book, this is the place to come. There are nine restaurants on the island; if you want a nice seafood lunch, check out That Place in Apalach—The Owl Cafe on Avenue D. (Save room for dessert!) Visit a few of the shops, then head back to town. For dinner, order oysters, fresh from Apalachicola Bay—maybe the best in the world. You can get grand ones at That Place on 98.

SIGHTSEEING HIGHLIGHTS

★★★★ APALACHICOLA NATIONAL FOREST
Bounded by SR 375, SR 20, and U.S. 319, 850/926-3561
Here is one of North Florida's most impressive natural areas—the forest stretches across four counties and contains pine flatwoods, hardwood hammocks, swampland, and two wilderness areas. Canada geese and a wide variety of songbirds like to spend the winter here. Animals of the forest include the rare red-cockaded woodpecker, osprey, and alligator. You may also see bald eagles, sandhill cranes, wild turkeys, and even panthers and bears. Beginning at U.S. 319 there are about 60 miles of Florida National Scenic Trail for you to explore.

Details: Forest accessible from several roads: SR 20, SR 65, SR 67, SR 267, SR 375, SR 379, and U.S. 319. Scenic trail starts on U.S. 319. For maps and more information, write to Forest Supervisor, Woodcrest Office Park, 325 John Knox Rd., Bldg. E, Tallahassee, FL 32303. (3–5 hours)

★★★ APALACHICOLA HISTORIC DISTRICT
Market St. between 17th St. and Waterfront, 850/653-9419
Although Apalachicola escaped the wrecking-ball and bulldozer mentality that engulfed Florida some years back, it had almost become a

The Red-Cockaded Woodpecker

One of the very first creatures to receive federal protection when the Endangered Species Act became law in 1973 was the red-cockaded woodpecker. This bustling little bird measures about eight inches long, and wears a neat black cap and snowy white cheek patches. Its high-pitched squeak has been compared to a baby's squeeze toy.

The practice of clear-cutting—that is, cutting every tree on a selected forest tract—along with the red-cockaded's extreme pickiness when it comes to house hunting, have landed this little guy on the endangered species list. While other birds can tap out a comfy little cavern in a couple of weeks, the red-cockaded may take as long as five years to prepare what he and his mate consider a proper roost cavity! And that's not the only problem. The tree in question must be at least 60 years old, and he really prefers that it be infected with heart rot fungus, which makes the excavation process a little less arduous.

Florida's Apalachicola National Forest holds the world's largest population of red-cockaded woodpeckers, with upwards of 700 clans (a "clan" is a communal group of two to nine birds who live within 1,500 feet of each other.) Big clans, too, nest in Blackwater River State Forest, Big Cypress National Preserve, Collier-Seminole State Park, and Withlacoochee State Forest. Even populations as large as these, though, can't be taken for granted. In 1989 when Hurricane Hugo blasted across South Carolina's Francis Marion National Forest, more than half its red-cockadeds were

ghost town, with many fine old buildings shuttered and boarded up. Yet, because of careful planning and some imaginative renovation, today's visitor can stroll among a wealth of nineteenth-century commercial structures that now house a number of shops, galleries, and antique stores.

Don't miss the **Grady Market**, 76 Water St., 850/653-4099. This beautiful old brick building was once the Grady Hardware Store, but now—lovingly restored—it houses an elegant fashion boutique, art gallery, and antiques shop. There are luxury apartments upstairs in the same building available for short-term stays (800/642-3964). The **Market Street Emporium**, 75 Market St., 850/653-9889, offers a killed outright. Hurricane Opal took a heavy toll on Florida's red-cockaded population in 1996.

How will you recognize a red-cockaded woodpecker tree when you see one? The nest's "front door" is nothing more elaborate than a round hole in the bark, but a sharp-eyed observer will notice that numerous small holes are scattered about near the cavity entrance. These are called "resin wells," and the resultant resin flow keeps predators such as rat snakes from slithering up the tree and dining on the occupants.

If you are going to look for these interesting but elusive birds, you'll need comfortable hiking boots, good binoculars, and patience. Look in open longleaf pine forests with wiregrass, but no hardwood trees or shrubs. The birds are known to be in the Apalachicola National Forest north on Highway 65 from Apalachicola town and west of State Route 20 from Tallahassee, and at Big Cypress National Preserve, where State Route 84 (Alligator Alley) and U.S. 41 (Tamiami Trail) traverse the preserve. Collier-Seminole State Park, off U.S. 41 about 17 miles south of Naples, and Withlacoochee State Forest, west of Bushnell on SR 301 and SR 48 about 40 miles south of Ocala, each have considerable populations.

Hopefully, environmentalists, industrialists, and the government will come up with ways to preserve these unique woodpeckers, which, like the spotted owl of the Pacific Northwest and the wood stork of the Florida Everglades, is considered an "indicator species" that testifies to the health of an ecosystem.

fine selection of items produced by local artists and craftspeople, as well as souvenirs, T-shirts, and collectibles.

Details: Pick up a self-guided walking tour brochure at the Apalachicola Chamber of Commerce, 57 Market St. Grady Market open Mon–Sat 10–5:30 and Sun 12:30–4. Market Street Emporium open Mon–Sat 10–8. (2 hours)

★★★ JOHN GORRIE STATE MUSEUM
Corner of Sixth St. and Ave. D, 850/653-9347

John Gorrie must have been quite the hero back in 1851. That's the year in which he was granted the first U.S. patent for mechanical refrigeration. He invented an ice-making machine that really worked. The original is at the Smithsonian, but a replica is on display here, along with displays documenting the good doctor's prototype of today's air conditioners, his significant work with victims of yellow fever, and much more.

Details: Thu–Mon 9–5. $1 adults, free 6 and under. (1 hour)

★★★ ST. GEORGE ISLAND
Off U.S. 98 at Eastpoint, 850/927-2111

This quite-accessible barrier island is a geologically fascinating place, with considerable windswept beauty. The eastern end of the island is protected from development and forms the St. George Island State Park. Gracious vacation homes, shops, restaurants, and clubs occupy the developed portion of the island. St. George Island is often the site of music festivals and other cultural and entertaining events. Call the above number for information.

Details: Turn south off U.S. 98 at Eastpoint, about six miles east of Apalachicola. (6–8 hours)

★★ *GOVERNOR STONE* GULF COAST SCHOONER
Apalachicola Maritime Museum, 268 Water St., 850/653-8700

This historic 1877 vessel sails on a regular schedule during the spring, summer, and fall. Occasional sunset or moonlight cruises are also offered.

Details: Tue–Sun, no Sun sails during winter. Call ahead for sunset and moonlight cruise times. $20 adults, $10 children. (2 hours)

★ ST. VINCENT WILDLIFE REFUGE
Offshore from the mouth of the Apalachicola River, 850/653-8808, www.fws.gov/r4eao

This refuge is managed especially for more than 270 species of wildlife. You're allowed to hike along 14 miles of beach or 80 miles of sand roads, where you may see sambar deer (a kind of elk native to Southeast Asia), white-tail deer, bald eagles, wild turkeys, and even alligators. You may also shell and fish here. This is one of several southeastern coastal islands where endangered red wolves are bred before being released into other compatible environments.

Details: Daylight use only. Carry all litter away with you—no trash receptacles on the island. No pets allowed. (3–5 hours)

FITNESS AND RECREATION

As you might guess, the main recreational draw here is fishing. You'll see people fishing everywhere. They fish along the shore, from piers and bridges, in marshes, and from boats. Canoeing is popular, or if you don't want to paddle your own, you can take a boat tour. Apalachicola Estuary Tours, Water St. at Ave. G, 850/653-2593, will carry you through the marsh, deep into the swamps, or across the bay to the barrier islands for a close-up look at plant and animal life unique to the area. The Apalachicola National Forest features the Munson Hills Off-Road Bicycle Trail, 850/926-3561, where you can choose a 7.5-mile loop or a 4.25-mile shortcut through scenic, albeit challenging, national forest lands. Walkers will enjoy taking a self-guided tour of the 2.5-mile historic district, lined with more than 200 historically and architecturally significant houses. Shelling is good on the east end of St. George Island. Jennie's Journeys will take you there by boat, 850/927-3259.

FOOD

You can't go wrong with the restaurant at the **Gibson Inn**, Market St. and Ave. C, 850/653-2191. The food—especially the seafood—is consistently good, and the Victorian surroundings are delightful. The big dark carved-wood bar is of museum quality. The **Rainbow Inn**, 123 Water St., 850/653-8139, right on the shore of the river, has good seafood along with a view of the vessels that bring it to you. The **Magnolia Grill**, 133 Ave. E., 850/653-8000, is recognized as one of Florida's finest restaurants in a little out-of-the-way cottage. The snapper Pontchartrain is to die for. A more casual dinner atmosphere (and very good chowder) is at **That Place on 98**, 500 U.S. 98 in Eastpoint, 850/670-9898.

That Place in Apalach—The Owl Cafe, 15 Ave. D, 850/653-9888, has an old-Florida fish-house ambiance and offers fresh seafood imaginatively prepared. They call it casual-elegant dining, and rightly so. Although the food presentation is elegant, the surroundings and dress are casual. The breads are homemade, and the dessert menu always has some special goodies. Look around at the photos displayed on the walls. They're local and very good.

Check out **Harry A's**, 10 Bayshore Dr., 850/927-9810, on St. George Island. It's the oldest building out there, and has a nice big porch, enclosed now, with a fine view of the bay. The rustic walls are covered with antiques and oddities, most of them gifts from customers. A new addition is the outdoor courtyard, with a stage for entertainers to use when the weather is fine. The menu is simple but good—big burgers, wings any way you like them, and other standard pub grub.

APALACHICOLA REGION

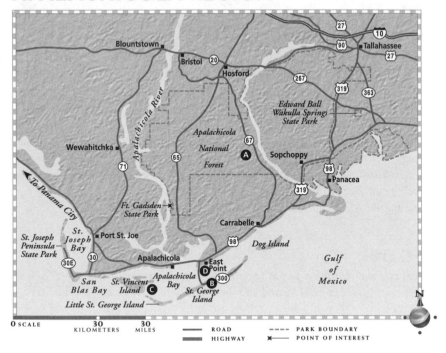

SIGHTS
- Ⓐ Apalachicola National Forest
- Ⓑ St. George Island
- Ⓒ St. Vincent Wildlife Refuge

FOOD
- Ⓑ Harry A's
- Ⓓ That Place on 98

LODGING
- Ⓑ Inn at Resort Village

Note: Items with the same letter are located in the same area.

LODGING

The Gibson Inn, Market St. and Ave. C, 850/653-2191, is a wonderfully restored turn-of-the-last-century Victorian inn. Each room is decked in furnishings and color schemes reminiscent of the Victorian era. The inn offers affordable rates with senior and military discounts. For a really elegant B&B,

the **Historic 1905 Coombs House Inn**, 80 Sixth St., 850/653-9199, www.coombshouseinn.com, is sure to impress. The Victorian mansion accommodations are plush and perhaps not as pricey as you might think. You can stay right on St. George Island at the **Inn at Resort Village**, 1488 Leisure Ln., 800/824-0416, www.fla-beach.com; it offers both beachfront and island-view rooms, some with kitchenettes.

Best Western Apalach Inn, 249 U.S. 98, 850/653-9131, is the newest and probably the most modern of the lodgings hereabout. It's a two-story, outside corridor–style building with a good fenced pool and comfortable lounge chairs. There's no restaurant, but they offer free continental breakfast.

CAMPING

Apalachicola National Forest, 850/926-3561, has 15 campgrounds within its 600,000 acres. They offer basic facilities and all but two of them are free. Silver Lake and Wright Lake require a small fee, but offer a little more in the way of creature comforts. The family campground on St. George Island, 850/927-2111, is in the center of the island, away from the beach, but a boardwalk leads to the beach.

4
TALLAHASSEE

Tallahassee is perhaps best known as Florida's seat of government. It's been the state capital since 1824. Before that, in the 1500s when Hernando de Soto first showed up on these shores, it was the capital of the Apalachee Indian nation. The name evolved in the 1700s when some Creek Indians came here and called the place Tallahassee, which translates as "old town."

Tallahassee is just 25 miles north of the Gulf of Mexico and only 14 miles south of the Georgia border. It rests between the foothills of the Appalachians and the juncture of Florida's "Big Bend." This is a surprising city. In some ways, Tallahassee feels more like it belongs in Georgia than Florida, with its canopy roads, antebellum mansions, snowy dogwood blossoms, and picturesque churches. Yet things Floridian are evident, too. The capital city is a veritable showcase of Florida's history, boasting a stunning 145 properties listed on the National Register of Historic Places. Fishing is fine, beaches are conveniently nearby, and shopping is plentiful and varied. Tallahassee is also a college town. Both Florida State University and Florida A&M University are located here.

The rich confluence of history and people makes for fine entertainment. In March keep an eye out for the Jazz and Blues Festival, featuring nonstop jazz, blues, gospel, and local singing talent. When May rolls around, Tallahassee turns into a slice of Renaissance England with the Southern Shakespeare Festival (850/671-0742), and fair goers are treated to games, mime performances, food, and Shakespeare in the Park. There's so much to see and do here, you can keep busy every minute if you want to. But, if keeping busy isn't what you have in mind, this can be a fine place to relax, too.

A PERFECT DAY IN TALLAHASSEE

Get started early on Apalachee Parkway with a tasty breakfast at The Mill, where the coffee is freshly ground and the bread is homemade. Now head west, toward the center of town. Notice the Union Bank Building at 295 Apalachee—it's the oldest bank building in Florida. Go to the new capitol building and take the elevator up to the 22nd floor for an amazing panoramic view of the whole city. If there's a legislative session going on in the building, you're free to walk right in and listen. Maybe you'll want to grab a burger at Andrew's Capital Bar & Grill. Then it's off to Governor's Square to check out the wares of the area's biggest selection of specialty shops and high-tone push-cart vendors. Next, a relaxing drive down some of the area's famous canopy roads where towering, centuries-old trees form green tunnels. At night listen to blues and sample some great southern barbecue at Dave's CC Club.

ORIENTATION

Tallahassee Regional Airport serves the area with national and regional airlines. If you're driving up from Apalachicola on U.S. 98, you have two options for reaching Tallahassee. Before Carabelle Beach, U.S. 98 also becomes U.S. 319. Past Lanark Village, you can either follow U.S. 319 north toward Tallahassee, going past the Ochlockonee River State Park, or continue on U.S. 98 along the coast through Panacea (about 38 miles south of Tallahassee), and then merge onto U.S. 319 at Medart. Or you can continue east on U.S. 98, and take State Route 61 north, which is Monroe Street, right to the center of the city. The downtown area is pretty compact. The Apalachee Parkway (U.S. 27) takes you right up to the front of the old Capitol Building. I-10 runs north of the city. U.S. 90 (Tennessee Street) passes Florida State University.

SIGHTSEEING HIGHLIGHTS

★★★★ **FLORIDA STATE CAPITOL BUILDING**
400 S. Monroe St., 850/413-9200
This is an imposing 22-story tower, one of only five "tower capitols" in America. There's an excellent Florida information center here, but visit it on your way out. You don't want to carry all those brochures

TALLAHASSEE

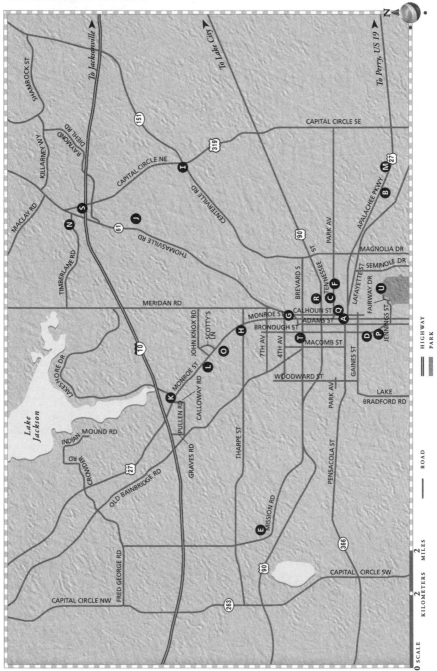

around with you! Now head for the elevators and go all the way up to the 22nd floor. The house and senate chambers are both up there and each has public viewing areas for the benefit of those who like to keep track of what the legislators are up to. Go to the observation deck and take a look around. Be prepared for a jaw-dropping view of this city of gently rolling hills, canopy roads, and the Gulf of Mexico sparkling in the distance. **Details:** *Mon–Fri 8–5, Sat–Sun 9–3. Free. (1 hour)*

The Sunshine Law of Florida requires that all government meetings are open to the public. Be sure to take advantage of this right when legislature is in session.

★★★★ **MACLAY STATE GARDENS**
3540 Thomasville Rd., 850/487-3711
Back in the '20s this used to be the home of wealthy businessman Alfred B. Maclay. The 308-acre park features the most astonishing gardens—more than 200 kinds of flowering plants are here. Huge pine trees and oaks tower over flowering dogwoods and redbuds. There are about 150 different varieties of camellias here and dozens of kinds of azaleas. Lots of native Florida plants add balance to the arrangement. Take a stroll along the nature trails you can follow,

SIGHTS
- Ⓐ Florida State Capitol Building
- Ⓑ Governor's Square
- Ⓒ Knott House Museum
- Ⓓ Museum of Florida History
- Ⓐ Old Capitol Museum
- Ⓔ San Luis Archaeological Site
- Ⓕ Union Bank Building

FOOD
- Ⓖ Andrew's Capital Bar & Grill
- Ⓗ Barnacle Bill's
- Ⓘ The Buckhead Brewery & Grill
- Ⓓ Chef's Table
- Ⓙ Chez Pierre
- Ⓚ Julie's Place
- Ⓛ The Melting Pot
- Ⓜ The Mill
- Ⓝ The Mustard Tree
- Ⓞ Silver Slipper
- Ⓟ Sloppy Joe's
- Ⓠ Sparta Club & Grill

LODGING
- Ⓚ Cabot Lodge
- Ⓡ Calhoun Street Inn
- Ⓖ Doubletree Hotel
- Ⓖ Governor's Inn
- Ⓢ Hilton Garden Inn
- Ⓚ Ramada Inn Tallahassee
- Ⓣ Ramada Limited
- Ⓤ The Riedel House

Note: Items with the same letter are located in the same area.

TALLAHASSEE'S CANOPY ROADS

Certain Tallahassee roads have been designated canopy roads, and the reason is clear once you drive or stroll down them—because they're arched by towering, century-old oaks draped with lacy Spanish moss. The early settlers planted these roadways with live oaks, and today they offer a glimpse into how it might have looked here back when settlers traveled on dirt roads heading for their new Florida homesteads. There are 60 miles of these roadways, named among "America's Ten Most Scenic Byways" by *Scenic America.* The effect is dramatic, especially on a sunny day when the diffused light through the branches gives off an emeraldlike glow.

Be sure to take a drive on one or more of these special roads while you're here. The designated roads are Miccosukee, Old St. Augustine, Meridian, and Magnolia. For a good map and more information, call the Tallahassee Area Convention and Business Bureau, 850/413-9200, and ask for the brochure "Canopy Roads and County Lanes," or visit www.co.leon.fl.us/visitors/index.htm.

where you're likely to see and hear some of the many birds and animals that share this tranquil and beautiful place. The Maclay house, which you can visit, is still furnished as it was in the 1920s. If you want to spend more time here than it takes for just the sightseeing tour—and well you might—there are facilities for swimming, boating, and fishing. You may decide to make a day of it.

Details: *Daily 8 a.m.–sunset. $3.25 per vehicle with up to eight people. Jan–Apr additional garden fee $3 adults, $1.50 children. (1–2 hours)*

★★★★ **OLD CAPITOL MUSEUM**
5 S. Monroe St., 850/487-1902
This museum is just across from the new capitol. This is a real architectural gem, restored between 1978 and 1982 to its 1902 appearance. It was, in fact, one of the most meticulous capitol restoration projects in the nation. They've even replaced the red and white–striped awnings, which early legislators deemed necessary to

shade offices from the intense Florida sun. There's a wonderful curving staircase and a remarkable stained-glass dome. Look closely above the columned porticos at the entrances. There are pressed-metal reliefs that incorporate details from the Florida state seal. They're painted the same color as the rest of the building because, although the governor wanted them to be in color, the architect insisted that the building was a "plain subject." He thought the architectural effect of the building would be lost if the reliefs were more colorful.

Details: Mon–Fri 9–4:30, Sat 10–4:30, Sun & holidays noon–4:30. Free. (1 hour)

★★★ MUSEUM OF FLORIDA HISTORY
500 S. Bronough St., 850/488-1484
Here is a precious time tunnel to Florida's past. Did you know that mastodons once lived in Florida? At the museum you'll meet a nine-foot-tall skeleton of one that was pulled from nearby Wakulla Springs. (The local kids call him Herman.) Discover a trove of real Spanish treasure, and climb right aboard a steamboat just like the ones that navigated Florida's rivers long ago. Inside the museum you can get an up-close peek at one of the Tin Can Tourist Camps (the great-granddaddy of today's RV parks), a reconstructed riverboat, and a display of a citrus packing house from the 1920s.

Details: Mon–Fri 9–4:30, Sat 10–4:30. Free. (1 hour)

★★★ SAN LUIS ARCHAEOLOGICAL SITE
2020 Mission Rd., 850/487-3711
If archaeological digs fascinate you, check out this ongoing excavation/exhibit at the original site of a Spanish mission and an Apalachee Indian village. From 1656 to 1704 Spanish Franciscans ministered to the local Christian Indian population at this site. The investigation of those long-ago people and their lives is the focus of this active archaeological site. Living history demonstrations and interpretive displays help to bring the subject to life.

Details: Mon–Fri 8–4:30, Sat 10–4:30, Sun noon–4:30. Free. (1–2 hours)

★★ GOVERNOR'S SQUARE
1500 Apalachee Pkwy., 850/671-INFO,
www.governorssquare.com

This is the area's biggest shopping center, featuring plenty of specialty shops, upscale pushcart vendors, full-service restaurants, and a 500-seat food court. Browse Abercrombie & Fitch, Eddie Bauer, The Gap, Wet Seal, Victoria's Secret, and many more shops. Major stores—Dillard's, Burdines, J.C. Penney, and Sears—anchor the mall.

Details: Located one mile east of the capitol on Apalachee Pkwy. Open Mon–Sat 10–9; Sun 12:30–5:30. (2 hours)

★★ KNOTT HOUSE MUSEUM
301 East Park Ave., 850/922-2459

This is a lovely antebellum mansion home, chock-full of Victorian antiques. It's been carefully restored to 1928 condition, so it looks as it did when politician William Knott and his family lived here. Knott's wife, Luella, was moved to write bits of poetry about the various furnishings in the home, and tied the quirky little odes to each piece for the enjoyment of guests. They're still there for you to read.

Details: Wed–Fri 1–4, Sat 10–4. $7 family, $3 adults, $1.50 children. (1 hour)

★★ UNION BANK BUILDING
295 Apalachee Pkwy., 850/487-3803

This imposing structure is the oldest bank building in Florida. First opened in 1833, the bank closed in 1843. From there, the building served as a ballet school and a bakery, among other businesses, undergoing various refurbishings—some of them unfortunate. Happily it's been restored to its original appearance, and now it houses the Black Archives Extension from Florida A&M University.

Details: Open Mon–Fri 8:30–4:30. Free. (30 minutes)

★ BRADLEY'S 1927 COUNTRY STORE
Centerville Rd., 850/893-1647

You don't find many stores listed on the National Register of Historic Places, but this one is. It's a real, working store—not a museum. The Bradley family has been operating the place, which still looks about the same way it did when their great-grandparents opened it in 1927. It's located on one of those famed canopy roads; they sell groceries, canned goods, and the like, along with hardware and hats. There's fresh produce, private-label jams and jellies, homemade grits, and homemade cane syrup, Tupelo honey, and hot sauces. The Bradleys are mostly famous, though, for their sausage links. (They sell a whopping 70,000 pounds of it every year!) The family uses the same recipe their great grandmother Mary Bradley used in 1910.

Details: Located near the intersection of Mocassin Gap Rd. on Centerville Rd. Open Mon–Fri 9–6, Sat 9–5. (1 hour)

★ **TALLAHASSEE ANTIQUE CAR MUSEUM**
3550A Mahan Dr., 850/942-0137, www.tacm.com
See some really rare wheels here, including some award-winning Chevys, a 1956 T-bird, a DeLorean, and a 1931 Dusenberg, along with some famous movie and TV cars. Check out the 20-foot-long "Batmobile" from the movie *Batman Returns*. They even have Abraham Lincoln's horse-drawn funeral hearse.

Details: Mon–Sat, Sun noon–5. $7.50 adults, $4 children. (1 hour)

FITNESS AND RECREATION

Tallahassee has plenty of places to play. Charter a boat, play a few holes of golf, rent a bike or in-line skates, play tennis, hop aboard a horse, wet a line, or go swimming. At Edward Ball Wakulla Springs State Park and Lodge, 550 Wakulla Park Dr., Wakulla Springs, 850/922-3633, you'll see plenty of 'gators

Wakulla Springs State Park

WAKULLA SPRINGS

from the glass-bottom–boat tours—or in the parking lot, for that matter. It's a great place for bird-watchers and there are swimming areas, too. A number of local lakes are famous for record-breaking and trophy-sized catches. Lake Talquin, Cook's Landing Rd., 850/875-2605, just west of the city, yielded the state-record black crappie a few years back. At Lake Seminole, 45 miles northwest of the city on SR 271 at Three Rivers State Recreation Area, 850/482-9006, there's a 100-foot fishing pier arranged so that even landlubbers can reel in the big ones. Hikers, bikers, strollers, and skaters will enjoy St. Mark's Historic Railroad Trail, U.S. 319 and SR 363, 850/922-6007, where pavement now covers a 16-mile trail laid over a historic railroad bed. There are lighted tennis courts at Myers Park, Myers Park Dr., 850/891-3866, along with a covered pool, weight room, and showers. Hilaman Park, 2737 Blairstone Rd., 850/891-3935, offers 18 holes of golf, a putting green, driving range, clubhouse, and restaurant. At Cross Creek, 6701 Mahan Dr., 850/656-GOLF, try the nine-hole, par-3 lighted course, the three-tiered driving range, and putting area. For family fun, take the gang to Fun Station Inc., 2821 Sharer Rd., 850/383-0788. Play 36 holes of miniature golf, ride the bumper boats, play laser-tag, and test your skills in batting cages and at arcade games. Top it all off with pizza, of course. For more outdoor fun, visit the 678-acre Phipps Park, N. Meridian Rd., 850/891-3866, for its horse and bike trails.

FOOD

With the Gulf only 25 miles away, Tallahassee has easy access to the freshest seafood. A number of downtown restaurants specialize in Apalachicola oysters. Nearby Panacea—"blue crab capital of the world"—supplies plenty of that tasty commodity. Vidalia onions grow near here, and so do Quincy mushrooms and Jefferson County watermelons.

The Mill, 2329 Apalachee Pkwy., 850/656-2867, is a favorite Tallahassee spot. Locals and visitors line up here every day to feast on yummy breakfasts featuring freshly baked breads and muffins, luncheon specials of hefty sandwiches and imaginative salads, and dinner entrées of steak, seafood, and pizza. There's outdoor seating for fine weather and indoor décor is country-bright. Beer lovers say that the hand-crafted beer is special. **Nicholson's Farmhouse Restaurant**, on SR 12 about 3 1/2 miles northwest of Havana (Ha-VAY-na), 850/539-5931, is a favorite with both locals and visitors. In a 1820 farmhouse approximately seven miles north of Tallahassee, the fourth-generation Nicholsons specialize in old-fashioned Southern cooking. Their hand-cut juicy steaks come from their own cattle and the freshly baked bread is prepared in the family kitchen. Enjoy boiled peanuts served as appetizers.

Silver Slipper, 531 Scotty's Ln., 850/386-9366, is where you're apt to spot Florida legislators and famous guests. Look! Is that the Governor over there? This is a special-occasion kind of place, famous for steak, seafood, and some awesome Greek specialties. At **Posey's**, on U.S. 98 in the village of Panacea, 850/984-5799, enjoy local seafood in cozy surroundings. Mullet is a specialty, along with frog's legs, oysters, and fresh Gulf fish. For a quick lunch or breakfast, you can join the downtown crowd at **Chef's Table**, 500 S. Borough St. (the R. A. Gray Bldg.), 850/224-7441, for soups, salads, sandwiches, and hot homemade goodies that change daily. If you're there at noon on Tuesday or Wednesday, you get live entertainment.

You wouldn't expect a Golden Spoon Award–winning restaurant to be tucked in the basement of a nondescript downtown building, but that's where you'll find **Andrew's Capital Bar & Grill**, 228 S. Adams St., 850/222-3444. Andrew's is *the* downtown sports and political gathering place for the Capital City crowd. There are 17 TVs to keep the sports lovers happy, and outdoor seating for people-watchers. Open Monday through Saturday for lunch and dinner. Brunch is on Sunday only. **Sloppy Joe's**, 301 S. Bronough St. at Kleman Plaza, 850/222-7575, is modeled after its Key West counterpart, with a breezy relaxed atmosphere, Tropical Keys décor, and friendly wait staff. Try sloppy joe sandwiches and other casual island fare.

Waiters and waitresses usually get 15 to 20 percent, depending on the quality of the service. Generally tips aren't necessary in cafeterias unless your tray is carried to your table. Some places automatically add a gratuity to your restaurant bill, so check to see if they have before you figure the tip.

Julie's Place, 2905 N. Monroe St., 850/386-7181, is popular with the people who live here and with visitors, too. It's filled with lots of greenery, etched glass, and antiques. The onion soup alone is worth the trip, and the prime rib is arguably the best in town. **The Melting Pot**, 2727 N. Monroe St., 850/386-7440, is an intimate sort of place, kind of romantic actually, where they prepare your Swiss fondue tableside. Dunk in filet mignon, teriyaki sirloin, chicken, seafood, veggies, whatever. There's even chocolate fondue for dessert. The **Sparta Club & Grill**, 220 S. Monroe St., 850/224-9711, is a long-time favorite with Tallahasseans. They specialize in Greek-accented seafood dishes, along with traditional Greek fare like souvlaki and *pastitsio*.

The Buckhead Brewery & Grill, 1900 Capital Circle NE, 850/942-4947, doesn't look like a Florida restaurant at all. It more resembles a lodge in

TALLAHASSEE REGION

N

Georgia
Florida

Ashville ■

221

90   10

27

Greenville ■

221

Perry ■

19

Sirmans ■

27   19

98

Monticello ■

19

90

19

Wacissa ■

Miccosukee ■

Lloyd ■

Nutal Rise ■

St. Marks National Wildlife Refuge

142

A

151

Bradfordville ■

10   27

59

Edward Ball Wakulla Springs State Park

98

Gulf of Mexico

C

D   E

319   Tallahassee

319

Wakulla ■

267

319

H

B

Lake Jackson

363

12

319

263   319

I

Wakulla Springs

Medart ■

Havana ■

12

27

F

20

267

Crawfordville ■

319

Panacea ■   G

Quincy ■

12

Jackson Bluff ■

Sanborn ■

10

375

90

0 SCALE   25 MILES   25 KILOMETERS

POINT OF INTEREST   ★

STATE BOUNDARY   ■■■

HIGHWAY

ROAD

the mountains, replete with dark wood and stag horns. Wild game is on the menu as well as in the décor, and handcrafted beer complements steaks and seafood. You can go on a tour of the microbrewery if you like. **The Mustard Tree**, 1415 Timberlane Rd., Market Square, 850/893-8733, has a nice casual feeling to it, even though the food presentation is quite sophisticated. There's quite an impressive wine list, and they do interesting things with seafood. You can dine outside when the weather is fine. **Barnacle Bill's**, 1830 N. Monroe St., 850/385-8734, claims to have the best fried shrimp in town, and judging by the number of locals who order it, they may be right. And Barnacle Bill's serves the best smoked seafood dip in the whole state according to *Florida Trend Magazine*. Sports followers like the big screen and satellite TVs positioned amid the crab traps and pilings, and everybody likes the seafood pastas.

Chez Pierre, 1215 Thomasville Rd., in Historic Lafayette Park, 850/222-0936, has the ambiance of a "great house" with the charm of a French café. Roast duck, *tournedos*, quiche, homemade soups, and chicken crepes are served with style by the knowledgeable wait staff. But save room for the gorgeous pastries. The restaurant offers patio dining, if you like. **Lucy Ho's**, 2814 Apalachee Pkwy., 850/878-3366, and 1700 Halstead Blvd., 850/893-4112, offers both Chinese and Japanese cuisine, but on separate menus. There's a hibachi steak and tatami room and a Japanese cuisine and sushi bar. **Marie Livingston's Texas Steak Restaurant and Saloon**, 3212 Apalachee Pkwy., 850/877-2986, features Midwestern corn-fed beef in a Texas-saloon atmosphere. They have chicken and fish, too, but the claim to fame here is definitely the hand-cut steaks.

LODGING
Florida's capital city offers a pretty wide spectrum of accommodations. There are restored historic B&Bs, country club golf course suites, beachside cottages, and familiar chain and corporate hotels. An interesting historic B&B in a convenient downtown location is the **Calhoun Street Inn**, 525 N. Calhoun St.,

SIGHTS
Ⓐ Bradley's 1927 Country Store
Ⓑ Maclay State Gardens
Ⓒ Tallahassee Antique Car Museum

FOOD
Ⓓ Lucy Ho's
Ⓔ Marie Livingston's Texas Steak Restaurant and Saloon
Ⓕ Nicholson's Farmhouse Restaurant
Ⓖ Posey's

LODGING
Ⓗ The Inn at Killearn Country Club
Ⓘ Wakulla Springs Lodge

850/425-5095. Enjoy a full breakfast amid antique furnishings and cozy ambiance. The **Ramada Inn Tallahassee**, 2900 N. Monroe St., 850/386-1027, puts you just minutes from the downtown attractions. Check out the interesting collectibles displayed in the lobby. **Cabot Lodge**, 2735 N. Monroe St., 850/386-8880, isn't far from the downtown area, yet it's surrounded by lovely woods where you can enjoy a jogging trail. Inside, guests relax in the living room/library of this large, attractive B&B. There are 160 guest rooms. Everybody enjoys the generous continental breakfast and the evening cocktail, too. **The Riedel House**, 1412 Fairway Dr., 850/222-8569, is an older B&B in a white brick, federal-style home built in 1937. You'll spend the night in a pretty bedroom, and in the morning you'll enjoy fresh fruit and homemade muffins with your coffee in the elegant dining room. **Doubletree Hotel**, 101 S. Adams St., 850/224-5000, is within walking distance of the state capitol and all the other major downtown attractions. It has recently renovated guest rooms and, of course, those fresh-baked Doubletree chocolate chip cookies. From the moment you walk in through beveled glass–paned doors of the **Governor's Inn**, 209 S. Adams St., 850/681-6855, you know you are entering a very special place. There are only 41 rooms and suites, so book early. Created from the remains of an old livery stable on a brick-lined street, the inn belies its humble beginnings with sumptuous suites, fluffy bathrobes, whirlpool baths, and the like.

Ramada Limited, 1308 W. Brevard St., 850/224-7116, overlooks the Florida State University campus. The rooms are neat and clean, and you're only a mile from the capitol. There's a complimentary breakfast and a bar on the premises. One of the newer hotels, **Hilton Garden Inn**, 3333 Thomasville Rd., 850/385-3553, is a Hilton "value-priced" venue. Business travelers like the guest rooms with two-line phones, data ports, big desks, and ergonomic chairs. Everybody likes the pool and the fitness room. **The Inn at Killearn Country Club**, 100 Tyrone Cr., 850/893-2186, is located at one of the city's leading golf courses, but even non-golfers enjoy this contemporary resort in a woodsy setting. No cookie-cutter rooms here. Each one is uniquely decorated and some have original paintings, plush furnishings, and wide balconies. There's an Olympic-sized pool, an excellent restaurant, tennis courts—and, of course, 27 holes of golf.

Wakulla Springs Lodge, 550 Wakulla Park Dr., Wakulla Springs (15 miles south of Tallahassee on SR 267), 850/224-5950, has some lovely and unusual accommodations. Founder Edward Ball built this 27-room lodge in 1937, using hand-wrought iron, marble, and handmade imported tile. There's a lobby with a fireplace, marble floors, and cypress-beamed ceiling, and a full-service restaurant, too.

THE LEGENDARY WAKULLA SPRINGS

Wakulla Springs—home to one of the world's deepest freshwater springs—is the stuff from which folklore is made. When Ponce de León visited these parts in 1513, he thought he'd finally found the Fountain of Youth. And the old Tarzan films were shot on location at Edward Ball Wakulla Springs State Park and Lodge.

CAMPING

Tallahassee is famous for its tall, spreading oak trees, and most campgrounds have some of them to provide cooling shade and privacy. One campground is even named for its trees. Big Oak RV Park, 4024 N. Monroe St., 850/562-4660, is close to a grocery store and restaurant, but doesn't have any tent sites or cabins to rent. Those who like to fish upon rising may want to check out Red & Sam's Fish Camp on Lake Jackson, 5563 N. Monroe St., 850/562-3083, www.cpddlab.fsu.edu/rednsams. The camp has RV and tent sites as well as cabins. You can also rent a boat or canoe, buy bait and tackle, and hire a fishing guide from here.

NIGHTLIFE

Dooley's Down Under, 2900 N. Monroe St., 850/386-1027, is a nightclub with an Australian theme. It's downstairs at the Ramada Inn Tallahassee. The décor is Aussie casual with boomerangs and such sprinkled amid the neon. Entertainment is bluesy-jazz, and innovative comedy acts sometimes take the stage on weekends. Satisfying pub grub stars on the limited but good menu. Dave's C.C. Club, Sam's Lane off Bradfordville Road, 850/894-0181, is a mecca for blues aficionados, and some folks travel for miles to be on hand when some notable blues performers play this well-known room. (Some of the best blues artists in the world show up here on Friday and Saturday nights.) The Moon, 1105 E. Lafayette St., 850/878-6900, is a glitzy, multilevel club replete with laser lights and state-of-the-art sound equipment, with a high-energy D.J. presiding over it all. Wednesday, Friday, and Saturday night happenings, along with occasional special events and concerts, keep the Moon rocking year-round.

Scenic Route: The Native Trail

You've heard about the wonderful canopy roads of Tallahassee and now you're going to experience some of them. At the same time, you'll learn something about the Native Americans who roamed these hills long, long ago. For a good background in where you're going, start at the Museum of Florida History in the R. A. Gray Building at 500 S. Bronough Street. Spend some time among the giant mastodon bones, arrowheads, and native pottery. See the dugout canoes and the Spanish doubloons, and come away with a better understanding of the ghosts you may meet today along the Native Trail.

Head east from the Museum to Duval Street and turn left onto Duval. Take another left at the light on Tharpe Street. Go eight miles, and then turn right on old Bainbridge Road. This lovely road is one of the five in Leon County that have been designated as official canopy roads. All of the massive live oak trees you see on either side are protected by law, which prohibits any new development within 100 feet of them.

When you get to Fred George Road, turn right. (It becomes Crowder Road after a while.) Turn right onto Indian Mound Drive. You're going to visit the Lake Jackson

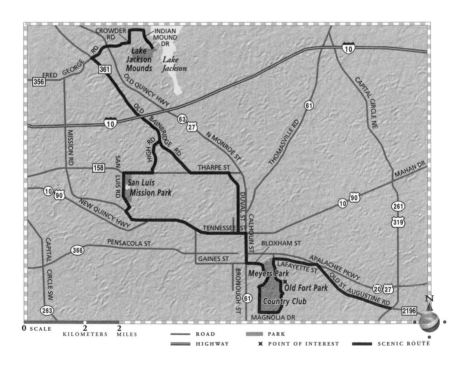

Mounds. These mounds mark a major ceremonial center for this region's Apalachee Indians who lived here back in the 1500s. Once there were six temple mounds here, as well as a large village with a spacious plaza. Temples and houses of priests and rulers were built atop the mounds. Small farms surrounded the village. Imagine what it was like here, all those centuries ago.

Now retrace your route via Crowder Road and turn left onto Old Bainbridge. Turn right on High Road and then right at Tharpe Street. After about five miles, turn left on San Luis Road. At the end of the road, turn left on Mission Road. You're going forward in time now to Mission San Luis de Apalachee. This is the spot the Spaniards chose for their mission capital when, in the 1630s, they came here to convert the Apalachee natives to Christianity. You'll explore the remains of this old mission and the surrounding village where archaeologists continue to unearth exciting clues about life here in the 17th century.

Turn left coming out of the parking lot and, at Ocala Road, turn right. Turn left on Tennessee Street, then right on Calhoun Street. Go left on Bloxham Street. You're going to Cascades Park, where in pre-Columbian times Native Americans lived beside a dramatic waterfall. By the 1900s the cascade was blocked off to make way for industrial development. In this park you'll find the Prime Meridian Marker. From this spot all Florida land surveys are calculated. Continue on Bloxham and turn right on Gaines Street. This is Myers Park, where they've located part of Anhaica. This was the capital village of the Apalachee Province before the Europeans arrived. As many as 30,000 Indians once lived here. Can you picture it?

Turn right on Golf Terrace, left on Magnolia Drive, then left on Country Club Drive, going around the golf course. This is such a lush beautiful place to live, it's no wonder the Indians—and later the Spanish—chose to build their homes here. When you get to the stop sign, turn right on Santa Rosa Drive. You've moved ahead in time to the Civil War, and here, at Old Fort Park, you'll see the remains of the fortifications that Tallahasseans built to protect the city from Union attack. (The closest Union troops ever came to Tallahassee, though, was Natural Bridge in southern Leon County, about 10 miles southeast.)

Return, going straight on Santa Rosa Drive, then right on Myers Park Drive. Turn right on Lafayette Street, and then right onto De Soto Park Drive. In the 1980s archaeologists made a remarkable discovery on this hilltop. They found olive jar fragments, coins, chain mail, and some other artifacts. They were from the 1539–40 winter encampment of Hernando de Soto and his soldiers. (Every holiday season volunteers reenact America's first Christmas Mass here, which was celebrated on this site in 1539.)

Turn right on Lafayette Street; it turns into Old St. Augustine Road. This is another designated canopy road. It's not only very beautiful but historically important as well. This same road dates back to at least the 1600s when it linked the Spanish missions of Leon County to St. Augustine. Back then they called it the Royal Road. The road later served as the foundation for Florida's very first American road, the Pensacola–St. Augustine Highway. Prosperous cotton plantations lined both sides.

Today travelers enjoy the beauty of these lovely canopy roads, remembering as they move along in the dappled shade of those massive live oaks, how many others have been here before them.

5
CEDAR KEY

The village of Cedar Key is actually perched on a couple of keys—little islands dotting the Gulf shore—about three miles out in the Gulf of Mexico. In its early days Cedar Key was important as the southern terminus for the first cross-Florida railroad. That opened up an immense lumber and turpentine industry. Cedar Key enjoyed a timber boom, and cedar from this area was considered the world's finest for the manufacture of pencils. Fishermen have always kept the docks here busy, and they still do today, providing fresh fish to the hotels and restaurants of the area. Cedar Key oysters still are sought for their distinctive flavor, and mullet, blue crab, and stone crab are all welcome catches.

In recent years Cedar Key has gained something of a reputation as an art colony. Though art galleries and shops have replaced fish-packing plants and timber mills, the town still has the look of yesterday. The houses have wooden clapboards, porches, gables, and tin roofs. Seabirds perch on columned wharves. Your camera will love this place, and, chances are, so will you.

Cedar Key is a small place with fewer than 700 year-round inhabitants. It's been a close-knit community for so many years that you may notice a general disregard for address numbers. Seems that everybody has known where everything was for so long, no one ever got around to consistently using a numbering system. So if some of the addresses seem a bit vague, don't worry. The streets aren't very long and you'll find your way around just fine.

CEDAR KEY

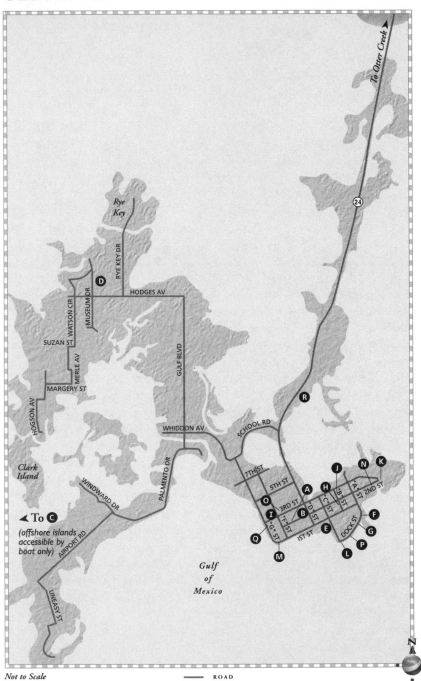

To Otter Creek

Rye Key

RYE KEY DR

D

HODGES AV

WATSON CIR

MUSEUM DR

SUZAN ST

MERLE AV

GULF BLVD

MARGERY ST

HOGSON AV

R

WHIDDON AV

SCHOOL RD

Clark
Island

WINDWARD DR

PALMENTO DR

7TH ST

5TH ST

J **N** **K**

◀ To **C**

(offshore islands
accessible by
boat only)

AIRPORT RD

O

3RD ST

A **H**

B ST

A ST

2ND ST

I

C ST

B

D ST

F

F ST

DOCK ST

Q

G ST

E

G

1ST ST

P

M

L

UNEASY ST

*Gulf
of
Mexico*

Not to Scale

━━━ ROAD

N

To get to Cedar key from Tallahassee, take U.S. 19 south and head west on SR 24 for about 20 miles. You'll come to a picturesque series of small bridges that lead across a series of keys to your destination.

A PERFECT DAY ON CEDAR KEY

Have breakfast at Cook's Cafe, and just before you polish off your homemade waffles, perhaps you'll want to toss a crumb to the neighborhood egret that seems to have declared the patio here his personal territory. Then walk across the street and rent a bike from the bait store at Salty's Plaza. You're going to do some exploring. Start with a leisurely ride down Second Street, and perhaps a stop at Cedar Key Bookstore to pick up a copy of *The Naturalist's Guide to Cedar Key*, written and self-published by local writer Harriet Smith. It's small enough to tuck into a pocket and will help you identify some of the birds and animals you may encounter. Now head west toward the shore and follow the coast north toward the Cedar Key State Museum. When you get there, park the bike and stroll through the grounds, enjoying the cool and quiet as you identify the various species of Florida plants and trees. The museum itself houses what may be the most beautiful collection of shells ever assembled. Then go back to town and check out all those tempting shops on the dock. If there's time, take an afternoon cruise aboard the *Island Hopper Queen*. It's been a busy day, so you'll really enjoy your seafood dinner at The Captain's Table. After dinner, change back into your jeans and head over to the L&M Lounge where you'll join the local folks and maybe dance a little to that good old rock 'n' roll music!

SIGHTS
ⓐ Cedar Key Bookstore
ⓑ Cedar Key Historical Society Museum
ⓒ Cedar Key National Wildlife Refuge
ⓓ Cedar Key State Museum
ⓔ Dock Street Shops and Galleries

FOOD
ⓕ The Brown Pelican
ⓖ The Captain's Table
ⓗ Cook's Cafe
ⓘ Crabby's
ⓐ The Heron
ⓙ The Island Hotel Restaurant
ⓚ The Island Room at Cedar Cove
ⓛ Seabreeze on the Dock

LODGING
ⓜ Beachfront Hotel
ⓝ Cedar Cove Beach & Yacht Club
ⓞ Cedar Key Bed & Breakfast
ⓟ Dockside Motel
ⓠ Faraway Inn
ⓙ The Island Hotel
ⓡ Mermaid's Landing Cottages

Note: Items with the same letter are located in the same area.

SIGHTSEEING HIGHLIGHTS

★★★★ **CEDAR KEY HISTORICAL SOCIETY MUSEUM**
SR 24 and Second St., 352/543-5350
This museum is a little like Cedar Key itself—a quirky collection of things from the past. There are Indian relics here and some antique furniture, a rock collection, lots of photos, and old newspaper clippings—bits and pieces of old Florida all displayed in an interesting late 1800s house. It's a little like being in a really great attic of some wonderful old family home, one where no one for generations ever threw anything away. Here's a place to learn about not only the architectural history of Cedar Key but also about the social history of generations of islanders.
Details: Mon–Fri 11–4, Sat 1–4. $1 adults, 50 cents children. (1 hour)

★★★★ **CEDAR KEY NATIONAL WILDLIFE REFUGE**
Offshore islands, access by boat from Cedar Key, 352/493-0238
This historic refuge comprises 12 offshore islands located in the Gulf within five miles of the town of Cedar Key. The islands range in size from 1 to 165 acres. This sanctuary was established in 1929 when President Hoover set aside three keys as refuge and breeding grounds for colonial birds. Four of the islands—Snake, Bird, North, and Seahorse Keys—are now officially designated as Wilderness Areas. The interior of all of the islands is closed to the public in order to protect the plants and creatures, but the beaches are open for shell collecting, bird watching, and photography during daylight hours. You can rent a boat or join a scheduled cruise from the City Marina at Cedar Key.
Details: There's no admission charge to visit the islands. For boat rental prices and cruise schedules, call the City Marina 352/543-5904. (3–4 hours)

★★★★ **CEDAR KEY STATE MUSEUM**
1710 Museum Dr., 352/543-5350
If you've become fascinated by the color and variety of Florida's seashells, don't miss this museum. Here you'll find what is arguably the finest shell collection ever assembled. It belonged to longtime resident St. Clair Whitman, to whom the museum is dedicated. Some

MANGROVES—FLORIDA'S WALKING TREES

"No one likes the mangroves," John Steinbeck once wrote. And in Florida until fairly recently, he was probably right. You can understand that sentiment when you first view mangroves propped up in often-smelly mud by their tangled reddish roots. These strange, aerial roots look like spiders' legs, and to some folks it looks as if they trees are about to walk off on these leglike roots—hence the nickname "walking trees."

Over the past few years, the red mangroves have made lots of friends. It's been amply demonstrated that the much-maligned tree is, in fact, the basis of a most remarkable food chain, one that supports much of coastal Florida's unique and wonderful animal, marine, and bird life.

Mangrove trees drop leaves into the water daily—a lot of them. An acre of trees, on the average, deposits three tons of leaves per year. The leaves quickly decompose and are eaten by myriad tiny crabs, worms, and other small aquatic creatures. In turn, these critters become food for larger fish and birds.

Florida's mangroves are tropical species, so they're sensitive to cold. You'll come across them on the Gulf Coast as far north as Cedar Key. State law says that mangroves cannot be removed, pruned, or disturbed without a special permit. These trees are truly part of the state heritage and one of its most valuable—albeit ungainly—coastal resources.

wonderful old photographs record Civil War activity in Cedar Key in 1862. A bronze plaque on the museum's beautifully landscaped 19 acres pays tribute to conservationist John Muir and his "Thousand-Mile Walk to the Gulf," which ended in Cedar Key in 1867. "Today I reached the sea and many gems of tiny islets called keys," Muir wrote in his journal upon his arrival here. There are Indian artifacts here as well, and some fascinating bits of folklore carefully preserved along with artifacts relating to the area's natural history.

Details: *Open Thu–Mon 9–5, closed Tue and Wed. $1 admission. (1 hour)*

★★★ CEDAR KEY BOOKSTORE
310 Second St., 352/543-9660
This interesting old-fashioned bookstore is the kind that makes you want to spend hours investigating every shelf, every stack, every rack. They have cards and gifts, too. Maybe you'll pick up a copy of John Muir's *A Thousand-Mile Walk to the Gulf* (Houghton-Mifflin, 1998), or if you're in the mood for fiction get John D. MacDonald's Cedar Key–based thriller *The Empty Copper Sea* (Fawcett, 1996).
Details: *Mon–Sat 10–5, Sun noon–5. (30 minutes)*

★★ DOCK STREET SHOPS AND GALLERIES
Along Dock St. between First and C Sts.
This street has some good little shops with unusual items. Art galleries are beginning to proliferate here, too. These businesses sometimes seem to come and go, but some of them that have been here for years are **Ibis Gallery** (352/543-6111), with a good selection of arts and crafts gifts, and **The Water's Edge** (352/543-5710), with lots of sea-related memorabilia and souvenirs including a lovely display of real seashells. At **Rustic Woods** (352/543-9400), admire the sturdy, good-looking, handcrafted furniture. Satisfy a sweet tooth with some old-fashioned homemade fudge at **Sweet Memories** (352/543-6230). Some contemporary artists from the region show their works in oil, watercolor, and photography at **Island Arts** (352/543-6677), **The Sawgrass Gallery** (352/543-5007), and the **Wild Women Gallery** (352/543-9888).
Details: *Most shops open daily 10–6, some stay open later on weekends. (2 hours)*

FITNESS AND RECREATION
Cedar Key is so relaxing that you'll probably keep your recreational activities pretty low-key while you're here. There are miles of nature trails, and many bird-watchers make regular visits to Cedar Key's wilderness areas where, on average, more than 50,000 nesting birds may be observed during a year. Cedar Key National Wildlife Refuge is comprised of offshore islands within five miles of the town. The refuge contains an interesting 1850s lighthouse. Access is by boat only. You can rent one from Island Hopper at the City Marina, or if you prefer to have someone else operate the boat, take a cruise on the *Island Hopper Queen* at the same location, 352/543-5904. Shell Mound Park is a prehistoric Indian mound and nature trail. It's just off SR 347 on County Rd. 326. There are camp-

ing, boating, and picnicking facilities amid some typical northwestern Florida scenery. Cedar Key is a great place for exploring. Grab your camera or sketch pad and rent a bicycle at Salty's Plaza from Cedar Key Bait & Tackle on the corner of Third St. and SR 24, 352/543-9700, or a golf cart at Dock on the Bay, 352/543-9143. (If you feel up to doing some paddling, you can rent a kayak at the same place.) There's a small public beach just opposite the City Dock, a playground for the kids, and some picnic tables. (Sand here isn't of the soft, powder variety though, so you may want flip-flops on tender feet.)

FOOD

It's not by any means an official statistic, but it certainly seems to regular visitors to Cedar Key that there are more good restaurants per square mile here than anyplace else. You can hardly go wrong, no matter which of the dozen or so dining spots you'll discover. **Cook's Cafe**, Second St., 352/543-5548, is a local landmark, serving breakfast, lunch, and dinner. Fresh seafood is a specialty here, and breakfast is a made-to-order treat. Watch for "Spike," the resident great egret. For a quick bite, try **Crabby's**, 509 Third St., 352/543-9143, for steamed clams, crab, or shrimp—all from local waters. You can take out or eat on the patio. **The Captain's Table**, 222 Dock St., 352/543-5441, has been here just about as long as anyone can remember, still serving fabulous crab bisque and stuffed flounder, among other good things. **The Brown Pelican**, 450 Dock St., 352/543-5428, has been here for years, too, with its lovely water view and imaginative treatments of seafood. Don't be afraid to try the alligator appetizers.

    Seabreeze on the Dock, Dock St. (no street number because it's literally on the dock), 352/543-5738, sits atop weathered, sturdy pilings right out over the Gulf. There are spectacular water views from virtually every table, and moderately priced seafood dishes along with steak and chicken tastefully prepared for landlubbers. Interesting nautical charts, coins, shells, and such are imbedded in the tabletops, and nets and crab traps give a seafaring touch to the décor. **The Heron**, at the corner of SR 24 and Second. St., 352/543-5666, gets its Victorian ambiance from the fact that it's set in a late nineteenth-century building dating back to when Cedar Key was a thriving lumber community. There's seafood, of course, but that's not all. For those who don't like seafood, it offers chicken and steak dishes. It's a casual, comfortable place, and the kids are welcome. **The Island Room at Cedar Cove**, 10 E. Second. St., 352/543-6620, overlooks the Gulf from its yacht club location. You don't have to join the yacht club to eat here, though. Everyone enjoys the excellent prime rib and, of course, the seafood. There's an attractive cocktail lounge, too, overlooking the Gulf where you can eavesdrop on the conversations of yachtsmen and boat skippers from all around the coast. **The Island Hotel Restaurant**, corner of Second and B Sts., 352/543-5111, is housed in an 1850 building that's listed on the National Register of Historic Places. The architecture is reminiscent of Jamaica, and a pot-bellied stove and other antique items furnish the rooms. The bar has a faint scent of cedar, and the seafood is fresh as can be. Prices are surprisingly moderate.

LODGING

Faraway Inn, corner of Third and G Sts., 352/543-5330 or 888/543-5330, www.cedarkeyfla.com/faraway, was built on the site of the nineteenth-century Eagle Pencil Mill, and it has an Old Florida look and feel about it. The Gulf sparkles outside the ground-floor windows, from which you can watch birds dive and soar. Perhaps Cedar Key's most famous lodging place is **The Island Hotel**, at the corner of Second and B Sts., 352/543-5111 or 800/432-4640, www.gnv.fdt.net/-ishotel/. Built in 1859, this authentic country inn is listed on the National Register of Historic Places. It was once a general store and post office, and retains all of its charm. There's a gourmet restaurant here, and guests enjoy a full breakfast. **Cedar Cove Beach & Yacht Club**, 192 Second St., 352/543-5332 or 800/366-5312, is one of the newer properties, and it's right on the Gulf. A swimming pool, Jacuzzi, and sauna, along with exercise equipment, are available for your use. All the units are efficiencies with private balconies. **Cedar Key Bed & Breakfast**, at the corner of Third and F Sts., 352/543-9000 or 800/453-5051, was built in 1880 by Eagle Cedar Mill as a guest house. It's been beautifully restored and offers a restful Victorian ambiance, with homemade breakfasts every morning and tea and baked goods every afternoon. **Dockside Motel**, 491 Dock St., 352/543-5432, is small but right in the heart of things. It's literally dockside, so you can walk to downtown and most of the restaurants and the shops. **Beachfront Hotel**, Corner of First and G Sts., 352/543-5113, has its own curvy but rocky beach. Most of the rooms offer good views of the Gulf. The 23 rooms are comfortable and fairly new, and some are efficiencies. **Mermaid's Landing Cottages**, SR 24, Back Bayou, 352/543-5949, is far enough away from the dock area (about eight blocks) that you may want to rent a bike to get around. If you're bringing the family along, this is a good choice. You can get a two-bedroom cottage with a full kitchen for about the same price as you'd pay for a moderate-range motel room.

For a very nice color brochure listing other accommodations in Cedar Key, call the Cedar Key Area Chamber of Commerce at 352/543-5600 and ask for "Places to Stay in Cedar Key."

BIKING ALONG THE COAST

Lee Island Coast Convention and Visitors Bureau

CAMPING

Cedar Key RV & Trailer Park, at Seventh and G Sts., 352/543-5150, overlooks the harbor and is within walking distance to the beach and downtown. They have 29 sites, all with full hookups. Rainbow Country RV Campground, 311951 SW Shiloh Rd., 352/543-6268, offers boating and saltwater fishing, nice wide sites, and full hookups. There's a little grocery store, too.

NIGHTLIFE

After dark, most of the local folks and visiting fishermen head for the L&M Lounge, 433 Second St., 352/ 543-5827. It's a friendly, laid-back neighborhood bar, and sometimes there's a local band playing good old rock 'n' roll music in the big back room. There's a dance floor, if you're in the mood to cut a rug.

6
CRYSTAL RIVER, HOMOSASSA, AND WEEKI WACHEE

Chamber-of-commerce types call this part of West Coast Florida "the Nature Coast," and it surely is a showcase for much of what's real and natural about Florida. Sometimes visitors who have only seen the big-city side of Florida are especially surprised and usually delighted when they encounter the slower-paced, less-congested counties that make up this unique portion of the coastline. Absent are the bright brochures promising "miles and miles of sugary white sand." Gulf of Mexico beaches here are few and far between. Instead, there are miles and miles and acres and acres of salt bays and estuaries and brackish marshes, fringed with hardwood swamps. You won't meet up with a lot of surfers here. But you might see lots of great blue and little blue herons; green herons; black-crowned and yellow-crowned night herons; common, snowy, and cattle egrets; and the graceful white ibis. You might come across ospreys and alligators, mink and raccoons, bald eagles and wild turkeys. You also might encounter a whole flock of white pelicans, a flock of roseate spoonbills, a Florida panther, a gray wolf, or a black bear. And when you see them, they won't be in cages, cases, aviaries, or aquariums. They'll be free, because they all live here.

Don't think because there aren't a lot of Gulf-front beaches that you won't be swimming. You will indeed-because here are some of Florida's most magnificent freshwater spring-fed rivers. Several of these springs are known as "first-magnitude" springs. That means they have a flow rate of 100 cubic feet or more per second. This makes for some of the purest and clearest water you've ever experienced. Why, the springs at Weeki Wachee are so pure that they have mermaids swimming here. You'll see!

The area is well acquainted with the concept of ecotourism. The region's many parks and wilderness preserves are laced with well-marked trails for hiking, bicycling, and, in many cases, horseback riding. And visitors and locals alike have learned to enjoy these natural wonders responsibly.

A PERFECT DAY AROUND CRYSTAL RIVER, HOMOSASSA, AND WEEKI WACHEE

The best time to look for manatees is early morning, so take the first sightseeing boat from the marina at Plantation Inn. It will take you to famous King's Bay where the gentle giants will be looking for breakfast. Vegetarians all, manatees spend their time munching their way along the river and near-shore waters. (Each one can eat as much as 100 pounds of hydrilla, water hyacinths, and other submerged green goodies in a single day.) When the boat returns you to the marina, hop into the car and head for Spring Hill. That's where the Weeki Wachee Spring attraction is: mermaids! You'll marvel—as have generations of viewers—at the graceful way the young women maneuver through the spring water. When the "curtain" of bubbles signals the end of the show, head up U.S. 19 to Highway 490 and take West Yulee Drive to Old Homosassa Village. Stroll among the art galleries and crafts shops until you spot the perfect memento of this perfect day.

ORIENTATION

U.S. 19 passes through Crystal River, Homosassa, and Weeki Wachee. It's not a pretty route—lots of fast-food places and shopping malls—but it'll get you there. Just west of Crystal River is King's Bay, which is part of the Crystal River Wildlife Refuge. Homosassa is eight miles south of Crystal River, and Weeki Wachee is 20 miles south of Homossassa.

SIGHTSEEING HIGHLIGHTS

★★★★ BUCCANEER BAY
U.S. 19 at SR 50, Weeki Wachee, 352/596-2062
Adjacent to Weeki Wachee Spring (described below), is this natural-spring water park where visitors splash and swim in pleasantly fresh, cool water (always 74 to 77 degrees). A smooth sandy beach, three

CRYSTAL RIVER AND HOMOSASSA

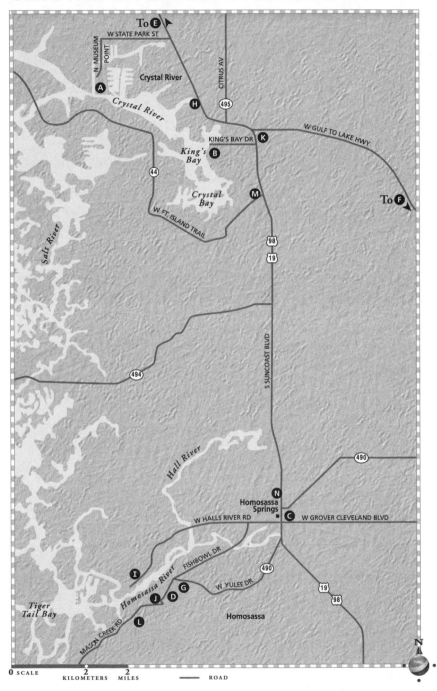

different flume rides and rope swings, a variety of floats and big inner tubes to rent, and a game room keep everyone happy. Someone has thoughtfully placed lounge chairs around on both the sand and the grassy areas for your comfort. Wooden picnic tables are in the shade for a comfortable lunchtime break. There's a small gift shop, a snack bar, and an ice-cream stand, or you can bring your own picnic.

Details: Open late March until Labor Day and a few weekends on either end of that time frame, generally 10–5. Hours extended during the summer months. $11.95 adults, $9.95 children. (3–4 hours)

★★★★ **CRYSTAL RIVER STATE ARCHAEOLOGICAL SITE**
North of Crystal River, off U.S. 19 at Museum Point, 352/795-3817

This is an important site of prehistoric archaeological significance. It's a National Historic Landmark and is listed on the National Register of Historic Places. As far as anyone can tell, the earliest inhabitants of Crystal River belonged to what's known as the "Deptford Culture." These Native Americans did their seasonal food gathering here and occupied this 14-acre site for about 1,600 years—beginning in around 200 B.C. Through the complex is a half-mile paved walking trail leading visitors past several mounds. (Mounds are simply the accumulation of Indian refuse, and they yield fascinating artifacts like the tools and pottery of these ancient Floridians.) Park personnel are on hand to answer your questions.

SIGHTS

- **Ⓐ** Crystal River State Archaeological Site
- **Ⓑ** Crystal River Wildlife Refuge
- **Ⓒ** Homosassa Springs State Wildlife Park
- **Ⓓ** The Olde Millhouse Gallery and Printing Museum
- **Ⓔ** The Power Place
- **Ⓓ** River Works Studio and Copper Art Gallery

SIGHTS *(continued)*

- **Ⓕ** Ted Williams Museum and Hitters Hall of Fame
- **Ⓖ** Yulee Sugar Mill Ruins State Historic Site

FOOD

- **Ⓗ** Crackers Bar & Grill
- **Ⓘ** K. C. Crump
- **Ⓙ** Yardarm Restaurant

LODGING

- **Ⓚ** Best Western
- **Ⓛ** Howard Johnson's Riverside Inn and Marina
- **Ⓛ** MacRae's of Homosassa Fishing Resort
- **Ⓜ** Plantation Inn & Golf Resort
- **Ⓝ** Ramada Inn Downtown

Note: Items with the same letter are located in the same area.

OLD HOMOSASSA VILLAGE

Old Homosassa Village is one of the oldest residential communities found along Florida's Gulf Coast. Stroll around and admire the historic buildings, many of them dating back to the early nineteenth century. Before the Civil War, Homosassa supported a thriving sugar-growing and refining industry, and homes built here at that time reflect the prosperity. Now Old Homosassa has become a favorite spot for artists, galleries, and shopkeepers.

Details: *Visitors center open daily 9–5, grounds open 8–sundown. $2 per car. (2 hours)*

★★★★ HOMOSASSA SPRINGS STATE WILDLIFE PARK
4150 S. Suncoast Blvd., Homosassa, 352/628-2311
The main attraction here is the remarkable Spring of 10,000 Fish. As far back as Indian times, people have known about the strange spot in the spring-fed Homosassa River where many species of fish would congregate. The oddest thing is that there are both freshwater species and saltwater species, all swimming and eating together. You can view this strange phenomenon from an underwater "fish bowl," where the viewers are on the inside looking out at the fish. Manatees will peek in the windows at you, too. This is one of the few spots where manatees may be observed at close range every day of the year. Bring your camera. You'll get some good underwater shots without getting wet. There are other creatures here, too, and the nature trail offers opportunities to see deer, bobcats, otters, and cougars at close range. Colorful wood ducks, flamingos, herons, and egrets also live here.
    Details: *Main entrance on U.S. 19 in Homosassa. Daily 9–5:30 (ticket counter closes at 4). $7.95 adults, $4.95 children. (4 hours)*

★★★ CRYSTAL RIVER WILDLIFE REFUGE
1502 SE King's Bay Dr., Crystal River, 352/795-3149
Crystal River is the winter home for at least 200 manatees. Between September and March the gentle giants seek the warm, 72-degree

water here at King's Bay. The bay, created by Florida's second-largest spring head, is a special place where our endangered West Indian manatees like to congregate in the winter, and it's one of the few places in the state where you're allowed to swim with them. Although manatees can grow to be huge, they are extremely gentle. Some of the older ones are so accustomed to swimming with humans that they'll roll over and "ask" to have their tummies scratched. You'll need to find a guide to take you to the right spot to view the creatures—and you'll have to go by boat. The refuge doesn't provide tours or boat rentals. Your hotel can recommend a guide, or try **Captain Larry Campbell's Aquamarine Images**, 888/732-2692, www.aquamarineimages.com, which specializes in manatee tours and underwater photography. The captain gives scuba instruction, too.

Details: Office open Mon–Fri 7:30–4, refuge open Mon–Fri 9–4. For information on guides, contact the Nature Coast Chamber of Commerce, 28 U.S. 19 NW, Crystal River, 352/795-3149. (3 hours)

★★★ **WEEKI WACHEE SPRING**
U.S. 19 at SR 50, Spring Hill, 352/596-2062
This underwater spring has long been famous for its live mermaids. In 1947, Navy Frogman Newton Perry began teaching young women the techniques of rudimentary snorkeling—breathing through hoses so that they could remain underwater for long periods of time. These women became the first mermaids. The attraction continues to delight visitors year-round with underwater performances. You can view the mermaids from a cool underground amphitheater through four-inch-thick plate-glass windows. The beautiful young mermaids flip shimmering tails and move easily through sparkling clear water as the story unfolds. Productions change from time to time. Recent offerings have included *The Little Mermaid* and *Pocahontas.*

While at the spring, you can also take the **Wilderness River Cruise** along the river to the **Pelican Preserve**, where sick and injured birds are brought to recuperate. There's also a petting zoo where you're allowed to pet a pygmy deer, a llama, and even an emu. Trained birds will entertain you with remarkable feats at the **Exotic Bird Show**.

Details: Daily 10–5:30 (last admission one hour before closing). $16.95 adults, $12.95 children. (3–4 hours)

★★★ YULEE SUGAR MILL RUINS STATE HISTORIC SITE
10470 W. Yulee Dr., Old Homosassa, 352/795-3817
This small wooded area, not far from the Homosassa Springs State Wildlife Park, was once the setting of a thriving sugar mill. All that's left now is a partially restored section that houses the boiler and some of the grinding machinery, but one can imagine how it must have been in 1851 when David Yulee's 5,100-acre sugar cane plantation, handsome home, and bustling mill stood here. Yulee, who later became Florida's first U.S. senator, also developed the Homosassa orange in his citrus groves. You can still enjoy these tasty treats today. To take the self-guided tour, follow the signs explaining the mill and its history.
Details: Open daily 8 a.m.–sunset. Free. (30 minutes)

★★ THE OLDE MILLHOUSE GALLERY AND PRINTING MUSEUM
10444 W. Yulee Dr., Old Homosassa, 352/628-1081
This museum will give you a firsthand look at the old way of art printing. Letterpress methods from the mid-1800s up to the present are graphically displayed. Sometimes local artists are on hand to give a live demonstration, and works by regional artists are on sale in the gallery.
Details: Open Thur–Sat 10:30–3. Free. (1 hour)

★★ THE POWER PLACE
15760 W. Power Line St., Crystal River, 352/563-4490
This is a presentation by the Florida Power Corporation, offered at the Crystal River Energy Complex. Energy exhibits, video presentations, and educational lectures help visitors understand how things work in Florida. Climb aboard a bicycle generator and test your pedal power. Learn just how much power it actually takes to run a portable TV or a curling iron. An animated display explains how a nuclear power plant works, and you can take charge of a nuclear power plant simulator, raising and lowering the control rods to regulate nuclear chain reaction. In "A Celebration of Light," you'll meet Benjamin Franklin, Thomas Edison, and the father of the atomic age, Enrico Fermi. Travelers with kids will find the makings for a great science project here.
Details: 3.8 miles west of U.S. 19 and 2.5 miles north of Crystal River. Open Mon–Fri 9:30–4. Free. (1–2 hours)

Antiquing in Historic Mount Dora

Florida visitors interested in things antique will surely hear about Mount Dora! Although it's too far inland to qualify as a Gulf Coast destination, any antiquer worth his or her salt will set aside a day (or more) and make the trek to this delightful town where the antique is celebrated every day. More than a hundred antique and memorabilia dealers are within walking distance of each other in this charming historic village overlooking beautiful Lake Dora. There are delightful cafés, tea rooms, and bed-and-breakfasts. Most of the stores are open seven days.

If you're here on a weekend, you'll probably want to go to **Renninger's Twin Markets**, an enormous flea market where hundreds of dealers show their wares every weekend. In November, January, and February, watch for announcements for Renninger's Mount Dora Extravaganzas. These are truly huge events; more than 1,000 dealers from all over the country set up in a big outdoor market. Plan on spending a whole day and wear comfortable shoes. For information and dates, call 352/383-8393.

Don't spend all your time at Renninger's though. This is a wonderful little town—not a touristy re-creation but a genuine small town with a sense of its own history. The roads in and out of Mount Dora still look like what country lanes are supposed to look like. There are woods and gardens and both grand and modest houses. In the little downtown area, antique shops are arrayed among hardware and apparel stores. The old Atlantic Coast Railroad Depot now houses the chamber of commerce, and across the street Mount Dora's active oldsters play at shuffleboard courts right smack in the middle of the retail district. Everyone drops in at the **Windsor Rose English Tea Room** for high tea, British style (114 W. Fourth Ave., 352/735-2551). If you visit the chamber of commerce, pick up a self-guiding Mount Dora Historic Tour brochure.

To get to Mount Dora from the Weeki Wachee area, take SR 50 to U.S. 98 to I-75 North. Take the U.S. 441/U.S. 27 exit to Leesburg and stay on U.S. 441 through Eustis until you see the signs for Mount Dora. This trip could take you all day. If you'd like to stay overnight, contact the Mount Dora Chamber of Commerce at 352/383-2165 for accommodations recommendations.

ADOPT A MANATEE

Manatees have had a tough time surviving the onslaught of human encroachment on their habitat. Some 170 manatees meet their demise each year along the Florida coast, many from collisions with boat propellers. As Florida's waterways attract more and more crafts every year, those numbers may very well rise. Environmental factors play a role, too. In 1996, more than 300 of these creatures were killed by an algae bloom known as "red tide."

You can "adopt" a sweet-natured manatee in its own Florida habitat, and though you may not be able to cuddle her in your arm-chair at home, you will be contributing to the effort to save these en-dangered mammals. The Save the Manatee Club's Adopt-A-Manatee program will send you a manatee adoption certificate, a photo, and bio of your manatee, along with quarterly updates. It's a great way for kids to help an endangered animal while learning about environmental issues. It costs $20 a year. Call 800/432-JOIN for more information. Do what you can to promote the survival of these Florida treasures.

★★ **RIVER WORKS STUDIO AND COPPER ART GALLERY**
10844 W. Yulee Dr., Old Homosassa, 352/628-0822
River Works houses a remarkable assemblage of large-scale copper art pieces. Giant copper fish—some of them six or seven feet long—and copper fountains are among the outstanding works on display. If you have an idea for a copper sculpture, you can get one custom made here.
Details: Open by appointment only. (1 hour)

★ **TED WILLIAMS MUSEUM AND HITTERS HALL OF FAME**
SR 486 and Citrus Hills Blvd., Hernando, 352/527-6566
It's all here except the roaring crowds and fresh popcorn. Shaped like a baseball diamond with eight galleries, the museum takes on much of the character of Boston's Fenway Park. See rows and rows of bats, awards, uniforms, and pictures from Williams's illustrious career. In the 85-seat theater hear Williams, in a recording, talk about the "old

days" when he hit 521 home runs and finished a 21-year career with a lifetime .344 average, the sixth highest ever. (You'll wonder what it would have been if he hadn't taken four and a half years to serve his country as a United States Marine.)

Details: *Take I-75 to SR 200 Exit; continue west on SR 486. Tue–Sun 10–4, closed major holidays. $3 adults, $1 children. (1 hour)*

FITNESS AND RECREATION

Not long ago, the World Wildlife Fund named Withlacoochee State Forest, 352/754-6777, one of the "Top 10 Coolest Places You've Never Seen." The Withlacoochee River forms the heartline of the forest, rising from the Green Swamp. The forest has more than 113,000 acres of longleaf pine, scrub oak, and slash pine. The newly opened Withlacoochee Trail, 352/394-2280, transverses eastern Citrus County, parallel to the Withlacoochee River, for 57 miles through the Withlacoochee State Forest from the village of Trilby in the south to Citrus County's northern boundary. The trail is designed to accommodate hikers, bicyclists, and equestrians. Trailheads, campsites, corrals, and picnic areas are available at scenic points along the trail. Also check out the Chassahowitzka National Wildlife Refuge, along the coast between the towns of Homossassa and Chassahowitzka. Not only does it offer good camping, but canoeing and a yoga retreat center as well. Maps of the trails and access information can be obtained from the Nature Coast Chamber of Commerce, 352/795-3149.

Fishing is a big deal here. It always has been. After all, you have the waters of seven different spring-fed rivers all emptying into the Gulf of Mexico. The great, silvery tarpon is a favorite game fish, and participants in local tournaments seem to catch record-sized ones—150 pounds and more—every season. Bass fishermen also love to explore the many miles of riverbanks, streams, and bays. River Safaris, 5297 S. Cherokee Way, Homosassa, 352/628-5222, will take you fishing or rent you a boat so you can find your own way to the big ones. So will MacRae's of Homosassa, 5300 S. Cherokee Way, Homosassa, 352/628-2922.

Dive shops, large and small, abound here. The clear water and many underwater caves make this a favorite place for diving and underwater photography. Experienced divers will want to ask local experts about diving Blue Sink, Devil's Den, and Hospital Hole. A full-service dive center in the Weeki Wachee area is Dive Center, 4648 Commercial Way, Spring Hill, 352/597-0101. They can fix you up with rental equipment, and they organize monthly dive trips. For dive charter service, call Captain Gary Stambaugh, Adventurer, 4211 Shoal Line Blvd., Spring Hill, 352/597-1476.

Golfers aren't neglected here either. There are a dozen or so courses in the

WEEKI WACHEE

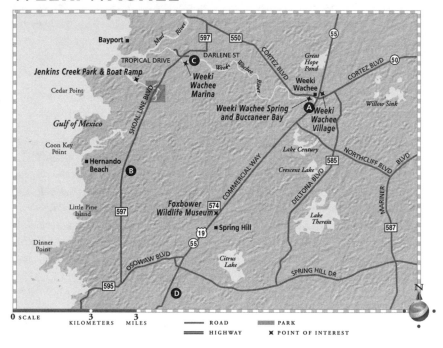

SIGHTS

- **A** Buccaneer Bay
- **A** Weeki Wachee Spring

FOOD

- **B** B. J. Gators on the Canal
- **C** Otter's

LODGING

- **D** Best Western Weeki Wachee Resort

Note: Items with the same letter are located in the same area.

Nature Coast area. Plantation Inn & Golf Resort, 352/795-4211, is in Crystal River; World Woods Golf Club, 352/796-5500, is in Brooksville; and Oak Hills Golf Club, 352/683-6830, is in Spring Hill.

FOOD

With the Gulf nearby and rivers and springs at every turn, it figures that seafood is going to be prominent on local menus. And it is. Most travelers eventually wind up at the **Yardarm Restaurant**, 5295 S. Cherokee Way, Old Homosassa Village, 352/628-3327, which is on the banks of the Homosassa. Yardarm has been here as long as anyone can remember, and the antiques on the walls and in the entrance hall remind us of that fact. Once a hunting and fishing lodge, it now serves up good seafood and steak dinners, but only on Friday and Saturday nights. Yardarm serves breakfast, too, on Saturday and Sunday. Just across the river from the Yardarm is **K. C. Crump**, 11210 W. Hall's River Rd., Homosassa, 352/628-1500. This was an old fishing camp, but it's been lovingly restored. You'll enjoy fresh seafood and hand-cut steaks in the handsome dining room, the more casual lounge, or even dock-side at the bar. (You can take a boat tour of the river from K. C. Crump's dock with Captain Warren, 352/527-0898.)

    Crackers Bar & Grill, 502 NW Sixth St., Crystal River, 352/795-3999, is a favorite with families for its hefty burgers and fresh salads. And it's right on King's Bay—what a view.

    On the banks of the Weeki Wachee is **Otter's**, 5386 Darlene St. (off Shoal Line Blvd.), 352/597-9551. There's a boat dock if you come by sea and plenty of parking if by land. If you like, take advantage of the open-deck seating, just across from a neat little community beach. Sunday brunch during the season is good, and they serve great chicken-salad sandwiches at lunch every day. You'll meet a lot of local folks at **B. J. Gators on the Canal**, 4054 Shoal Line Blvd., Spring Hill, 352/596-7160. They do a nice Sunday brunch, along with everyday lunch and dinner specials, burgers, sandwiches, wings, and more.

LODGING

There are plenty of places to stay along U.S. 19, which runs right through the Nature Coast. Many of the national chains are present, as are several well-established independent hotels and motels.

    The **Howard Johnson's Riverside Inn and Marina**, 5297 S. Cherokee Way, Old Homosassa Village, 352/628-2474, is a favorite spot with visiting fishermen and vacationers alike. It's always been fun, but now it's been recently rehabbed by new owner, HoJo, and is even better than before. **MacRae's of Homosassa Fishing Resort**, 5300 S. Cherokee Way, Old Homosassa Village, 352/628-2602, offers not only motel accommodations, but boat rentals, fishing guide services, a bait and tackle store, and a fuel dock.

    In Crystal River the old Southern atmosphere of **Plantation Inn & Golf Resort**, 9301 W. Fort Island Tr., Crystal River, 352/795-4211, attracts repeat visitors among travelers and locals alike. A championship golf course is part of the action here, along with full-service boating and diving facilities. At Crystal

River there's a **Best Western**, 614 NW U.S. 19, 352/795-3171, close to King's Bay and its fascinating manatee population. There's a marina right next door, where you can get aboard a boat for a dive-with-the-manatees adventure. **Ramada Inn Downtown**, 4076 S. Suncoast Blvd., Crystal River, 352/628-4311, is kind of a plain-Jane motel, but the beds are comfortable, the location is good, and it allows pets. Of note are a playground for the kids, tennis courts for you, and a restaurant on the premises.

Directly across U.S. 19 from the Weeki Wachee Spring mermaid attraction is the **Best Western Weeki Wachee Resort**, 6172 Commercial Way, Spring Hill, 352/596-2007. Check with the manager for special weekend deals and for discounted tickets to both Weeki Wachee and Buccaneer Bay.

CAMPING
Anyplace that calls itself the Nature Coast is bound to have some nice, scenic campgrounds. A lovely one close to King's Bay and all the manatee action is Crystal Isles RV Resort, 11419 W. Fort Island Tr., Crystal River, 352/795-3774. It has 250 sites, offering the usual amenities, on a canal leading to the main river. Also on site are a pool, tennis courts, fishing, boating, and game room for the kids.

Citrus County Chassahowitzka River Camp Grounds, 8600 Miss Maggie Dr., Homosassa, 352/382-2200, is within walking distance of the wonderful Chassahowitzka National Wildlife Refuge, so nature lovers are in for an exciting time here. You'll have manatees, bald eagles, otters, deer, and black bears for neighbors. But you have to keep your pets on leashes, and there's no alcohol allowed. It's a quiet park and the folks running the place—and staying here—like to keep it that way. Boat and canoe rentals are available on site.

Weeki Wachee locals recommend Mary's Fish Camp, 8092 Mary's Fish Camp Rd., Spring Hill, 352/596-2359. Mary's is a no-frills spot, perfect for serious fishermen. Bring your own RV or rent a trailer from Mary.

7
TARPON SPRINGS

Back in 1882, Philadelphia entrepreneur and developer Hamilton Disston took a steamer ride along the Anclote River. The steamer passed a charming bayou—a tiny settlement the local folks called "Tarpon Springs." Enchanted by the beauty of the place, Disston decided then and there to build a town on the site. (Just a year earlier Disston launched Florida development by buying four million acres in the Everglades for 25 cents an acre, so this was a man who knew a real estate bargain when he saw one.) A year later, two hotels and a long pier marked the spot, and winter visitors began to arrive. Before long, some of Disston's Philadelphia friends showed up to build fine homes, and the town began to grow.

Inevitably, the railroads came, and by 1887 Tarpon Springs was on its way to becoming a popular winter resort, attracting sportsmen and wealthy vacationers. In 1891 the Anclote and Rock Island Sponge Company chose the little resort town for one of its offices, since the Gulf waters around Tarpon Springs were among the few places in the whole world where live sponges were readily accessible. In 1900 the company hired a young Greek sponge expert named Jon Cocoris, who then introduced the diving suit to the fledgling sponge fleet. Soon hundreds of Greeks flocked to Tarpon Springs, bringing their considerable boat-building and diving skills along with them.

Today the sponge-fishing trade is mostly gone, but its legacy still draws visitors to sample the ethnic pleasures of Tarpon Springs. The festive notes of

TARPON SPRINGS

the mandolinlike bouzouki spill out from speakers in restaurants and shops along Dodecanese Boulevard. Couples sip retsina at outdoor tables, and passers-by peer into streetside windows and watch cooks slice roasted lamb for gyro sandwiches.

Every year traditional Greek events draw thousands of spectators. Each January the town and its guests celebrate the Feast of Epiphany with a colorful procession to Spring Bayou, where young Greek Orthodox boys brave the chilly waters to retrieve a cross, the winner earning special blessings for the year. Fishing tournaments and arts and crafts shows are regular happenings here, too, and with the many Greek restaurants—both large and small—eating is an every-day celebration of wonderful flavors.

A PERFECT DAY IN TARPON SPRINGS

Start the day with a cup of strong Greek coffee and a lovely square of baklava (that catastrophically caloric Greek pastry made with honey and walnuts) at the Taste of Greece Bakery and Restaurant. Now you can begin to explore the shops along Dodecanese Boulevard. It's a bit of old Athens, complete with intriguing crafts items, lovely embroidery, even authentic copper and brass diving helmets. Just for fun, drop in and see the live sharks being fed at the Konger Coral Sea Aquarium, as the theme from *Jaws* plays in the background. Head for downtown now and visit the remarkable St. Nicholas Greek Orthodox Cathedral. The rich Byzantine architecture, stained-glass windows, and sculptured marble make this a true historic gem.

SIGHTS
- **Ⓐ** Dodecanese Boulevard Shops
- **Ⓑ** George Inness Jr. Paintings
- **Ⓒ** Historical Society Museum
- **Ⓓ** Konger Coral Sea Aquarium
- **Ⓐ** Spongeorama Exhibition
- **Ⓔ** St. Nicholas Boat Line
- **Ⓕ** St. Nicholas Greek Orthodox Cathedral

SIGHTS (continued)
- **Ⓖ** Tarpon Springs Antiques District
- **Ⓓ** Tarpon Springs Sponge Exchange

FOOD
- **Ⓗ** Costa's Restaurant
- **Ⓓ** Hellas
- **Ⓘ** Pappas Restaurant
- **Ⓙ** Plaka Restaurant
- **Ⓘ** Riverside Cafe
- **Ⓚ** Taste of Greece Bakery and Restaurant

LODGING
- **Ⓛ** Best Western Tahitian Resort
- **Ⓜ** Gulf Manor
- **Ⓝ** Holiday Inn Tarpon Springs
- **Ⓞ** Sheraton Four Points Hotel
- **Ⓟ** Spring Bayou Inn
- **Ⓠ** Tarpon Springs Days Inn
- **Ⓡ** Westin Innisbrook Resort

Note: Items with the same letter are located in the same area.

Check out a few of the many antique shops along Tarpon Avenue in the beautifully restored Historic Downtown. Head back toward the sponge docks, stopping at the Unitarian Universalist Church for a peek at the outstanding collection of George Inness Jr. paintings. Go to Pappas Restaurant and order a Greek salad for lunch, stop at Catherine's Linen Shop and treat yourself to a pair of handmade Madeira pillowcases, then board an authentic 1900s sponge-fishing dive boat at 693 Dodecanese Blvd. and see for yourself how sponges were harvested in the old days. The original sponge markets have made way for shops and boutiques aplenty, enough to fill an afternoon with shopping bliss. Tonight go to Zorba's, sip Metaxa, and watch the belly dancers.

ORIENTATION

The city of Tarpon Springs is sometimes called the "Venice of the South" because it has so many lakes and bayous. It's located on the Gulf of Mexico, approximately 15 miles north of Clearwater, 30 miles north of St. Petersburg, and about 30 miles northwest of Tampa. The historic downtown area encompasses several city blocks, all accessible from Alternate U.S. 19 (U.S. 19-A). Beautiful Victorian homes stand on the edge of the business district, offering a pleasant setting for a stroll around Craig Park and Spring Bayou. The famous Sponge Docks are north of downtown, mostly on Dodecanese Boulevard.

SIGHTSEEING HIGHLIGHTS

★★★★ DODECANESE BOULEVARD SHOPS
Dodecanese Blvd. between U.S. 19-A and the Anclote River
These six sun-drenched blocks look, feel, and sound a lot like Athens. Shops and restaurants abound here, next to the century-old Sponge Docks. **Catherine's Linen Shop**, on the corner of Dodecanese Blvd. and Athens St., 727/934-0432, offers a wonderful selection of imported embroidered linens as well as Greek clothing, shell crafts, and religious icons. Open every day 10 to 6.

At **Sunshine Gifts & Jewelry**, 514 and 516 Dodecanese Blvd., 727/937-5927, find souvenirs and T-shirts, shells and sponges, and a great selection of Greek music. (Pick up a tape or CD by Nana Mouskouri and take a bit of Greece home with you!) Open daily 9 to 8.

The **Athens Gift Shop**, 703 Dodecanese Blvd., 727/937-3514, is the place for Grecian pottery, statues, and dolls. Open daily 10 to 9.

The Museum Shoppe, 822 Dodecanese Blvd., 727/934-6760, www.museumshoppe.com, isn't a bit Greek, but it's still a really neat shop for very unusual gifts. It's a "brass rubbing center," too, where you can make your own beautiful wall decorations. Open daily 10 to 7. *Details: Most shops open daily. (2 hours)*

★★★★ ST. NICHOLAS BOAT LINE
693 Dodecanese Blvd. at the Sponge Docks, 727/942-6425
Frequent daily sailings aboard a vintage sponge-fishing vessel give visitors a taste of what it was like in the old days. A guide narrates the history of local sponge fishing while a diver wearing authentic gear descends into the Gulf waters. Although antiquated now, the diving gear—complete with an orange rubber and canvas inflatable diving suit, 12-pound "Frankenstein" shoes, 70-pound shoulder weights, and a circular 22-pound windowed helmet attached to an air hose—was state of the art around the turn of the last century. And, believe it or not, the diver always comes up with a sponge.

Details: Half-hour round trips run daily, year-round. $5 adults, $2 children. (30 minutes)

★★★★ ST. NICHOLAS GREEK ORTHODOX CATHEDRAL
36 Pinellas Ave., 727/937-3540
This outstanding example of Byzantine architecture is a replica of St. Sophia's Cathedral in Istanbul. St. Nicholas is the patron saint of ships and sailors, and this jewel of a church is an important focal point in this seafaring community. Stained-glass windows filter the light spilling onto traditional icons and luminous marble carvings. One of the most venerated articles here is an icon of the saint, framed in glass and housed just inside the main entrance. It is said that the image occasionally weeps and hundreds of people have witnessed this unusual phenomenon. Each January 6 the church bell rings to announce the Epiphany festival and the entire congregation marches—singing and dressed in traditional garb—through town to Spring Bayou, where local boys compete to retrieve a gold cross tossed into the water.

Details: Daily 9–5. Donations accepted. (1 hour)

★★★ GEORGE INNESS JR. PAINTINGS
Unitarian Universalist Church, 230 Grand Blvd., 727/937-4682
Here you can see 11 paintings by landscape artist George Inness Jr.

STONE CRABS: A FLORIDA DELICACY

Each year between October 15 and May 15, Florida diners consume the better part of three million pounds of stone crab claws. The tasty crustaceans are unique among Florida's considerable marine resources. Because the crabs are capable of re-growing their claws, fishermen remove only the largest claw, then return the creature to the water. This conservation measure means that even though some 1.1 million crab traps are fished during the season, the stone crab fishery has not yet experienced the stock depletion so many other fisheries have suffered.

Noted for his skill in portraying light and depth, Inness created some of the larger works specifically to replace the church's arched stained-glass windows, which had been damaged during a hurricane in 1918.

Details: *Paintings on display Oct–May Tue–Sun 2–5, closed holidays. A docent is on hand to guide you around. $1 donation requested. (30 minutes–1 hour)*

★★★ TARPON SPRINGS SPONGE EXCHANGE
735 Dodecanese Blvd.

This was the spot where, back in the early 1900s, sponge sellers and buyers met to sell and warehouse the many varieties of sponges for which this city was famous. After a sponge blight during the 1940s, the old buildings fell into disrepair. Today the sponge exchange houses mostly a modern cluster of shops and eating places. A few of the old warehouse stalls remain, however, so visitors can see how things used to be at this bustling locale. Have your photo taken with the great white shark or the giant turtle. Check out **Cotton Patch Casuals** (No. 35), 727/938-8489 for a big selection of sportswear and accessories. Open Monday to Saturday 10 to 7; Sunday 11 to 6. **The Pelican** (No. 29) has those great-looking Greek fisherman's hats and lots of locally made gifts, lamps, and home décor. It's open Monday to Saturday 10 to 6; Sunday noon to 6. **CJ's Nature Shop** (No. 17) specializes in various nature-related items, including T-shirts, toys, and jewelry. The shop is open Monday to Saturday 10 to 8; Sunday 10 to 5.

Details: *Across from the Sponge Docks on Dodecanese Blvd. Most shops open daily. Call Tarpon Springs Chamber of Commerce at 727/937-6109 for more information. (2 hours)*

★★ SPONGEORAMA EXHIBITION
510 Dodecanese Blvd., 727/943-9509
This special exhibition at the Sponge Factory screens a film that gives a brief history of sponge fishing and explains uses for various types of sponges. In the factory showroom you can buy the sponges you've just learned about. Little wooden cottages house gift shops and a café.

Details: *Open daily 10–7:30. Free. (1 hour)*

★ HISTORICAL SOCIETY MUSEUM
Corner of Safford and Tarpon Aves., 727/938-3711
The museum is housed in a wonderful old building that used to be the Tarpon Springs Railroad Station when the Atlantic Coast Line ran through these parts. At the south end of the building is a model railroad exhibit featuring miniature buildings of historic Tarpon Springs.

Details: *Tue–Thu 2–4, Sat 12–4. Free. (1 hour)*

★ KONGER CORAL SEA AQUARIUM
850 Dodecanese Blvd., 727/938-5378
A reef tank with live coral, sponges, fish, and sharks is the focus of this marine exhibit. The 100,000-gallon tank is the scene of shark feedings several times daily. Watch as divers hand-feed live sharks.

Details: *Mon–Sat 10–5, Sunday noon–5. Feeding times are 11:30, 1, 2:30, and 4. Admission $4.75. (1 hour)*

★ TARPON SPRINGS ANTIQUES DISTRICT
Tarpon Ave. and U.S. 19-A, 727/944-3364
In 1991 this main street district was chosen to be included on the National Register of Historic Places. There are dozens of shops, and since some of them are multiple-dealer operations, you'll see items from more than a hundred dealers. Tree-shaded brick sidewalks, green benches, and nostalgic street lamps make browsing around this neighborhood of antique stores, specialty shops, art galleries, and cafés a delightful diversion. Some gems include **Carter's Antique Asylum**, 106 E. Tarpon Ave., 727/942-2799, which has a stunning

selection of Civil War items, a goodly amount of Victoriana, as well as old clocks, lamps, and jewelry. Open Monday to Saturday 10 to 5; Sunday 1 to 5; evenings by appointment. **Vintage Department Store**, 167 E. Tarpon Ave., 727/942-4675, is an eclectic place full of oldies but goodies. Take your time and browse amid the china, glass and porcelain items, jewelry, gifts, and collectibles. The district is also home to the annual **Blues on the Bayou Festival** in October. Call the main number for more information.

Details: Most shops open Mon–Sat 10–5, Sun 1–5. (1–4 hours)

FITNESS AND RECREATION

Boats, both commercial and recreational, have long been a major focus in Tarpon Springs. Several prestigious boat builders are headquartered here. Visitors interested in fishing, diving, snorkeling, swimming, or shelling will find boats available for hire. There are island cruises that offer trips lasting an hour, a day, overnight, or over the weekend. You can rent powerboats, or, if you prefer, you can go with a group aboard the 40-foot pontoon boat *Helios*, 600 Dodecanese Blvd., 727/934-0606, for a four-hour trip to Anclote Key. You also can take a short sightseeing excursion around the harbor. Deep-sea fishermen will seek out the 85-foot vessel *Two Georges*, Dolphin Dock, 727/937-8257, for half-day trips. Charter boat *Get-A-Lot*, docked behind Pappas Restaurant, 727/937-5938, takes private all-day or half-day fishing charters.

There are some wonderful state and county parks here for other outdoor activities. Fred Howard Park, 1700 Sunset Dr., 727/937-4938, is a 150-acre county facility with a mile-long causeway connecting the offshore swimming area with the mainland. Barbecue grills, sheltered pavilions, children's playgrounds, rest rooms, and showers make this an excellent choice for family fun. The county also manages A. L. Anderson Park, 39699 U.S. 19, 727/937-5410. It's on Lake Tarpon and there's boat access to the lake and a nature trail. Highland Nature Park is a little gem of a park, showcasing a great variety of Florida foliage. Kids will enjoy Discovery Playground with its facilities for softball, baseball, volleyball, soccer, basketball, and more. Call 727/938-3711 for information on these smaller city-owned parks.

Winding through town is the Pinellas Trail, the paved roadway created just for bicyclists, joggers, skaters, and walkers, which extends all the way to St. Petersburg. Tops with golfers is the plush Westin Innisbrook Resort. Ninety holes of golf, driving ranges, and putting greens await your pleasure. The resort is located off U.S. 19 south of Klosterman Road.

FOOD

Tarpon Springs holds fast to its Greek traditions, and this is nowhere more evident than on the menus of the many cafés and restaurants. Diners and snackers are confronted by choices like spanakopita (spinach and cheese pie), pastitsio (ground beef, macaroni, cheese sauce), and dolmades (stuffed grape leaves)—all wonderful choices. **Pappas Restaurant**, 10 W. Dodecanese Blvd., 727/937-5101, is perhaps the most famous dining spot in town. The Pappas family has been in the restaurant business in Tarpon Springs since 1925, and they know what they're doing. Try blackened grouper and a Greek salad. Waterside view, romantic lighting, and tasteful décor add to the dining pleasure. Pappas has added a new dining area to its existing restaurant—**Riverside Cafe** (same address and phone)—that offers a special menu featuring Mediterranean cuisine with a Caribbean flavor Thu–Sun. During the rest of the week, the café offers the same fare as Pappas.

The county's number-one Greek restaurant is **Hellas**, 785 Dodecanese Blvd., 727/943-2400. The extensive menu includes traditional Greek dishes and plenty of local seafood, and the décor is pure Athens. The folks who manage Hellas also run **Taste of Greece Bakery and Restaurant**, 709 Dodecanese Blvd., 727/938-0088. The menu is similar to that of Hellas, but here there's a bakery. The bakery opens at 9 a.m., so this is a fine spot to stop for coffee and a baked treat in the morning. **Costa's Restaurant**, 521 Athens St., 727/938-6890, is located on a charming side street, where a good many of Tarpon Springs's oldest shops and businesses still thrive. With its rustic fish-house décor and good Greek cooking, Costa's is popular with lunch and dinner crowds. The **Plaka Restaurant**, 769 Dodecanese Blvd., 727/934-4752, claims to be "the Greek answer to McDonald's." Here passers-by can watch the cooks slice the lamb and build gyro (pronounced YEAR-oh) sandwiches.

LODGING

Accommodations in Tarpon Springs range from large resorts and well-known chains to homey B&Bs. The 600-acre, elegant **Westin Innisbrook Resort**, off U.S. 19 south of Klosterman Rd., 727/942-2000, www.westinnisbrook.com, has 1,000 units to rent, all with kitchens. Some are townhouses; all are roomy—and pricey. Restaurants, saunas, pools, tennis courts, and a golf course are all on the premises. The **Sheraton Four Points Hotel**, 37611 U.S. 19 N., 727/942-0358, has Mediterranean décor and a lakeside locale. There's a fitness center, a business center, and a waterfront dining room. Rates are moderate to expensive, depending on the season. The **Best Western Tahitian Resort**,

2337 U.S. 19, 727/937-4121, has, as the name suggests, a South Seas ambiance. Tropical plants abound amid thatched roofs and tiki gods, and rates are moderate year-round. **Spring Bayou Inn**, 32 W. Tarpon Ave., 727/938-9333, is a large, comfortable home within walking distance of the antique district and close to peaceful Spring Bayou. Kids over 12 are okay. Rooms with shared bath are in the $60–$70 range; rooms with private bath are around $100. **Gulf Manor**, 548 Whitcomb Blvd., 727/937-4207, is an interesting place to stay—close to all of the downtown sights and the antique district, and within a short drive of the golf course. Bring a boat if you want: the Manor has a dock on one of those famous Tarpon Springs bayous. Rooms are comfortable and homey, and the grounds are abloom with flowering plants shaded by moss-draped oaks.

Holiday Inn Tarpon Springs, 38724 U.S. 19 N., 727/934-5781, is a big, modern hotel with lots of sybaritic amenities. The contemporary décor is luxurious, and many of the suites have full home-away-from-home kitchens. Balconies and patios bring the outdoors in. Even the corridors bear a decorator's touch. A restaurant and cocktail lounge are in the building, and there's a playground for the kiddies and a steam room for you. **Tarpon Springs Days Inn**, 40050 U.S. 19 N., 727/938-8000, is well located for day-trippers. You're just off I-75, yet not too far from the beaches and the Tarpon Springs Sponge Docks. There's an International House of Pancakes on the property, too.

CAMPING

There aren't a lot of campgrounds in Tarpon Springs. The closest one to the waterfront action and the Sponge Docks is Bayshore Cove RV Park, 403 Riverside Dr., 727/531-7998. The Cypress Pointe Campground, 4600 U.S. 19, 727/938-1966, www.rvresorts.com, on lovely Lake Tarpon is a highly rated RV resort with tree-shaded lots and all the expected amenities. The Clearwater/Tarpon Springs KOA, is on U.S. 19 about two miles south of Tarpon Springs, 727/937-8412. Kids will enjoy the recreation room and the playground. There's a general store for basics and souvenirs and a heated swimming pool for year-round fun.

The Florida Association of RV Parks and Campgrounds has a Web site at www.florida-camping.com.

NIGHTLIFE

Tarpon Springs has so many excellent restaurants, lots of folks make an evening out of lingering over dinner. For those who like a real "nightclub" atmosphere though, there are some attractive options. At the elegant Westin Innisbrook on U.S. 19, 727/942-2000, check out the Turnberry Pub for casual nighttime entertainment, or the colorful Jimmy Guana's, where the musical entertainment is often live and lively. (Same phone number for both places.) The place for live Greek music and belly dancers is Zorba's, 508 Athens St., 727/934-8803. They also serve traditional Greek food and beverages.

If you'd like to do a little gambling while you're here, head for the Sun Cruz Casino, where you can enjoy poker tables with the highest table limits in Florida. There are roulette and Odyssey slot machines, too. You'll arrive at the casino via one of two fast "water taxis," which leave from behind Pappas Restaurant on the Sponge Docks. For schedules and boarding information, call 727/848-DICE.

Another option might be a live stage performance at the Tarpon Springs Performing Arts Center, 324 Pine St., 727/942-5605. Performances and curtain times vary with the seasons, so be sure to call ahead or pick up a copy of *Weekly Planet*, a free local weekly with news on what's happening after dark.

Scenic Route: Dunedin

You can take the big highways here to take you from point A to B, but sometimes it's just more fun and more relaxing to take one of the older, more scenic routes to get where you're going. Besides, there are usually some neat places between "here" and "there" that you would bypass if you took the highway. Such a place is Dunedin (pronounced dun-EE-din).

U.S. 19-A takes you along the Gulf from Tarpon Springs all the way south to the St. Petersburg barrier islands. Along the way, you'll pass through Dunedin. It was almost 150 years ago that two Scots settled here, naming it after a town they liked in their homeland. This Gulf-side city celebrates its heritage every April with the **Highland Games**, *a citywide event complete with plaids, pipes, and kilts. In addition, Dunedin is home to the spring training camp of the Toronto Blue Jays, and locals and visitors (particularly those from Canada) like attending exhibition games at* **Dunedin Stadium** *(727/733-9302).*

Drive along the coast U.S. 19-A until you come across the Dunedin Beach Causeway. Continue along to Honeymoon Island State Recreation Area, 1 Causeway Blvd., west of U.S. 19-A, 727/469-5942. Maybe you'll stop to picnic or swim or

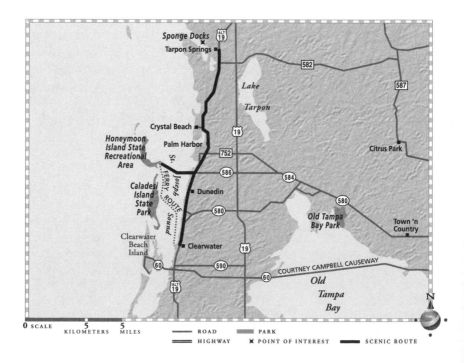

catch the ferry to **Caladesi Island State Park**, 727/469-5918. This unique park is located three miles offshore from Dunedin, just north of Clearwater Beach. It's one of the few undeveloped barrier islands left in the state, and this 600-acre park is accessible only by boat. (From Honeymoon Island, fares are $4 for adults and $2.50 for children. There's a park entrance fee per vehicle.) A self-guided nature trail winds through the island's interior and park rangers are there to answer your questions. Caladesi Island State Park is open 8 a.m. to sunset daily.

Continue along U.S. 19-A. Pause when you reach Dunedin's Main Street. Here are some really interesting shops and eating places. Sometimes you'll encounter one of the town's frequent outdoor downtown events. Open-air antique shows, crafts fairs, and art events are often in evidence here. The Pinellas Trail passes through Dunedin, and hikers, bikers, and skaters may whiz past as you stroll through town. Perhaps you'll stop for a bite at **Sea Sea Riders**, 221 Main St., Dunedin, 727/734-1445. It's a pretty wood-framed house close to the water, with a big porch and seafood that's wonderful. Another super place for breakfast, lunch, or dinner is **Kelly's for Just About Anything**, 319 Main St., 727/736-5284, with its fun décor, smiling service, and special desserts. The **Old Feed Store**, 785 Railroad Ave., 727/734-4705, has been converted to house a big antique mall. (Lots of other antique shops are in the area, too.)

To get to Clearwater, three miles south of Dunedin, take U.S. 19-A as it skims along the bay past tall palms and rolling expanses of elegant lawn as you pass by some stately "old Florida" homes—and quite a few stately new ones.

8
CLEARWATER/
ST. PETERSBURG

If you had never been to Florida and were trying to imagine what it ought to look like, you'd probably think up a place that looks a lot like the Clearwater and St. Petersburg area.

For starters, you'd expect plenty of sunshine—and here the sun shines an average of 361 days a year. Add some wide clean beaches, unspoiled islands, clear sparkling water, and gentle surf. Throw in some major attractions nearby, but not too close (90 minutes to Walt Disney World, 30 minutes to Busch Gardens). Imagine a relaxed family atmosphere; good things to eat; and antiques, boutiques, and malls for shopping excursions; along with festivals, shows, and museums. Add outdoor fun galore, with 41 golf courses, a 47-mile hiking and jogging trail, and 35 miles of beach. Of course, this picture of the ideal Florida wouldn't be complete without palm trees silhouetted against a brilliant sunset and reflected in the turquoise Gulf waters. Got that, too. It's no wonder this area is such a popular destination for vacationers from all over the world.

A PERFECT DAY IN ST. PETERSBURG

Start with an early morning walk on the beach. The sea birds will be making a racket, coming ashore from their island rookeries searching for breakfast. Walk along the water's edge and see what treasures the tide may have brought in during the night. Find a perfect shell and put it in your pocket—something to remember this day. Take Gulf Boulevard to Redington Beach. You're going to have breakfast at the Frog Pond. Portions are huge, but that's okay. You're going to have a busy day.

Now cross the Treasure Island Causeway to St. Petersburg to see the Salvador Dalí Museum and its over $125-million collection of paintings, drawings, and sculpture. Awesome! For lunch, dine *al fresco* in the shaded courtyard at The Garden, a Mediterranean Bistro, on Central Avenue. Check out the antique district, then to St. Petersburg's famous landmark, the Pier. Walk up to the observation deck for a good view of the city and the Gulf. Relax. When it's almost time for the sun to set, head south on Gulf Boulevard to Pass-a-Grille Beach and the Hurricane Lounge. Go straight to the top deck, face west, listen to jazz, and drink a toast to a spectacular sunset and a perfect day.

ORIENTATION

Clearwater and St. Petersburg are both located in Pinellas County (pronounced pin-NELL-as), a peninsula with Tampa Bay to the east and the Gulf of Mexico to the west. Clearwater is situated on some of the highest land on the peninsula, and the downtown area, with its moss-draped oak trees, has a feeling of a quiet old Southern town. Adjacent to downtown Clearwater is a wide public beach. From there the Memorial Causeway joins the city to the tropical setting of Clearwater Beach. Clearwater's marinas and yacht clubs shelter all kinds of pleasure boats, as well as one of the largest charter sport-fishing fleets in the country.

From Clearwater go south on U.S. 19 to reach St. Petersburg. If you prefer a more leisurely route, take the Memorial Causeway in Clearwater to U.S. 19-A, which meanders through the Gulf beach communities of Clearwater Beach, Indian Rocks Beach, Redington Beach, Madeira Beach, Treasure Island, St. Pete Beach, and Pass-a-Grille.

On the eastern side of U.S. 19 is St. Petersburg's downtown, where visitors enjoy museums, restaurants, shops, and historical landmarks. The western edge is dotted with barrier islands connected to the mainland by causeways. Here are miles of beaches, quiet parks, and laid-back beach communities and fishing towns. The founding fathers of St. Petersburg planned the city pretty well, with wide streets and a neat grid pattern. Avenues run east and west; streets run north and south. Central Avenue divides north and south St. Petersburg, with numbered avenues beginning on either side of Central (e.g., First Avenue South and First Avenue North). The only problem one might encounter is a hard-to-figure-out system of one-way streets here and there. Just watch the road signs. If there's a Devil Rays baseball game at Tropicana Field

CLEARWATER BEACH

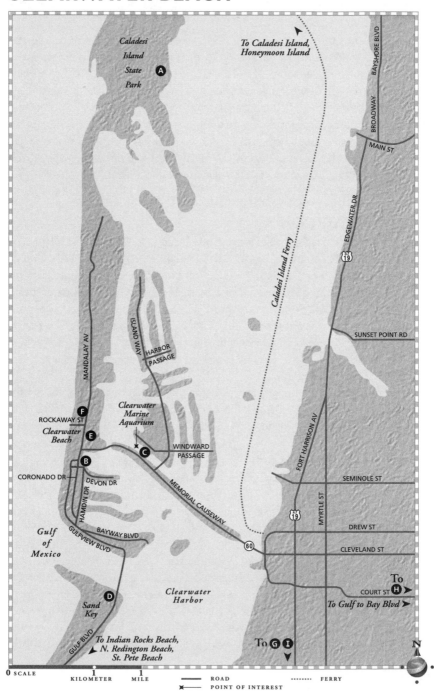

Caladesi Island State Park **A**

To Caladesi Island, Honeymoon Island

BAYSHORE BLVD

BROADWAY

MAIN ST

EDGEWATER DR

19

SUNSET POINT RD

Caladesi Island Ferry

ISLAND WAY

HARBOR PASSAGE

MANDALAY AV

Clearwater Marine Aquarium

ROCKAWAY ST **F**

Clearwater Beach **E**

WINDWARD PASSAGE

C

FORT HARRISON AV

SEMINOLE ST

B

CORONADO DR

DEVON DR

HAMDIN DR

MEMORIAL CAUSEWAY

MYRTLE ST

19

DREW ST

Gulf of Mexico

GULFVIEW BLVD

BAYWAY BLVD

60

CLEVELAND ST

To **H**

COURT ST

D

Sand Key

Clearwater Harbor

To Gulf to Bay Blvd

GULF BLVD

To Indian Rocks Beach, N. Redington Beach, St. Pete Beach

To **G** **I**

N

0 SCALE   1 KILOMETER   1 MILE   —— ROAD   ·········· FERRY
✕— POINT OF INTEREST

on Central Avenue, things get slowed down a lot before and after the game, so check the sports pages before you head downtown during baseball season. Trolleys connect all the downtown museums, hotels, and the Pier, making the rounds every half-hour.

CLEARWATER BEACH SIGHTSEEING HIGHLIGHTS

★★★★ CALADESI ISLAND AND HONEYMOON ISLAND STATE PARKS
North of Clearwater Beach, 727/469-5942, www.dep.state.fl.us/parks
Caladesi and Honeymoon Islands are among the very few unspoiled barrier islands left in Florida. They each give visitors a chance to see what Florida looked like back before the bulldozers came. The near-pristine beaches offer a fine place to picnic, swim, fish, or just goof off. You can drive to Honeymoon Island; Caladesi requires a boat ride. Honeymoon Island is a romantic place, as the name suggests—sugary white sand, waving palm trees, and gentle sea breezes. It's a lovely swimming and sunning spot, and there are showers and snack bars available. You can even bring your dog for a stroll on "Dog Beach." Caladesi Island was rated second best beach in the United States in 1995. It's pretty remote, and you can walk for miles along the beaches or explore the nature trails. There are picnic tables and a concession stand, but this island is mostly unspoiled.

Details: Caladesi Island ferries depart from two places. From the Drew Street Dock in downtown Clearwater, fares are $4.95 for adults and $3 for children ages 3 to 12, plus $1 park entrance fee for each person over age 5. From Honeymoon Island at the end of Dunedin

SIGHTS	FOOD	LODGING
Ⓐ Caladesi Island and Honeymoon Island State Parks	Ⓔ Bob Heilman's Beachcomber	Ⓘ Belleview Biltmore
Ⓑ Captain Memo's Pirate Cruise	Ⓕ Frenchy's	
	Ⓖ The Pepper Mill	
Ⓒ Clearwater Marine Aquarium	Ⓗ Tio Pepe	
Ⓓ Sand Key Park		

PLUMES ON THE BEACH

You'll probably notice sea oats on the Gulf Coast's beaches, with their feathery flags waving in warm breezes. These grassy plants are vital to stabilizing beaches. They have long roots and rough stems, both of which help trap and collect sand into piles that eventually become dunes. State law protects sea oats, so don't pick them.

Causeway, fares are $4 for adults, and $2.50 for children ages 3 to 12, plus $3.25 park entrance fee per vehicle. The Clearwater Municipal Marina is at Clearwater Beach, and the ferry makes a stop there, too. Take U.S. 19 N. to Curlew Rd. Turn left to Honeymoon Island. Follow signs for ferry to Caladesi, or catch ferry from Clearwater Marina, 727/442-7032. Park open 8–sunset. (3–4 hours)

★★ CAPTAIN MEMO'S PIRATE CRUISE

Clearwater Beach Marina #3, 25 Causeway Blvd., 727/446-2787, www.pirateflorida.com

Everybody loves the pirate cruise. It's a true fantasy world for kids and grownups, complete with swashbucklers and pirates on-board. The good vessel *Pirate's Ransom* (custom designed and built to U.S. Coast Guard specs) cruises within cannon-shot of Captain Memo's deserted island along the Intracoastal Waterway and out into the Gulf of Mexico. Sometimes playful dolphins leap along side to add to the fun.

Details: *Board at Dock 3 at the end of U.S. 60 on Clearwater Beach. Regular cruises depart Mon–Sat at 10, 2, 4:30, and 7; Sun 2, 4:30, and 7. $27 adults, $20 seniors and children. For champagne/sunset cruises call 727/446-2587. (2 hours)*

★★ CLEARWATER MARINE AQUARIUM

249 Windward Passage, Clearwater, 727/447-0980, CMA@cftnet.com

This well-maintained aquarium is a nonprofit facility dedicated to the rescue, rehabilitation, and release of sick or injured sea creatures. It's not as fancy, perhaps, as some of the big attraction-type aquariums,

---

but it's fascinating in terms of environmental education and research. Visitors get a good look at rescued dolphins, otters, and sea turtles during animal care and training presentations, which are offered hourly. Kids of all ages like the "touch tanks," where there's a hands-on exhibit. Feel the silky stingrays and the pebbly starfish. You can even try on a giant sea turtle shell for size.

Details: *Take I-275 to SR 60 west toward Clearwater Beach; turn right on Island Way, then left on Windward Passage. Mon–Fri 9–5, Sat 9–4, Sun 11–4; closed major holidays. $6.75 adults, $4.25 children. (1–2 hours)*

★★ SAND KEY PARK
Gulf Blvd., Clearwater Beach, 727/595-7677
A rock jetty, extending out into the Gulf, shields the waters off Sand Key park. This makes for ideal swimming and fishing conditions. This 65-acre park has a very wide beach with lovely white sand. There's also a landscaped park, a boardwalk, playground, grills, and picnic tables.

Details: *Sand Key Park is located on Gulf Blvd., just south of the Clearwater Pass Bridge. Open daily 7 a.m. to dark. Lifeguard on duty 9:30–4:30. Metered parking. (1 hour–all day)*

ST. PETERSBURG SIGHTSEEING HIGHLIGHTS

★★★★ FLORIDA INTERNATIONAL MUSEUM
100 Second St. N., St. Petersburg, 727/822-3693, www.floridamuseum.org
This sprawling facility was once a major department store encompassing a whole city block. It now houses blockbuster artistic and historical exhibitions from around the world on an annual basis. Dates vary slightly from exhibit to exhibit, but shows usually open in October and end in late spring. These events are hugely popular with visitors and residents, so it's best to make reservations if you want to be sure to get in. Previous big shows have included "Treasures of the Czars," which featured Russian imperial jewels and artifacts; "Alexander the Great;" and "Titanic, the Exhibit," with actual items from the sunken ocean liner. On permanent display is the Robert L. White John F. Kennedy Collection, a fascinating exhibit of photos and articles associated with the late President and Mrs. Kennedy. There are even doodles JFK made on White House stationery and a gold

ST. PETERSBURG

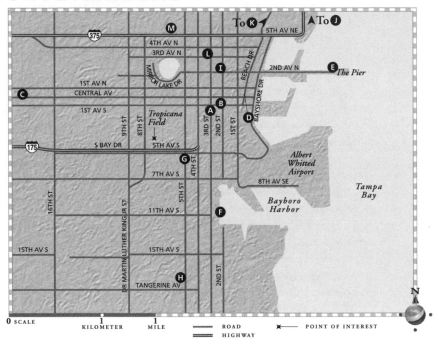

SIGHTS

Ⓐ American Stage
  Company
Ⓑ Florida International
  Museum
Ⓒ Haslam's New and
  Used Books
Ⓓ Museum of Fine Arts
Ⓔ The Pier

SIGHTS (continued)

Ⓕ Salvador Dalí Museum
Ⓖ Tampa Bay Holocaust
  Memorial Museum and
  Educational Center

FOOD

Ⓗ Basta's Ristorante
Ⓘ Heritage Grille

LODGING

Ⓙ Bayboro House
Ⓚ Bay Shore Manor
Ⓛ Heritage Inn
Ⓜ Renaissance Vinoy
  Resort

---

locket Mrs. Kennedy often wore. JFK's wallet is here, with his
Massachusetts driver's license, in addition to many other artifacts.

 Details: *Daily 9–8, Sat 9 a.m.–10 p.m.; closed Thanksgiving and
Christmas. Tours start every 15 minutes, with last tour at 6. Admission
varies with shows, adults usually $15, students $6. (2 hours)*

★★★★ THE PIER
800 Second Ave. NE, St. Petersburg, 727/821-6164

Perhaps St. Petersburg's most recognizable landmark, the Pier is a five-story inverted-pyramid building situated, logically enough, on a pier jutting out into Tampa Bay. The view is—dare we say it?—peerless. Inside you'll find a sizable marine aquarium, the wonderful and kid-friendly **Great Explorations Hands On Museum** (727/821-8885; open Monday to Saturday 10 to 8, Sunday 11 to 6), and lots of galleries and specialty shops. There's even a bait house, if you want to do a little fishing from the specially constructed catwalks. If you don't fish, just watch the pelicans and seagulls soaring and diving. Several good restaurants are on the premises, too. If you're at the Pier after dark, drop in at **Cha Cha Coconuts** (727/822-6655; Monday through Thursday 11 a.m. to midnight; Friday and Saturday 11 a.m. to 1 a.m.; Sunday noon to 10) for live music every night. From November to April MGM's historic **HMS *Bounty*** (727/896-5668) docks here and is open for tours daily 10 to 6, as well as day sails. A sightseeing boat makes four trips daily when the weather is fine. A seven-hour sail aboard the *Bounty*, including breakfast and lunch, can be arranged for $125 per person.

Details: Open daily 10–9. $2 parking per day. Admission charges to the museum is $4 for adults and $3 for kids. The Bounty admission is $6 adults, $5 seniors, $4 children. (1–4 hours)

★★★★ SALVADOR DALÍ MUSEUM
1000 Third St. S., St. Petersburg, 727/823-3767,
www.daliweb.com

This spacious facility adjacent to the waterfront Bayboro Campus of the University of South Florida (USF) houses what is arguably the largest collection in the world devoted exclusively to the Spanish surrealist master. The stunning collection contains 94 oils, numerous watercolors, sketches, jewels, sculptures, photographs, and more—over 2,500 items in total, displayed on a rotating basis. Dalí produced 18 masterworks, and six of them are right here. You'll see the huge *The Hallucinogenic Toreador* with its "hidden" images and *The Disintegration of the Persistence of Memory*—that's the famed "melting clocks" canvas.

Details: Mon–Sat 9:30–5:30, Thu 9–8, Sun noon–5:30; closed Thanksgiving and Christmas. $8 adults, less for children and seniors. (1–2 hours)

★★★ AMERICAN STAGE COMPANY
211 Third St. S., St. Petersburg, 727/822-8814,
www.americanstage.org
American Stage is an equity theater that presents four productions annually at its 130-seat main stage from November to June. Each spring the company puts on a Shakespeare in the Park performance, drawing more than 20,000 people annually. American Stage also hosts a children's theater season, a summer camp, and classes in theater arts.

Details: The annual outdoor Shakespeare festival usually runs from mid-April until mid-May at Demens Landing, a big, beautiful park on St. Petersburg's downtown waterfront. For dates and times, call American Stage Company. (2–3 hours, depending on show)

★★★ MUSEUM OF FINE ARTS
255 Beach Dr. NE, St. Petersburg, 727/896-2667,
www.fine-arts.org
This handsome museum is conveniently located in the downtown waterfront area on trendy Beach Drive. Noted particularly for its collection of French impressionist paintings, it also has an outstanding collection of European, American, pre-Columbian, and Far Eastern art, including an extensive glass sculptures exhibit. Special exhibits feature artwork on loan from other metropolitan museums. Period rooms feature antiques, and photographers will be delighted by the important collection of photographs by American masters.

Details: Tue–Sat 10–5, Sun 1–5. $6 adults, $2 students, $5 seniors (over 65), free Sun. Guided tours available for small donation. (2 hours)

★★★ TAMPA BAY HOLOCAUST MEMORIAL MUSEUM AND EDUCATIONAL CENTER
55 Fifth St. S., St. Petersburg, 727/820-0100,
www.tampabayholocaust.org
A new 27,000-square-foot center makes the Holocaust Museum the fourth largest of its kind in the United States. The centerpiece exhibit is a 30-foot by 15-foot boxcar that was used to transport people to Nazi concentration camps. Changing exhibits include art, photos, and historic documents. The goal of the center is to further education regarding the Holocaust and to promote the lessons of tolerance, respect, and responsibility.

TURTLE WATCHES

Giant sea turtles are among our coast's most fascinating creatures. Every year between early May and late August, these prehistoric reptiles, weighing 300 to 500 pounds, drag themselves up onto Florida beaches to lay their eggs in the darkness before returning to the water.

Sea turtle eggs must remain undisturbed in warm sand for about 60 days before they hatch. Coastal development hampers the nesting efforts, threatening sea turtles with extinction. If you visit Gulf Coast beaches during the nesting times, you may see chicken-wire fencing protecting known nests. Marine biologists and environmental groups are working hard to preserve these creatures, and many communities sponsor "turtle walks" or "turtle watches" that you can join. Watch for signs announcing turtle walks posted on fenced areas, or check with the nearest aquarium or marine science center.

Details: Some exhibits may be too graphic for children. Mon–Fri 10–5, Sat noon–5. $6 adults, $2 children. Free parking. (1 hour)

★ HASLAM'S NEW AND USED BOOKS
2025 Central Ave., St. Petersburg, 727/822-8616

The *Tampa Tribune* calls Haslam's "one of Florida's true treasures." It probably is. It's a big old rambling place with rows and rows of new, used, and rare books (more than 300,000, says Haslam's), arranged just so for your browsing pleasure. It's a real old-fashioned family-owned bookstore—a great place to visit on a rainy day.

Details: Mon–Sat 10–6:30, Sun 12:30–5:30. (1 hour)

SOUTHERN PINELLAS COUNTY SIGHTSEEING HIGHLIGHTS

★★★★ CENTRAL AVENUE ANTIQUES DISTRICT
600–1200 block of Central Ave., St. Petersburg

Central Avenue has long been a grand spot for antiquing, but it's only recently begun to look like a pleasant place to shop. The arrival of the Tampa Bay Devil Rays baseball team to downtown St. Petersburg's Tropicana Field has brought a welcome sprucing-up of the entire area, including dozens of antiques shops. **Gas Plant Antique Arcade**, 1246 Central Ave., 727/895-0368, is a huge mall right next door to Tropicana Field. It's housed in what used to be a major furniture store. There are four floors jam-packed with antiques, collectibles, and memorabilia. If you like the blond good looks of vintage Heywood-Wakefield furniture, visit **Echoes**, 1209 Central Ave., 727/898-3246. Baby boomers will love **Urbana**, 665 Central Ave., 727/824-5669. Furniture for the '50s and '60s shares space with Bakelite, chromeware, and all sorts of good vintage stuff.

> **Details:** *Most shops open Mon–Sat 10–5; Sun 12–5. To reach Central from I-75, take Exit 10. (2 hours)*

★★★ SUNCOAST SEABIRD SANCTUARY
188328 Gulf Blvd., Indian Shores, 727/391-6211,
www.webcoast.com/SeaBird
Known worldwide for its outstanding efforts in the preservation of wild birds, the nonprofit sanctuary displays more than 500 birds, including a large nesting colony of permanently injured brown pelicans. Some resident birds have called the sanctuary home for many years. Gabby the hawk, blinded by a bullet, has been here for 20 years. Visitors get a close-up look at sandhill cranes, white pelicans, varieties of owls, birds of prey, and more. Over 5,000 birds are treated here every year, and most of them are released back into the wild as soon as they recover.

> **Details:** *Gulf Blvd. runs the length of the beaches; Indian Shores is north of Madeira Beach, south of Clearwater Beach. Sanctuary open 9 a.m.–sunset. Guided tours and lectures conducted by knowledgeable volunteers Wed and Sun at 2. Donations appreciated. (30 minutes)*

★★ HERITAGE VILLAGE
11909 125th St. N., Largo, 727/582-2123,
www.co.pinellas.fl.us/bcc/heritag.htm
For a realistic look into Florida's pioneer past, traverse the old brick walkways of Heritage Village. Some of the county's oldest historic homes and buildings have been moved to this attractively arranged park, looking for all the world as though they've always been there.

Knowledgeable volunteer docents can show you around, or you can wander about on your own through the 22 buildings, including the oldest home extant in the county—a circa-1850 log cabin. Kids like the one-room schoolhouse, the railroad depot complete with caboose, and the operational blacksmith shop. There are occasional special events like sheep shearing, Civil War reenactments, and crafts fairs.

Details: From SR 688 in mid-county, turn south on 125th St. in Largo. Open Tue–Sat 10–4, Sun 1–4. Mostly free, but small admission to a couple of the houses. (2 hours)

★ JOHN'S PASS VILLAGE

John's Pass Bridge, Madeira Beach, 727/391-7373 or 800/944-1847, www.gulfbeaches-tampabay.com

Okay, so it's hokey and kitschy and has way too many T-shirt shops. But it's fun. And the food is good. And the boardwalk is interesting. You can shop till you drop in a hundred or so gift shops and galleries. **The Bronze Lady**, 12957 Village Blvd., 727/398-5994, features the paintings of Red Skelton, as well as the collectible lines of Armani, Swarovski, and Hummel. Open Monday to Friday 10 to 9; Saturday 10 to 5:30; Sunday 11 to 5:30. **The Fun & Sun Shop**, 12927 Village Blvd., 727/397-2046, offers a super variety of all sorts of things visitors like to see in a shop. T-shirts and shell craft share space with Native American crafts and Hawaiian fashions. Open daily 9:30 a.m. to 9:30 p.m.

Or you can just sit on a weathered bench, eat an ice-cream cone, and watch the boats, the people, and the pelicans. The area offers several restaurants (both the fast-food and sit-down varieties), parasail rides, fishing trips, watercraft rentals, and more. Each October, the village hosts the **Fall Seafood Festival**, a huge three-day event with entertainment, an arts and crafts show, and, of course, lots of seafood.

Details: Open daily. Merchant's hours vary shop to shop. For information on the Fall Seafood Festival, call John's Pass Village main number. (3 hours)

FITNESS AND RECREATION

Want to play some golf or fish in the Gulf, sail away or coast along on a bicycle, or go for a hike or play tennis? Or . . . but you get the idea. There's hardly anything one does out of doors that you can't do here.

Naturally, some of the best things for visitors to do involve miles and miles of beaches. On Clearwater Beach, the city maintains permanent nets for volleyball that are often used for professional, televised beach volleyball tournaments. If biking, hiking, and skating are your bag, you're going to love the Pinellas Trail. This 40-plus-mile path goes nearly the whole length of Pinellas County, from St. Petersburg to Tarpon Springs. Get information from the park department at 727/393-8909. Rent a bike at Lou's Bicycle Center, 8990 Seminole Blvd., Seminole, 727/398-2543, and get on the trail at nearby Seminole City Park.

Hooked on fishing? Try wetting a line off the fishing pier at beautiful, historic Fort De Soto Park, south of St. Petersburg on the Pinellas Bayway, 727/866-2662. For deep-sea fishing, check out Hubbard's Marina, John's Pass Village, Madeira Beach, 727/524-7999. Hubbard's offers half-day, all-day, and overnight trips. Feeling courageous? Try parasailing, where you'll hang beneath a parachute towed by a speedboat. Contact Gilligan's at John's Pass Village Boardwalk, 727/319-3731, for info on this activity.

Tennis is a popular pastime in Clearwater, where there are more than 60 public courts. Call Clearwater Parks and Recreation Department, 727/462-6532, for locations. There are too many golf courses to list—just check the Yellow Pages when you get here. One of our most famous, though, is Bardmoor, 7919 Bardmoor Blvd., Largo, 727/392-1234. If miniature golf is more your speed, visit Pirate's Cove Adventure Golf, 423 150th Ave., Madeira Beach, 727/393-8879. And, about that ice skating—Sunblades, 13940 Icot Blvd., Clearwater, 727/536-5843, has a full-sized rink for figure skating or ice hockey. Skate rentals are available. Some of the other ice rinks are in the middle of shopping malls. Try Tampa Bay Skating Academy at the Pinellas Park Side, 7200 U.S. 19, Pinellas Park, 727/527-2276.

FOOD

Dining out in the Clearwater/St. Petersburg area is truly cosmopolitan. Restaurants here serve foods of many national styles to visitors from many places—usually in a casual, resortlike atmosphere. Since the area is so water-oriented, you'll find most restaurants serving seafood delicacies from local waters—and lots of them have a water view or docking facilities for hungry yachtsmen. Florida is a top cattle-producing state, so you'll find a good share of steak houses, too. And with this climate, it goes without saying that the vegetables and fruits are farm fresh.

In Clearwater, **Bob Heilman's Beachcomber**, 447 Mandalay Ave., Clearwater Beach, 727/442-4144 serves generous, traditional-style meals.

Family fare includes wonderful fried chicken, fluffy whipped potatoes, fresh veggies, and hot, home-baked bread. **Frenchy's**, 7 Rockaway St., 727/446-0588, has a beachfront location and boasts "fish right off the boats." **The Pepper Mill**, 1575 S. Fort Harrison Way, 727/449-2988, is a busy place, and with good reason. Pepper Mill steak is a favorite and grilled fish dishes are specialties. Rich desserts and affordable wines round out a big menu. **Tio Pepe**, 2930 Gulf-to-Bay Blvd., 727/799-3082, is busy, noisy, and lots of fun. Locals adore Uncle Pepe's Spanish-style cuisine; so do visitors. Black bean soup is a must. Fresh sangria is made tableside and pumpernickel bread is warm from the oven.

In St. Petersburg, stop by **Basta's Ristorante**, 1625 Fourth St. S., 727/894-7880, an outstanding Italian restaurant that serves marvelous scampi, seafood dishes, and imaginative pastas. **Pepin Restaurant**, 4125 Fourth St. N., 727/821-3773, has been here for more than 20 years, serving grand Spanish food, such as *pompano en papillote,* and is famous with good reason. **Heritage Grille**, located in an old home, 256 Second St. N., 727/823-6382, is casual yet elegant. Try the roasted walnut, Dijon-crusted rack of lamb. Enjoy lunch or dinner indoors or outside in the banyan tree–shaded courtyard of **The Garden, a Mediterranean Bistro**, 217 Central Ave., 727/896-3800. The quaint historic building adds charm to tasty Mediterranean cuisine, and the late-night weekend Buster Cooper trio is a must-do for jazz fans. Authentic jerk chicken and curry dishes have made **Saffron's Caribbean**, 1700 Park St., 727/522-1234, a huge success with local island connoisseurs. It has a lovely junglelike setting and reasonable prices. **Ted Peter's Famous Smoked Fish**, 1350 Pasadena Ave. S. in South Pasadena, 727/381-7931, is an old-time favorite in these parts. Casual indoor/outdoor seating and hot smoked-fish dinners with all the trimmings make this place a favorite with visitors from all over the world. Giant burgers are popular fare, and they sell the justifiably famous smoked-fish spread by the pound.

Check out some of the spots along the Gulf beaches. **Hurricane Seafood Restaurant**, Ninth Ave. and Gulf Way, Pass-a-Grille Beach, 727/360-9558 is one of the oldest and most popular beach bars along these shores. Over the years the building and the menu have each undergone updating, but the old "beach bar" atmosphere remains intact. Have breakfast on the outdoor deck overlooking the beach, or party until late at night after a satisfying seafood dinner. Best place at sunset is the top deck. **The Friendly Fisherman**, 150 John's Pass Village Boardwalk, Madeira Beach, 727/391-6025, is a big, busy place. A window seat is worth waiting for. You can watch the commercial boats and pleasure yachts coming and going as you enjoy carefully prepared, moderately priced seafood-fried, broiled, baked as you like it.

SOUTHERN PINELLAS COUNTY

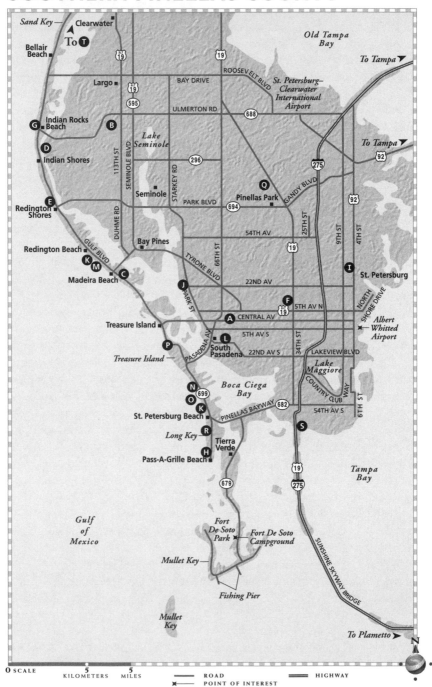

Dine indoors or out on the patio at **Guppy's on the Beach**, 1701 Gulf Blvd., Indian Rocks Beach, 727/593-2032. It's very casual, often crowded, maybe a bit noisy, and a tad pricey, but what good imaginatively prepared seafood—killer desserts, too. **Shell's** has two locations on the beaches, 6300 Gulf Blvd. at St. Pete Beach, 727/360-0889, and 17855 Gulf Blvd. at Redington Beach, 727/393-8990. Shell's regularly gets named in "Best of the Bay" listings and both visitors and local folks keep coming back for more. Take the name literally; everything they serve once lived in a shell.

Breakfast and lunch are generously served at the **Frog Pond**, 16909 Gulf Blvd. N., Redington Beach, 727/392-4117, amid the froggy ambiance. Amazing omelets, heaping fruit plates, and two-fisted sandwiches are served by pleasant wait staff every day. The **Wine Cellar**, 17307 Gulf Blvd., N. Redington Beach, 727/393-3491, is a winner of many awards for its European food, perfect service, and intimate atmosphere. The wine selection is vast. It's an elegant, albeit expensive, place to celebrate anything at all.

LODGING

When a place attracts millions of visitors every year, that place is very likely to have a great variety of lodgings to accommodate guests. That's certainly true of the St. Petersburg/Clearwater area. The beaches—those barrier islands along the western edge of the county—are always popular with vacationers. What could be nicer than having the surf and sand and sunshine just a few steps away from your window? But then, there's a lot to be said for the downtown locations, too—the museums, antique shops, galleries, restaurants, and

SIGHTS
Ⓐ Central Avenue Antiques District
Ⓑ Heritage Village
Ⓒ John's Pass Village
Ⓓ Suncoast Seabird Sanctuary

FOOD
Ⓒ The Friendly Fisherman
Ⓔ Frog Pond

FOOD (continued)
Ⓕ The Garden, a Mediterranean Bistro
Ⓖ Guppy's on the Beach
Ⓗ Hurricane Seafood Restaurant
Ⓘ Pepin Restaurant
Ⓙ Saffron's Caribbean
Ⓚ Shell's (2 locations)
Ⓛ Ted Peter's Famous Smoked Fish
Ⓜ Wine Cellar

LODGING
Ⓝ Alden Beach Resort
Ⓞ Best Western
Ⓟ The Bilmar
Ⓠ Day's Inn Getaway
Ⓡ Don CeSar Beach Resort and Spa
Ⓢ Holiday Inn Sunspree Resort—Marina Cove
Ⓣ Ramada Inn Clearwater Beach

Note: Items with the same letter are located in the same area.

clubs are right there, along with handy public transportation. Either way, visitors who plan ahead face a virtual smorgasbord of lodging possibilities.

Clearwater's crown jewel among lodgings has to be the **Belleview Biltmore**, 25 Belleview Blvd., 727/443-3701, www.belleviewbiltmore.com. Listed on the National Register of Historic Places, the Belleview Biltmore is one of the grand hotels built by railroad tycoon Henry B. Plant over 100 years ago. With 292 luxuriously appointed rooms, it's billed as the largest occupied wooden structure in the world. There's an 18-hole Donald Ross–designed golf course, and the ballroom has a Tiffany stained-glass ceiling. This hotel is totally posh. Even if you don't stay there, you'll enjoy joining a historical tour of the place. They hold one every morning at 11. There's a small fee for the tour, or for $15 you can have the tour and a buffet lunch, too. **Ramada Inn Clearwater Beach**, 521 S. Gulfview Blvd., Clearwater Beach, 727/447-6461, has your standard amenities.

The city of St. Petersburg offers a good variety of accommodation choices. If luxury in historic surroundings is appealing, check out the pleasures of the **Renaissance Vinoy Resort**, 501 Fifth Ave. NE, St. Petersburg, 727/894-1000, www.renaissancehotels.com. This is another of our 1920s vintage architectural treasures, one that has recently enjoyed a $100-million makeover. The imposing structure is listed on the National Register of Historic Places. There's even an 18-hole, par-70 golf course.

Listed among the Historic Hotels of America is **Heritage Inn**, 234 Third Ave. N., 727/822-4814. Within easy walking distance of all the downtown museums and attractions, this 1920s gem has traditional rooms, a pool, Jacuzzi, and the charm of a small inn (even though it is a Holiday Inn property).

Bed-and-breakfast places have enjoyed a resurgence lately as more folks visit downtown St. Petersburg's museums, attractions, and shops. The sprawling pink-and-white **Bay Shore Manor**, 635 12th Ave. NE, 727/822-3438, is located in a fine old building just across from a park and a small beach. Big German-style breakfast buffets are the rule here. **Bayboro House**, 1719 Beach Dr. SE, 727/823-4955, overlooks the bay. Wraparound verandahs replete with swings and wicker chairs invite the traveler to imagine turn-of-the-last-century St. Petersburg. This top-rated Queen Anne–style B&B features lovely antiques, classical art, and no telephones in the rooms. Adults-only ambiance is conducive to a restful bayside stay.

There are plenty of nationally known chains here that maintain locations both in town and on the beaches. In St. Petersburg, check out **Holiday Inn Sunspree Resort—Marina Cove**, 6800 Sunshine Skyway Br., 727/867-1151. Also in St. Petersburg is **Day's Inn Getaway**, 9359 U.S. 19 N., 727/577-3838.

If you mention hotels around the beaches bordering the St. Petersburg/

THE DREADED FIRE ANTS

Florida has not one but two kinds of fire ants: one native species and one imported one—a Brazilian variety brought here by accident in 1940. If you step on or disturb a nest, you'll never forget the experience. Though these ants are tiny, they swarm over an unwelcome visitor in seconds and deliver a sting that may burn and itch for hours. (An over-the-counter cortisone medication will help relieve the pain.)

Clearwater area, someone will surely mention the **Don CeSar Beach Resort and Spa**, 3400 Gulf Blvd., St. Pete Beach, 727/360-1881 or 800/282-1116, www.doncesar.com. This massive "pink palace," built in 1928, is listed on the National Register of Historic Places. The whole place is absolutely elegant—guest rooms, suites, penthouses, you name it. It's expensive, but service and amenities are always first rate. Don't be surprised to see a movie star or two, or even a president lounging poolside or working out in the spa. (You don't have to stay at the Don to enjoy dining at the delightful Maritana Grille, and you're welcome to drop in at the Lobby Bar or the Sea Porch Cafe.)

Another St. Pete Beach–front favorite is the **Alden Beach Resort**, 5900 Gulf Blvd., 727/360-7081 or 800/262-3464, e-mail alden@travelbase.com, www.travelbase.com/destination/st-pete/alden/. Suites offer homelike comforts with fully equipped kitchens, cable TV, and all the expected amenities. Resort fun includes tennis, basketball, and pools. Water-sport rentals are also available. **The Bilmar**, 10650 Gulf Blvd., 727/360-5531 or 800/826-9724, www.gotampabay.com/bilmar, has been a fixture on Treasure Island for a long time. Loyal vacationers return year after year for clean, comfortable rooms, great Gulf views, and a couple of nice pools, one only steps away from a wide sandy beach. It's moderately priced for such a primo location. The Bilmar is famous locally for good Dixieland jazz in the Beach Bar. A good **Best Western** is on 5390 Gulf Blvd., St. Pete Beach, 800/344-5999.

CAMPING

At the award-winning St. Petersburg/Madeira Beach Resort KOA Kampground, 5400 95th St. N., 727/392-2233 or 800/562-7714, families enjoy a waterfront resort with a private fishing dock. The famed Pinellas Trail runs nearby for biking and hiking adventures, and 60 neat little "Kamping Kabins" are available for campers without their own RVs.

A favorite campground with visitors and with locals who want to get away from it all for a few days is Fort De Soto Campground, in Fort De Soto Park on the Pinellas Bayway, St. Petersburg, 727/866-2662. Almost all of the 235 sites are on the waterfront, shaded by giant old oak trees or sheltering palms. This place is popular, and residents get preference, so call ahead to see what's available. Don't forget to take a quick walking tour of the fort while you're there.

Close to the Gulf beaches and fishing is Holiday Campground, 10000 Park Blvd., Seminole, 727/391-4960. Nicely situated on wooded acreage close to both St. Petersburg and the beaches, there's a heated pool and spa, and a golf course is nearby, too.

Conveniently located just off U.S. 19 is Travel Towne Travel Trailer Resort. It's a highly rated park, close to the ferry service to Caladesi Island. Visit a big shopping mall or go shelling on the beach. Both are close by. The park has paved roads and streetlights and is handy to some good restaurants, too.

NIGHTLIFE

Things have certainly changed on the after-dark scene in St. Petersburg. The coming of major league baseball to downtown Tropicana Field (locals call it "The Trop") has resulted in a proliferation of clubs—many of them sports themed. Extra Inning Ball Park Cafe, 1850 Central Ave., 727/896-9872, is just about a line drive away from Tropicana Field, where the Devil Rays play. Nineteen big-screened TVs guarantee plenty of sports talk while patrons eat and drink. Another club near the Trop, but without the baseball motif, is the very hip Budious Maximus, 1111 Central Ave., 727/898-8525. Marked by bright red doors, '40s décor, and a leopard-spotted sign, Budious rocks to DJ sounds every night.

Gator's Cafe and Saloon, 12754 Kingfish Dr., Treasure Island, 727/367-8951, is a party-down, bikini-okay, open-late, waterfront restaurant and sports bar. Come by land or by sea for the live music, the 15 appetizers, the sandwiches, and the burgers. You can climb to the top deck of the establishment's several tiers and view the most fabulous carved-mahogany bar you've ever seen.

Broadway hits, classical musicians, country singers, big bands, dancers, comedians, and top pop artists are standard fare at Ruth Eckerd Hall, 1111 McMullen Booth Rd., Clearwater, 727/791-7400. Entertainment runs from October to May.

For a memorable evening, take a dinner-dance cruise along the smooth inland waterway aboard either the *Starlight Princess*, Corey Ave. Causeway, St. Pete Beach, 727/462-2628, or the *Starlight Majesty* at the Clearwater Beach Marina, 727/462-2628. Full-course meals are prepared aboard ship.

For some Las Vegas–style casino action, hop aboard *Europa Sea Kruz* at John's Pass Village, 727/393-5110 or 800/688-PLAY. Every cruise features a buffet and live entertainment.

For dinner and a show without staying out until all hours, many visitors like Bill Irle's Early Bird Dinner Theater, 1310 N. Fort Harrison Ave., Clearwater, 727/446-5898. You'll get a hearty buffet and a stage show all for around $15. Call for times and reservations.

There are lots of other things to see and do after dark in the St. Petersburg/Clearwater areas. You'll find a couple of free tabloid-sized newspapers that will keep you up to speed. The *St. Petersburg Times* distributes *Weekend* every Friday, and the *Weekly Planet* puts out a Thursday publication listing happenings on both sides of the bay.

9
TAMPA

These days we often hear the term Tampa Bay used about this part of Florida: Tampa Bay Buccaneers football team, Tampa Bay Lightning ice hockey team, Tampa Bay Devil Rays baseball team. But Tampa Bay really is a body of water, with St. Petersburg and Clearwater on one side and the city of Tampa on the other. (So when you hear someone say something is in Tampa Bay—they probably don't mean it's underwater—just that it's in this general area.)

Tampa is quite different from its neighboring cities across the bay. In ever-increasing numbers, glass and steel towers glitter across the broad cityscape. Malls, office buildings, and sports facilities seem to sprout almost overnight as the area's stable economy, fine weather, and ready workforce continue to lure companies and individuals to this interesting and beautiful city.

But don't let all those skyscrapers and shiny new sports stadiums fool you. Tampa is actually a very old city. Hernando de Soto sailed into the bay way back in 1539. (He was searching for gold but didn't find it.) The natives who lived here at the time called the place something that sounded like "Tanpa." They said it meant "sticks of fire." Mapmakers of the time corrupted the spelling a little and it came out "Tampa." De Soto, being something of a diplomat, negotiated a treaty with the Indians beneath the shade of a big oak tree. That old tree still stands on the campus of the University of Tampa. It's known as the "Charter Oak."

In the 1880s, Tampa began to develop its identity as a multiculturally diverse business center. It was then that an entrepreneurial group of exiled Cuban cigar makers, led by Vincente Martinez Ybor (EE-bore), arrived and set up shop just northeast of today's downtown. At around the same time, railroad magnate Henry B. Plant oversaw the laying of the area's first railroad line, and Tampa began a boom of growth and prosperity.

Today Tampa boasts Florida's most active port, the seventh largest in the nation. Ybor's modest cigar factory is now the focal point of the two-mile-square neighborhood known as Ybor City, a center for Tampa's Hispanic culture and a favorite spot for antique shoppers and nightclubbers.

Millions visit Tampa every year, most of them heading for Busch Gardens, Tampa's wonderful 300-acre theme park where exotic animals, scary roller coasters, exciting water rides, and spectacular live shows enthrall visitors year after year.

Plant built a hotel here in 1891 as a resort to attract tourists, who—not coincidentally—would have to ride his train to get here. Plant spent a cool $3 million on the place, and it stands today as probably the finest example of Moorish architecture in the western hemisphere. The buildings, with their onion domes and silver turrets, now house the University of Tampa and a fine little museum.

One of America's fastest growing cities, business-oriented Tampa continues to reinvent itself. Museums, theaters, and art venues have achieved a new importance while shopping malls, antique districts, and flea markets lure shoppers from around the state and, indeed, from around the world.

A PERFECT DAY IN TAMPA

Tampa's Bayshore Boulevard is said to be the longest continuous paved walkway in the world. The six-mile sidewalk skirts the west side of Hillsborough Bay. Locals often walk, jog, or in-line skate here in the morning, and perhaps you'll join them for a brisk start to this perfect day. It's also a first-rate driving road, lined with mansions and handsome moss-draped oaks.

Pop over to nearby Old Hyde Park Village to check out the more than 50 upscale specialty shops, such as Williams-Sonoma, Chico, Sharper Image, and Godiva, nestled within this gracious historic district. Now for an up-close look at that fabulous old Tampa Bay Hotel. The south wing houses the Henry B. Plant Museum where, amid opulent turn-of-the-century furnishings, exhibits trace area history and give visitors a peek into Tampa's past. Have lunch at the famous Columbia restaurant, then off for a tour of the Ybor City Brewing Company and a sample of Ybor Gold lager. Scoot over to Ybor City where the Ybor State Museum offers free guided walking tours. Check out the unique

TAMPA

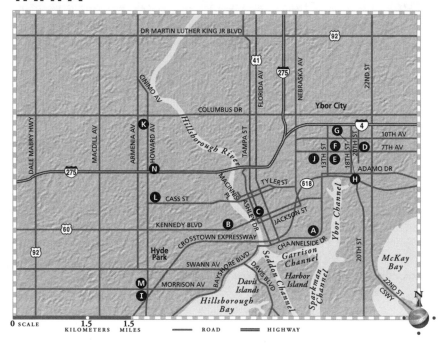

SIGHTS

Ⓐ Florida Aquarium
Ⓑ Henry B. Plant Museum
Ⓒ Tampa Museum of Art
Ⓓ Ybor City Brewery Company

SIGHTS (continued)

Ⓔ Ybor City Walking Tour
Ⓕ Ybor Square
Ⓖ Ybor State Museum

FOOD

Ⓗ Alessi Cafe Beignet
Ⓘ Bern's Steak House
Ⓙ The Columbia
Ⓚ Howards
Ⓛ Le Bordeaux
Ⓜ Sideberns
Ⓝ Tuscan Oven

galleries and boutiques and watch as cigars are hand rolled by skilled crafts people in the old manner.

Go back to the hotel for a dip in the pool. Relax, then dress for dinner. You'll be dining aboard the *Starlight Princess* riverboat. The filet mignon or seafood Alfredo will be lovely. Then go up to the top-level observation deck to watch the sun set on this perfect day.

ORIENTATION

Tampa International is one of the best airports in the world, and it's just seven miles northeast of downtown. Interstate highways provide access to the city. From St. Petersburg, take I-275 North—it'll take you right into town via the Howard Frankland Bridge. Or if you're coming from Clearwater, take SR 60, the Courtney Campbell Causeway.

Lots of one-way streets direct traffic flow, so watch the signs. Kennedy Boulevard dissects downtown into north and south, while Florida Avenue provides east and west access on the city's grid plan. Unfortunately, rush hours around here can be horrendous, so locals usually allow extra time going to and from work or when heading for any of the sports venues when a major game is scheduled.

The public bus company is HARTline (Hillsborough Area Regional Transit), and plainly marked stops are evident just about everywhere. There's a free shuttle bus running a downtown loop and the inexpensive Tampa-Ybor Trolley makes 17 stops at green-and-orange signs between Harbor Island (where the convention center is located) and Ybor City. Water taxis and the Tampa Ferry offer access to shore-side attractions.

SIGHTSEEING HIGHLIGHTS

★★★★ BUSCH GARDENS
3000 E. Busch Blvd., 813/987-5082, www.4adventure.com
Most everybody likes Busch Gardens. The animals are truly wonderful and the various environments are about as realistically true to nature as they can possibly be within a zoo setting. Zebras, antelopes, ostriches, and flamingos roam free along with other animals across the 80-acre "Serengeti Plain," which can be viewed from a unique safari walking tour where you can see the animals up close. Stanleyville recreates an African village where the Tanganika Tidal Wave awaits courageous adventurers. Don't miss the handsome and rare white Bengal tiger in the Congo exhibit. The kids will love the rides here. The Montu, Python, Scorpion, and Kumba are regularly listed among the world's best roller coasters by those who research such things. The park's newest attraction is an old-fashioned dueling wooden roller coaster.

Wear comfortable shoes and clothes you don't mind getting wet. There are plenty of restaurants, snack bars, and internationally themed souvenir shops. Strollers and wheelchairs are available.

Details: *Daily 9:30–6, with extended summer hours. $37 adults, $30 children. Single stroller is $7 (including a refundable $1 deposit), double stroller is $11 (including a refundable $1 deposit). Wheelchair is $7 (including a refundable $1 deposit). (6–8 hours)*

★★★★ **FLORIDA AQUARIUM**
701 Channelside Dr., 813/273-4000
A handsome, waterfront, three-story, glass-domed building houses this unusual aquarium, which tells the story of this state's unique freshwater, saltwater, and wetlands environments. See coral reefs, mangrove roots, and a cypress swamp as otters frolic in their own little river, and alligators and crocodiles lurk along shadowy creek banks. More than 5,000 creatures live here, artfully displayed and most in natural sunlight. The Florida Bays and Beaches Gallery spotlights both freshwater and saltwater displays, while the Florida Wetlands Gallery shows us a cypress swamp, mangroves, and a river. Lots of hands-on and interactive exhibits here, too.
Details: *Daily 9:30–5; closed Thanksgiving and Christmas. $10.95 adults, $5.95 children. (2–3 hours)*

★★★★ **MUSEUM OF SCIENCE & INDUSTRY (MOSI)**
4801 E. Fowler Ave., 800/998-MOSI or 813/987-6300, www.mosi.org
This is an interactive adventure with some quite remarkable effects and exhibits. Florida has a great interest in hurricanes and MOSI has a wind-tunnel exhibit that lets visitors experience a 74-mph Gulf Coast hurricane. There's a planetarium here, along with health and human body exhibits, flight and space displays, and more. An IMAX theater screens feature-movie presentations on an 11,500-foot screen. One exhibit called "Back Woods" is a 40-acre wilderness with three miles of hiking trails. There's a free-flight butterfly garden and an area especially for children under five. Major scientific special-effect displays change from time to time, but they are always quite spectacular.
Details: *Opens at 9 daily, closing hours are seasonal. $11 adults, $9 students and seniors, $7 children. (3–4 hours)*

★★★★ **YBOR CITY WALKING TOUR**
1901 N. 13th St., 813/247-6323
The Ybor State Museum and the Ybor City Chamber of Commerce

YBOR CITY NATIONAL LANDMARK DISTRICT

The 110-block area bounded by Columbus Dr., Fifth Ave., Nebraska Ave., and 22nd St., is one of Florida's three National Landmark Districts. Old cigar factories here have been transformed into shops and restaurants. Brick streets, gaslight-type street lamps, and ornate grillwork all add to the Hispanic ambiance. Pick up a walking-tour map at the Ybor Square Visitor Center on 14th Street. Early on Tuesday, Thursday, and Saturday afternoons, guided tours invite you along. Check out the antique shops. Nostalgia shops offer great selections of '40s, '50s, and '60s collectibles. At night, the whole place changes character when the many nightclubs begin to swing.

For more information, call Ybor City Chamber of Commerce, 813/248-3712, or visit www.ybor.org.

co-host this excellent walking tour. A hometown guide takes visitors behind the scenes and explains the history and recent happenings in this colorful neighborhood.

Details: *Available Jan–Apr, Thu and Sat at 10:30 a.m.; May–Dec, Sat 10:30 a.m. $4 per person. (1 1/2 hours)*

★★★★ YBOR STATE MUSEUM
1818 Ninth Ave., 813/247-6323
This interesting museum occupies the old Ferlita Bakery, which operated here at the turn of the last century. Displays highlight the history of the cigar industry, and adjoining buildings give an accurate picture of the lifestyle and working conditions of Cubans who worked in the cigar factors a hundred years ago.
Details: *Open daily 9–5. Admission $2. (30 minutes)*

★★★ HENRY B. PLANT MUSEUM
401 W. Kennedy Blvd., 813/254-1891,
www.plantmuseum.com
The Henry B. Plant is reputed to be the only museum in America housed in a former hotel. And what a hotel it must have been. Henry Plant was a railroad tycoon during the mid-1800s, and this five-story

BOK TOWER GARDENS

There comes a time during every Florida vacation when suddenly the main highways become absolutely claustrophobic. You're tired of pressing the gas pedal, jamming on the brake. You've had enough of cramped, bumpy lanes where there's road construction going on. Let's go to a place where you can rest your body and cleanse your mind.

You're headed for Lake Wales, about 55 miles east of downtown Tampa. From Tampa, take SR 60 east toward the town of Lake Wales. It's 250 feet above sea level—making it downright mountainous by Florida standards.

Just east of town is Bok Tower Gardens. Located three miles north of Lake Wales on County Road 17-A (Burns Ave.), off Alternate U.S. 27, 863/676-1408. Back in 1929, Edward Bok, an early editor of Ladies Home Journal and a Dutch immigrant, decided that he wanted to "make America more beautiful because he had lived in it." He selected the highest point he could find, a ridge with an elevation of 295 feet. Here he built a most amazing bell tower, surrounded by 128 acres of gardens, and then dedicated the whole thing to the American people.

William Lyman Phillips, a landscape architect, describes the places this way: "The gardens, once entered, affect the senses of the visitor gratefully, create a poetic mood, induce feelings of reverence, stir the mind to rapt admiration. A more striking example of the power of beauty could not be asked for."

The tower is made of pink and gray Georgia marble and coquina stone from St. Augustine. It rises 205 feet above the grounds and the town below.

museum was once the site of the Tampa Bay Hotel, which contained a glittering casino, two grand ballrooms, and an indoor swimming pool (back when that was an exotic novelty). Plant spent a cool $3 million making his hotel the place for society to see and be seen. The halls were so long and so wide, the story goes, that a fleet of rickshaws carried guests about. Rooms open to the public display the heavy furniture favored by the Victorians, accented by sumptuous rugs and monogrammed china. Bring your camera for a shot of the building. Gold crescent moons top silver onion domes, and arched windows feature carved wooden trim. A good gift shop features Victorian reproductions and unusual crafts items.

Housed within the tower is one of the world's great carillons, with 57 bronze bells ranging in weight from 17 pounds to 12 tons. It's know as the "Singing Tower," and every day at 3 p.m. visitors to the gardens are treated to a carillon recital. Shorter selections are played every half-hour beginning at 9 a.m. Sometimes there are moonlight concerts, too, and guest musicians often come from all over the world just to play these great bells for the enjoyment of garden visitors.

But wait until you see these gardens. Thousands of azaleas, camellias, magnolias, and other flowering plants provide seasonal splashes of color against a lush green background of ferns, palms, oaks, and pines. More than 127 species of birds are known to frequent the garden along with a variety of small wild animals. (Actually, none of the creatures is particularly wild. Squirrels will accept a treat from your hand if you offer it, but be careful.)

Bok Tower Gardens are open every day from 8–5. Guided tours depart at noon and 2, Jan 15–April 15. Admission is $4 adults and $1 children. There's a gift shop and café; picnic facilities are available, too.

As long as you're in Lake Wales, you may as well take another little side trip to visit Spook Hill. Talk about going from the sublime to the ridiculous! Spook Hill is a weird phenomenon. Kids love it. Grown-ups can't explain it. It's just off Alternate 27 at North Avenue. You'll have to watch for signs. You park you car at the bottom of the hill on the white line. Now release the brakes and clutch, and your car will roll uphill, all by itself! It's been written up by scientists for years, and there's still no explanation for it.

Details: *Tue–Sat 10–4, Sun noon–4. $3 adults, $1 seniors and children. (1–2 hours)*

★★★ LOWRY PARK ZOOLOGICAL GARDENS
7350 North Blvd., 813/935-8552, www.aza.org

This conveniently located city zoo is just five miles north of downtown Tampa. Well-planned environments house Asian animals, primates, jungle cats, and more. The children's petting zoo charms youngsters, and everyone likes the Florida wildlife exhibit, which includes alligators, snakes, red walruses, river otters, Florida manatee, and even the elusive Florida panther.

GASPARILLA WEEK

If you happen by a pirate ship docked next to the Platt Street Bridge on a stroll along Bayshore Boulevard, don't worry. Each February the *Jose Gasparilla*, crewed by costumed Tampa businessmen, "captures" the city as part of Tampa's Gasparilla Week. The "Gasparilla Invasion" is but one aspect of the annual citywide party, which also features balls and marathons. For information, contact the Tampa/Hillsborough Convention and Visitors Association at 813/223-1111.

Details: Daily 9:30–5; closed Thanksgiving and Christmas. $7.50 adults, $4.95 children. (3 hours)

★★ OLD HYDE PARK VILLAGE
Swann and Dakota Aves., 813/251-3500

Old Hyde Park is an unusual gathering of shops and restaurants in one of Tampa's most historic neighborhoods. Although the buildings are not old, they manage to capture the small town ambiance of long-ago Hyde Park.

Old Hyde Park Village is populated by a number of top-drawer, brand-name shops, such as Ralph Lauren, Mondi, Jacobson's, Restoration Hardware, and at least 60 others. It also features several sidewalk cafés as well as a movie theater.

Details: Two miles west of downtown. Take exit 24 off I-275 (Armenia-Howard Ave.). Go south on Armenia Ave. and turn left at Swann. Complimentary covered parking. Village hours Mon–Sat 10–9; Sun noon–5. (1–2 hours)

★★ TAMPA MUSEUM OF ART
600 N. Ashley Dr., 813/274-8130

This is a jewel of a museum that is gaining a reputation as one of Florida's best. Innovative presentations of thought-provoking exhibits have ranged from African gold jewelry to artistic creations made of chocolate. Fifteen changing exhibits are presented every year, along with a permanent collection of more than 7,000 choice pieces,

LAKELAND AND WRIGHT'S "CHILD OF THE SUN"

Did you know that when you're in Tampa you're only about 45 minutes from the largest integrated collection of Frank Lloyd Wright buildings in the world? It's true. Wright's "Child of the Sun" collection is located on the campus of Florida Southern College in Lakeland. A popular and prolific designer of buildings, Wright had many clients. Unfortunately, many of his outstanding efforts have vanished. Tokyo's Imperial Hotel has been demolished. Chicago's Midway Gardens fell to the wrecker's ball long ago. Sixty-seven Wright buildings have disappeared, and others are rapidly deteriorating. So it's no wonder that hordes of tourists troop across the campus of Florida Southern College admiring the 12 buildings Wright created, beginning with the **Annie Pfeiffer Chapel** designed in 1938.

Wright "fell in love with the site." He wanted the buildings to seem to grow from the earth, toward the light. Although his work was often termed "modern," Wright preferred the word "organic."

The steel-spired Annie Pfeiffer Chapel is renowned for its beauty today, but when it was completed in 1941, it didn't please everyone. Some of the donors, who had expected a traditional building, were dismayed when they saw the unconventional soaring structure. The **William H. Danforth Chapel**, completed in 1955, contains some stunning leaded-glass windows that have achieved worldwide fame. A notable feature of the Lakeland campus is the network of covered walkways, or "esplanades," as Wright termed them. The original plans called for 18 structures to be completed over a period of 20 years, but only the 12 now extant ever materialized. The **Polk Science Building**, with its white-capped planetarium, was the last one completed—in 1958.

Don't miss this opportunity to see for yourself this architectural treasure produced by the eccentric genius who was unquestionably the greatest American architect of his time. Maps for a self-guided tour are available outside the administration building.

Lakeland is about 45 minutes away from Tampa and is easily reached by taking I-4 to Exit 16, which is Memorial Boulevard. Head east on Memorial and then turn right onto Florida Avenue, which leads into the downtown area. Follow signs to Florida Southern College at Ingraham Avenue and McDonald Street. For information call 863/680-4118.

including Greek and Roman antiquities and some stunning pieces of contemporary art.

Details: Mon–Sat 10–5, Wed 5–7, Sun 1–5. Guided tours Wed and Sat at 1 and Sun at 2. $5 adults, $4 children. (30 minutes)

★★ YBOR CITY BREWERY COMPANY
2205 N. 20th St., 813/242-9222

The brewery is one of Ybor City's newest attractions, yet it's located in one of the oldest buildings. The three-story brick edifice was, back in 1894, home of the Seidenberg Cigar Factory. Now it's a micro-brewery. The popular Ybor Gold is among its beers. You can tour the brewery and learn about the brewing process—beer tastings are included.

Details: Tours Tue–Sat 11–3. Admission $2. (30 minutes)

★★ YBOR SQUARE
**Eighth Ave. and 13th St., 813/247-4497,
www.yborsquare.com**

These historic-landmark brick buildings once housed the world's largest cigar factory. Built in 1886 by Vincente Martinez Ybor, the three huge buildings were once the center of the Latin Quarter's political and social life. The place has been converted into a quaint enclave of shops and restaurants, but the brick walls and massive beamed ceilings still hold the sweet, faint scent of the cigars hand rolled years ago.

Antique Mini Mart, 813/247-1051, has an interesting assortment of baby boomer favorites—vintage costume jewelry, old radios, assorted collectibles. More nostalgia is evident at **Grandma's Attic**, 813/247-6878; and at **Chevere!**, 813/247-1339, you'll find all kinds of natural fiber clothing—incredibly comfortable stuff designed by the owners of this attractive shop. At the **Tampa Rico Cigar Company**, 813/248-0218, see how the fine art of handmade cigars is still being practiced in this historic factory.

Details: Most stores open daily. (1–2 hours)

★ TAMPA THEATER
711 Franklin St., 813/274-8981

This opulent old-time movie theater was opened in 1926 and deservedly is now listed on the National Register of Historic Places. Ongoing careful restoration has returned this crystal-and-marble

---

palace to its 1920s splendor, complete with Venetian lantern lights, a statuary of mythical and historical beings, spiral columns, and a refurbished 868-pipe Mighty Wurlitzer. Motion pictures, old and new, are shown here, and occasional concerts or magic shows delight audiences. Backstage tours include a brief organ concert.

Details: *Show times and prices vary; call for information. $5 donation requested for backstage tours. (Shows 2–3 hours, tour 1 hour)*

FITNESS AND RECREATION

This fine Florida weather means that there's always plenty of outdoor fun available—and people of all ages take advantage of that fact year-round. Bayshore Boulevard, 813/223-1111, south of downtown, is a 6.5-mile long sidewalk, which lays claim to being the longest paved sidewalk in the world. It curves along the banks of Hillsborough Bay, across the street from historic Hyde Park. It's a scenic place to walk, jog, or in-line skate through Old Hyde Park's handsome, tree-shaded residential neighborhood.

Some things you have to buy a ticket for; others you don't. Sometimes locals and visitors alike pretend they're selecting a place to go just to amuse the kids, when really they love it just as much themselves. One of these places is Adventure Island, 10001 Malcolm McKinley Dr. (40th St.), 813/987-5660, www.4adventure.com. Just next door to Busch Gardens, Adventure Island is an outdoor water park with every kind of pool-and-plunge gimmick you can imagine—from little kiddies' wading pools to the "Aruba Tuba," where visitors speed through a connecting set of enclosed water-filled tubes. For a quieter water adventure, try Canoe Escape, 9335 E. Fowler Ave., 813/986-2067 or 800/44-TAMPA, canuesc@tingley.net. Here's a 16,000-acre wilderness park where "real" Florida exists just minutes from downtown. Paddle downstream and say hello to birds, turtles, and even 'gators.

For an extraordinary, albeit pricey, sightseeing adventure, you can't beat Big Red Balloon, 16032 E. Course Dr., 813/969-1518 or 800/44-TAMPA, www.bigredballoon.com. It costs $160, but you get a 3-1/2-hour sunrise cruise over the Tampa area while enjoying a champagne brunch. If go-carts, bumper-boats, and batting cages are favorites with the family, you can't do much better than Celebration Station, 10230 Palm River Rd. (U.S. 60 and I-75), with its big video arcade and all those playland rides. There's a pizza restaurant, too. Kids love it. Grown-ups may find it a bit chaotic.

You'll notice that Florida is a little short of mountains, but it can still offer rock climbing. Vertical Ventures, 5402 E. Pioneer Park, 813/884-7625, www.verticalventures.com, is the south's largest indoor rock-climbing gym.

You can rent all the equipment you'll need and get instruction, too. Golfers find courses in Tampa challenging and exciting on both public and private courses. Try the public USF Golf Course, 4202 Fowler Ave., 813/632-6893. There are some companies in the area offering "golf packages," which can save you time by booking tee time reservations for you at several private and semiprivate courses. One is Stand-By Golf, 4815 E. Busch Blvd. #208, 813/899-BOOK. Many public parks around America offer "Vita Exercise Courses," which are pathways that have stops indicating types of exercises to do. Visitors often look for them. You'll find several of our parks that have these go-at-your-own-pace courses: Al Lopez Park, 4810 N. Himes Ave.; Lettuce Lake Park, 6920 Fletcher Ave.; MacFarlane Park, 1700 N. MacDill Ave.; Copeland Park, 11001 N. 15th St.; and University of South Florida, 4202 E. Fowler Ave. For more information call the recreation department at 813/274-8615. Rent in-line skates or bicycles at Blades & Bikes Bayshore, 201 W. Platt St., Ste. A, 813/251-0178. This is close to Bayshore Boulevard—a great place to skate or ride.

FOOD

Tampa folks love going out to eat, and no wonder. If you crave breakfast, brunch, lunch, afternoon tea, supper, dinner, late-night snacks—no matter what time of the day or night—there's a kitchen somewhere in town preparing just exactly what you want.

Florida's oldest Spanish restaurant, **The Columbia**, 2025 E. Seventh Ave., 813/248-4961, opened in 1905 in historic Ybor City. Operated by the fourth generation of the Gonzmart family, the 11-dining room establishment covers a city block. Seafood paellas are a favorite here, served over fluffy piles of yellow rice. **Bern's Steak House**, 1206 S. Howard Ave., 813/251-2421, is another Tampa landmark. *Wine Spectator* magazine called it "the best of all steak houses in America." For more than 40 years, Bern's has served its U.S. prime aged beef to delighted patrons. The 212-page wine list weighs eight pounds and lists more than 7,000 wines. Bern's grows all of its own vegetables organically at their farm, and the fish is so fresh you can pick one out still swimming in a special tank. Be sure to take the kitchen and wine cellar tour after your meal.

For a more casual atmosphere, **Alessi Cafe Beignet**, 1802 E. Eighth Ave., 813/241-2233, offers indoor/outdoor seating with a good view of what's happening in Ybor City. If you're near Busch Gardens, you have to sample **Mel's Hot Dogs**, 4136 E. Busch Blvd., 813-985-8000. These are what hot dogs used to taste like when you were a kid.

Tuscan Oven, 808 S. Howard Ave., 813/251-0619, offers lots of selections: wonderful wood-oven baked pizza and 11 different pasta selections, along with imaginative seafood specialties. Probably one of the best in-hotel restaurants you'll find is **Oystercatchers** in the Hyatt Regency Westshore, 6200 Courtney Campbell Cswy. (U.S. 60), 813/281-9116. It's in a 35-acre nature preserve on the shores of Old Tampa Bay. It's a great place to watch a sunset. The kitchen is open and you can watch preparation of your fish selection. It's expensive but very special. A good spot for a healthy lunch is **Howards**, 533 S. Howard Ave., 813/254-5431. Huge salads and colorful fruit plates are served amid spotless bright surroundings.

Sideberns, 2208 W. Morrison Ave., 813/258-2233, is just north of Bern's Steak House and is an easier-on-the-budget offshoot of the more famous Bern's. Eat in the courtyard or the large indoor dining room. Bring along a bottle of wine from the wine store next door if you want to. Cigar aficionados will enjoy the plush "cigar room." Sandwiches are served on homemade *focaccia* or roasted garlic-potato bread, and soups are rich and wonderful. They offer a big array of desserts. **Harry Harvey's**, 3333 S. West Shore Blvd., 813/835-7272, serves lunch and dinner daily except Mondays. Locally famed Chef Bradley named this restaurant after his father and hosts guests elegantly with such dishes as wild mushroom strudel with fresh spinach. And that's just an appetizer! **Landry's Seafood House**, 7616 Courtney Campbell Cswy. (U.S. 60), 813/289-7773, offers a view of the bay, along with a vast array of attractively presented seafood. You choose from all kinds of crab, tuna, flounder, catfish, grouper, oysters, and more, and then you decide which of their many sauces you want. Five different pasta dishes round out the menu. **Le Bordeaux**, 1502 S. Howard Ave., 813/254-4387, offers a spirited combination of French food and American jazz. A chalkboard menu reveals the day's specials. The food is French-country hearty, not frilly. Enjoy live jazz Wednesday through Saturday, and dinner every night.

LODGING

Just as knowledgeable visitors can seek out and find virtually any kind of food they desire within the Tampa Bay area, so can they also find the accommodations that best suit their needs. All of the major chains are here, along with charming guest houses, waterside retreats, and off-the-beaten-track B&Bs.

Families who are planning to go to Busch Gardens often gravitate to the **Holiday Inn Tampa Busch Gardens**, 2701 E. Fowler Ave., 813/971-4712. It's not fancy, but it's clean and comfortable and they welcome your kids and pets. Another hotel just a mile from Busch Gardens and Adventure Island is **Doubletree Guest Suites**, 11310 N. 30th St., 813/971-7690. They have a nice pool and give you warm chocolate chip cookies when you arrive. For

GREATER TAMPA

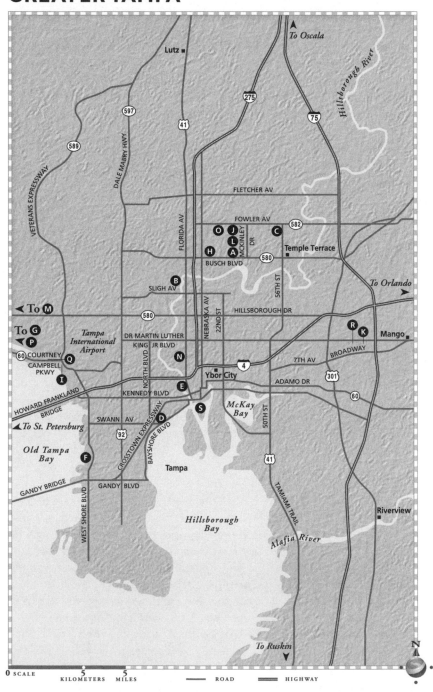

To Oscala

Lutz ■

Hillsborough River

597
275
41
75

589

VETERANS EXPRESSWAY

DALE MABRY HWY

FLETCHER AV

FLORIDA AV

FOWLER AV
582

O J
H L C
A
Temple Terrace
BUSCH BLVD
580

MCKINLEY DR

56TH ST

B
SLIGH AV

To Orlando

◄ To M

580
HILLSBOROUGH DR

NEBRASKA AV
22ND ST

To G
P

Tampa International Airport

DR MARTIN LUTHER
KING JR BLVD

R K
Mango ■

60 COURTNEY
CAMPBELL PKWY
I

Q

N

NORTH BLVD

7TH AV
BROADWAY

301

60

4
Ybor City

ADAMO DR

E
KENNEDY BLVD

HOWARD FRANKLAND BRIDGE

S
SWANN AV

D

McKay Bay

50TH ST

◄ To St. Petersburg

92

CROSSTOWN EXPRESSWAY

BAYSHORE BLVD

Old Tampa Bay

F

Tampa

41

GANDY BRIDGE

GANDY BLVD

WEST SHORE BLVD

TAMIAMI TRAIL

Riverview ■

Hillsborough Bay

Alafia River

To Ruskin

N

0 SCALE   5   5
    KILOMETERS MILES   ——— ROAD   ═══ HIGHWAY

something a little bit different, a place with a truly homelike atmosphere, check out the **English Rose Vacation Home**, 11266 W. Hillsborough Ave., 813/273-8980. It's a gracious, big, old house on a quiet inlet with a boat dock. It's filled with lots of comfy furnishings and flowers everywhere. There's even a tiny English pub on the premises.

The **Hyatt Regency Westshore**, 6200 Courtney Campbell Cswy., 813/874-1234, is located on a protected stretch of salt marsh overlooking Tampa Bay. Nature photographers love this place, and you'll love the many native birds and beasts just outside your window. **Wyndham Harbour Island Hotel**, 725 S. Harbour Island Blvd., 813/229-5000, is both in town and on the water. You can walk from here to the convention center, the Ice Palace, or the Florida Aquarium. Rooms and suites are on the elegant side, and you even get to use the well-appointed Harbour Island Athletic Club. The restaurant offers pricey but very good food and interesting inner harbor views of boats coming and going. **Sumner Suites**, 10007 Princess Palm Ave., 813/622-8557, offers surprisingly affordable suites (most under $100). There are no restaurants in house, but there are some nearby. It's an all-suite facility and they're big, comfortable ones.

The **Camberly Plaza**, 10221 Princess Palm Ave., 813/623-6363, www.camberlyhotels.com, was probably designed for business travelers, but families really enjoy the Olympic-sized pool, health club, and tennis courts. There are even nature trails within the 12 tropical acres. **Radisson Bay Harbor Inn**, 7700 Courtney Campbell Cswy., 813/281-8900, has a primo lo-

SIGHTS

- ⓐ Busch Gardens
- ⓑ Lowry Park Zoological Gardens
- ⓒ Museum of Science & Industry (MOSI)
- ⓓ Olde Hyde Park Village
- ⓔ Tampa Theater

FOOD

- ⓕ Harry Harvey's
- ⓖ Landry's Seafood House
- ⓗ Mel's Hot Dogs
- ⓘ Oystercatchers

LODGING

- ⓙ AmeriSuites Tampa–Busch Gardens
- ⓚ The Camberly Plaza
- ⓛ Doubletree Guest Suites
- ⓜ English Rose Vacation Home

LODGING (continued)

- ⓝ Gram's Place Bed, Breakfast & Music
- ⓞ Holiday Inn Tampa Busch Gardens
- ⓟ Hyatt Regency Westshore
- ⓟ Marriott Residence Inn Tampa Bay
- ⓠ Radisson Bay Harbor Inn
- ⓡ Sumner Suites
- ⓢ Wyndham Harbour Island Hotel

Note: Items with the same letter are located in the same area.

cation—just a couple of miles from the airport with a bayside view. They have a restaurant (Damon's Original Sports Restaurant) and a lounge, and there are suites available as well as regular rooms. There's an outdoor bar for poolside relaxation and even a basketball court. **Marriott Residence Inn Tampa Bay**, 3075 N. Rocky Point Dr. E. (on the Courtney Campbell Cswy.), 813/281-5677, is more like a waterfront home than a hotel. The one- and two-bedroom suites are fully equipped with not just a kitchen and living room but a fireplace, too. Guests are treated to complimentary breakfasts and afternoon cocktails. A less expensive all-suite hotel is **AmeriSuites Tampa–Busch Gardens**, 11408 N. 30th St., 813/979-1922. No fireplaces, but everybody gets a microwave and a refrigerator, and you're close to Busch Gardens and have handy access to I-75. **Gram's Place Bed, Breakfast & Music**, 3109 N. Ola Ave., 813/221-0596, http://members.aol.com/gramspl, is a laid-back eclectic-style place where guests are encouraged to bring along their guitars, CDs, and tapes and join in with the jazz, blues, rock, country . . . whatever the music of the day turns out to be. Two old (circa-1945) cottages form the nucleus of the place, and rooms come with private bath or shared bath. Guests enjoy sun decks, Jacuzzi, BYOB bar, and a couple of resident cats. It's not for everyone, but it's certainly interesting.

CAMPING

Tampa has campgrounds scattered here and there throughout the area—some close to the downtown action, some handy to major attractions, some out in the boonies. (To help you sort it all out, you can get a *Florida Camping Directory* from the Florida Association of RV Parks & Campgrounds, 1340 Vickers Dr., Tallahassee, FL 32303-3041, 850/562-7151; or check out their Web site at http://florida-camping.com.)

Big oak trees and lots of grassy areas make the Happy Traveler RV Park and Campground, off I-75 on Exit 54, three quarters of a mile east on Fowler Ave., 727/986-3094, happyrvl@gte.net, a friendly-looking place. It has full trailer hookups and is convenient to the zoo and Busch Gardens. Green Acres Campground & RV Park, east of Tampa off I-4 on Exit 9, one eighth of a mile south on McIntosh Rd., 813/659-0002, is about 15 minutes from Busch Gardens.

NIGHTLIFE

Tampa nightlife is a many-splendored thing. Just about every after-dark diversion you can think of is here. Comedy clubs are popular. Music spots are, too, with jazz, blues, big band, rock, pop, rap—whatever turns you on. Live theater is a year-round option, with musical offerings, stage plays, interactive mystery theaters, and dinner theaters. For a pretty complete listing of nighttime happenings, consult the *Weekly Planet*, a free tabloid newspaper you'll find stacked on just about every flat surface in town.

The Green Iguana Bar & Grill, 1708 Seventh Ave., 813/248-9555, www.greeniguana.net, has live music five nights a week. Jungle décor, a good sound system, and generous drinks make it a popular night spot. They have a limited food menu. Tampa Bay Brewing Company, 1812 North 15th St., 813/247-1422, is a casual brewpub with interesting beer complemented by excellent food. You can shoot a little pool or throw darts. At Side Splitters, 12938 N. Dale Mabry, 813/960-1197, stand-up comics take turns making audiences giggle. The Tampa Bay Performing Arts Center, 1010 N. MacInnes Pl., 813/229-STAR, www.tampacenter.com, has a deservedly earned reputation for bringing top-drawer Broadway theater to the Sunshine State. Lavish productions with well-known stars entertain in four theater centers. In addition to Broadway shows, the nonprofit center presents comedy, pop music, opera, dance, and plays.

Instead of whipping on I-75 South to get to Sarasota from Tampa, why not take a more scenic route? From Tampa, take I-275 west toward St. Petersburg and go south over the Sunshine Skyway bridge for a spectacular view of Tampa Bay (toll each way is $1). It's one of the nation's longest suspension bridges—and not for the faint-hearted. I-275 then merges back with I-75 and continues on to Bradenton, about 10 miles north of Sarasota.

*While in Bradenton, you can stop at the **Bishop Planetarium and Aquarium**, which features astrological shows and rooftop star demonstrations, laser light shows set to classic rock on weekends, and longtime resident, Snooty the manatee. Relax at **Lake Manatee State Recreation Areas**. And then check out the **Gamble Plantation State Historical Site**. When you're ready to get on your way, hop back on I-75 south to Sarasota.*

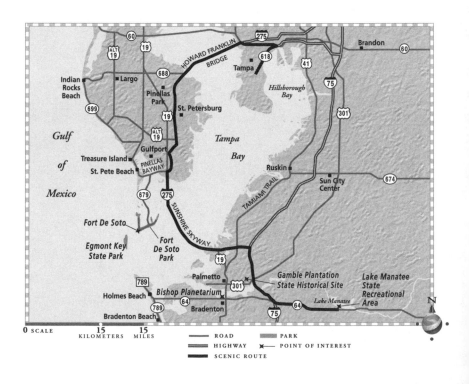

0 SCALE — 15 KILOMETERS — 15 MILES

ROAD — PARK — HIGHWAY — POINT OF INTEREST — SCENIC ROUTE

10
SARASOTA

Sarasota has justly acquired the title, "Florida's Cultural Coast." The area is home to a symphony, opera, ballet, four professional theater companies, and numerous arts and music festivals. The arts come to life at the Van Wezel Performing Arts Hall, known for its excellent acoustics and outstanding programming. The Sarasota Opera House is a lovely restoration of a 1926 theater. Professional theater companies often perform at the Asolo State Theater, originally built in 1798. A half-dozen or more smaller performance venues are here, too. In addition to the major art museum at the Ringling complex, scattered throughout downtown Sarasota are dozens of art galleries offering just about any kind of visual art a shopper could desire. Arts and music festivals are just about monthly happenings in the Sarasota area. If you'd like a listing of cultural events, contact the Sarasota Convention & Visitors Bureau, 655 N. Tamiami Trail, Sarasota, FL 34236; 941/957-1877, www.SarasotaFl.org.

With an average of 361 days of sunshine every year, it's not surprising that there's a major focus on outdoor activities here, too. Check out the 35 miles of dazzling Gulf Coast beaches, some of them have been rated among the best beaches in the world. You can spend a lot of hours doing water-related things around Sarasota—fishing, boating, surfing, parasailing on the bay, and canoeing, kayaking, and wetting a line in miles of waterways. There's plenty of land-based activity, too, notably on golf courses, tennis courts, hiking trails, and, of course, at shopping malls.

SARASOTA

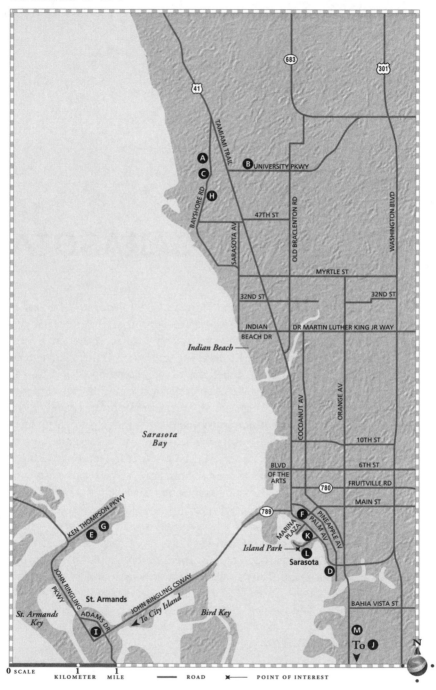

0 SCALE   1   1   ━━━ ROAD   ✕━━ POINT OF INTEREST
KILOMETER   MILE

Sarasota, including the barrier islands of Lido Key, Longboat Key, Siesta Key, and St. Armands Key, has long been known and loved by families on vacation. In fact, it was a Scottish developer, John Selwin Tait, who back in 1885 ran promotional ads stating that Sarasota was "the most beautiful and one of the healthiest" locations in the world. By 1902 Sarasota was home to a nine-hole golf course—maybe the first of its kind in America. When, in 1927, John Ringling selected Sarasota as the base of operations for his circus, people from all over the world came to see the fascinating home of "the greatest show on earth."

John Ringling did more than bring some circus performers and animals to town. He and his wife, Mable, made Sarasota their home, and the Ringling's mark on this community is indelible in a variety of ways. In the 1920s they built a magnificent Venetian-style estate on Sarasota Bay. Then they built an art museum to house their ever-growing collection of seventeenth-century Italian and Flemish art. Before long, using circus elephants to help with the heavy lifting, Ringling built the first bridge from the mainland to St. Armands Key. He'd purchased the island in 1917 from its original homesteader, Charles St. Amand. (The name was misspelled in land deeds, and the misspelling has stuck.) Today there are beautiful homes and a wonderful "shopping circle" on St. Armands.

Sarasota is still beautiful, healthy, and fascinating—and people still come from all over the world. One of the best things about Sarasota is the diversity of things to do and see. It's one of those cosmopolitan cities where it's nearly impossible for anyone to say, "I have nothing to do." And that's true whether the sun is shining or not.

A PERFECT DAY IN SARASOTA

Stop for coffee and fresh bagels at the Manhattan Bagel, then head right over to the Sarasota Jungle Gardens for a quiet stroll through the gorgeous gardens just

SIGHTS

- Ⓐ Asolo State Theater
- Ⓑ Cars & Music of Yesterday Museum
- Ⓒ John and Mable Ringling Museum of Art
- Ⓓ Marie Selby Botanical Gardens

SIGHTS *(continued)*

- Ⓔ Mote Marine Laboratory and Aquarium
- Ⓕ Palm Avenue Gallery District
- Ⓖ Pelican Man's Bird Sanctuary
- Ⓗ Sarasota Jungle Gardens

FOOD

- Ⓘ Columbia
- Ⓙ Manhattan Bagel
- Ⓚ Marina Jack
- Ⓛ O'Leary's Deck Restaurant

LODGING

- Ⓜ Holiday Inn Sarasota/Siesta Key

when hibiscus, azaleas, and bougainvillea are at their early-morning most beautiful. Stop and watch those amazing trained birds and maybe check out the gift shop, then it's back to the hotel where you'll hit the beach for a refreshing swim in the gulf. Then it's off on an art adventure. Head for Palm Avenue first. Here you'll see gallery after gallery of contemporary art of all kinds, from watercolors and sculptures to furniture and glass. Continue your adventure down U.S. 41 to Venice, a little town 18 miles south of Sarasota criss-crossed with canals. First, enjoy a fresh seafood lunch at Sharkey's on the Pier. Then go to Venice Avenue where galleries and antique shops abound. Maybe invest in an original work of art by Maxfield Parrish or Edna Hibel at the Parrish Connection Gallery. Head back to town to the Ringling Museum of Art and finish your art adventure by viewing one of the finest collections of Baroque, Italian, and Flemish Renaissance, and Old Master paintings in the world. Tonight attend a performance at the superb Asolo State Theater.

ORIENTATION

The Sarasota-Bradenton International Airport handles flights from virtually everywhere, and I-75 carries traffic smoothly and swiftly straight to several Sarasota exits. U.S. 41 takes a more leisurely route along the coastline and provides access to causeways and bridges leading to the barrier island towns of Lido Key and Siesta Key. Osprey is just south of Sarasota on I-75, and south of Osprey is Venice.

SIGHTSEEING HIGHLIGHTS

★★★★ JOHN AND MABLE RINGLING MUSEUM OF ART
5401 Bayshore Rd., 941/351-1660, www.ringling.org
This vast, U-shaped building was built in 1929 in the style of a grand fifteenth-century Italian Renaissance *palazzo*. The Ringlings, John and Mable, had it constructed to house their magnificent collection of Baroque masterpieces, totaling more than 600 items. (The Ringling collection of works by Peter Paul Rubens is thought to be the finest in the world.) Four of Rubens's giant paintings—known as tapestry cartoons—measure up to 14 by 19 feet. Between the museum's wings there's a handsomely landscaped courtyard graced with bronze replicas of Renaissance and classical sculpture. Adjoining the museum is **Ca'd'zan**, the 30-room Ringling mansion (Ca'd'zan means "house of John"). See how the rich and famous lived in the early 1920s. At

Museum of the Circus, also part of the Ringling complex, see some wonderful old, carved circus wagons, and fabulous sequined costumes, among the other significant circus memorabilia.

Details: Daily 10–5:30; closed major holidays. $9 adults, $8 seniors, children 12 and under free. (2 hours)

★★★★ **MOTE MARINE LABORATORY AND AQUARIUM**
1600 Ken Thompson Pkwy., 941/388-4441, www.mote.org
This is a real honest-to-goodness scientific research lab—but one that shares its activities with the public. Visitors are actually invited to watch as scientists do their work. Get a good look at sharks—big ones—and tarpon, barracuda, and other denizens of the Gulf of Mexico. See Sarasota's two favorite manatees, Hugh and Buffet, in their giant tank, which you view from ground level. You'll be looking up at these gentle giants, marveling at how they navigate with those powerful manhole-cover-shaped tails. Buffet is named for Jimmy Buffet, the Florida singer-songwriter who has long been active in the "Save the Manatee" movement. Hugh is named for all of us. Hu-manity—get it?

Details: Daily 10–5. $8 adults, $6 children. (1–2 hours)

★★★ **CARS & MUSIC OF YESTERDAY MUSEUM**
5500 N. Tamiami Tr., 941/355-6228
This is an attraction that draws visitors back year after year. Fully restored vintage and exotic automobiles are rotated regularly, so the displays are never quite the same. After checking out the gleaming Ferraris, Austins, and Rolls Royces, visit the Great Music Hall and see and hear more than 800 different music machines from calliopes to player-pianos. Play antique arcade games and try your skill at the shooting gallery.

Details: Daily 9–6. Group tours available. $9 adults, $5 children. (1–2 hours)

★★★ **PALM AVENUE GALLERY DISTRICT**
10–80 block of Palm Ave.
Just off Main Street in downtown Sarasota you'll find Palm Avenue. Back in the early 1900s, this was a bustling street full of elegant emporiums where Sarasota's early residents shopped. Today's visitors shop in fine emporiums here, too. Galleries, antiques shops, and specialty stores now also occupy this impressive palm tree–lined street.

Mediterranean-style architecture delights the eye, and interesting little courtyards invite investigation. So many interior decorators frequent these shops and galleries that Palm Avenue has earned the title of "interior designers row."

One of Palm Avenue's largest contemporary art galleries is **Chasen Galleries**, 16 S. Palm Ave., 941/365-4ART. International class artists are featured in rotating group shows. You'll see pottery, furniture, and tile works, in addition to unique paintings and sculpture. Down the street at **Apple and Carpenter Gallery of Fine Art and Antiques**, 64 S. Palm Ave., 941/951-2314, they approach art a bit more traditionally, specializing in nineteenth- and twentieth-century art. They also have an impressive selection of fine antiques.

More fine art is tastefully displayed at **Ziegenfuss Gallery of Fine Art**, 76 S. Palm Ave., 941/365-2366. Expect to view museum-quality originals, including oils and sculptures by nationally known artists. **Glass Reflections**, 55 S. Palm Ave., 941/955-3830, is the aptly named gallery where local, national, and international glass artisans exhibit their work. There's a glass-making studio for students on the premises as well.

Details: *Most galleries are open Mon–Sat 10–5. (2 hours)*

★★★ SARASOTA JUNGLE GARDENS
3701 Bayshore Rd., 941/355-5305

This is one of Florida's grand old garden attractions, where paths lined with literally thousands of palm trees and flowering plants wind through 10 lush acres. Exotic birds add even more color, as peacocks, flamingos, and parrots pose while cameras click. Delightfully scary creatures live here, too. Meet up with alligators, snakes, and leopards. The bird shows are amazing. How do they teach birds to do all those tricks? Kids will enjoy this—maybe even more than some of the big Orlando attractions—as they slide on the iguana slide or climb the haunted tree.

Details: *Daily 9–5. $9 adults, $5 children. (2 hours)*

★★ ASOLO STATE THEATER
5401 Bayshore Rd., 941/351-8000

There's probably no other theater in America to compare to this gold-and-white Baroque treasure. It was built in 1798 as an opera house in Denferline, Scotland, and later was moved to a castle in Asolo (pronounced ah-SO-lo), Italy. In 1949 the state of Florida pur-

SANDS OF MANY COLORS

Most Florida beaches have fine, white sand. That's because the sand is nearly 100-percent quartz. But some beaches appear more brown or tan in color, because those beaches contain broken pieces of colorful shells. The most unusual beaches in Florida are "black beaches." You can see some at Venice, near Sarasota. They usually contain minerals called *ilmente* and *rotile,* as well as quantities of phosphate material from shells and sea animal fossils.

chased the theater and had it disassembled and shipped across the Atlantic, where it was lovingly reassembled on the grounds of the Ringling estate.

It's small as theaters go—just 500 seats in the mainstage area. The horseshoe-shaped theater has gold-leafed boxes, ornately carved festoons, and candle sconces. Reportedly Robert Downing patronized the theater, and Eleanora Duse once graced its stage. Tours of the theater are available if you don't see a performance.

Details: *Professional theater companies perform here Nov–June. Show times vary; ticket prices range from $12–$40. Tours offered Nov–June, Wed–Sat at 10 a.m. for $3. (30 minutes–3 hours)*

★★ CRESCENT BEACH
Beach Rd., Siesta Key, 941/346-3207

Swim and play on the beach with the "whitest, finest sand in the world." At least that's how *Condé Nast Traveler* magazine hailed Crescent Beach in 1994. The beach is wide and long (2.75 miles). Snorkelers flock to the crystal-clear Gulf waters here, where they can easily view sea sponges, small fish, and other underwater wonders.

Details: *Take SR 789 from Sarasota to Siesta Key. The beach is mid-island. Parking is free. There are rest rooms, picnic tables, and a concession stand. Lifeguards on duty 9–5. (1 hour–all day)*

★★ G-WIZ HANDS-ON MUSEUM
8251 15th St. E., 941/359-9975

Explore the principles of science in a most entertaining manner. By all means, bring a child or two along to experience this learning adventure. Dig for fossils, touch live snakes, freeze your shadow, play a "laser harp," and much more. It's exhibits like these that make learning about science fun for the whole family.

Details: Tue–Sat 10–5; closed major holidays. Special events are held each Sat at 10:15 a.m. Admission $3 adults, $1.50 children. (1–2 hours)

★★ MARIE SELBY BOTANICAL GARDENS
811 S. Palm Ave., 941/366-5730, www.selby.org
Early Sarasotan Marie Selby left her elegant bayside property to the city "for the enjoyment of the general public." Today research, education, and conservation are part of the garden's mission. You'll marvel at the world-class display of orchid plants and other plant species from all over the world.

There are groves of trees, a waterfall garden, a hibiscus garden—even a very special hummingbird and butterfly garden. Exhibits also include displays of botanical art from the sixteenth to twentieth centuries.

Details: Open daily 10–5. Closed Christmas. Admission $8 adults, $4 children. (1–2 hours)

CHAMPION TREES
"Champion trees" are the largest trees in their respective species, as calculated by the American Forestry Association in Washington, D.C. (202/667-3300). The AFA reported 840 national champion trees a couple of years ago, and 145 of them are in Florida. Championship is determined by a tree's circumference, height, and crown spread.

You may get to see a few of these champion trees while you're here. The biggest blue pine cypress is in Bradenton, the biggest saw palmetto is in the Withlacoochee State Forest, and the biggest banyan tree is in Fort Myers. The champion white stopper tree is on Sanibel Island, and the biggest red mangrove is in the J. N. "Ding" Darling National Wildlife Refuge.

★★ PELICAN MAN'S BIRD SANCTUARY
1708 Ken Thompson Pkwy., 941/388-4444,
www.pelicanman.com

This is a much-needed haven for sick or injured birds, and visitors are invited to observe recovering birds awaiting release back into the wild. This is a permanent home, too, for 300 or so birds that can no longer survive without human assistance. Every year between 4,000 and 7,000 native and migratory species of birds are treated here. Nearly 60 percent of them are able to be released. Bring your camera. You may find some never-to-be-repeated photo opportunities.
Details: *Daily 10–5. Free, but donations welcome. (1 hour)*

★★ VENICE
18 miles south of Sarasota on U.S. 41, 941/488-2236

Venice is a small island city. Its main stretch of road, West Venice Avenue, is lovely. Palm trees line the street full of well-preserved historic buildings housing shops and eateries. Visit **Treasures in Time**, 101 W. Venice Ave., 941/486-1700, for quite a remarkable selection of antiques, collectibles, and gifts. **Mary's Memories and Mary's Too!**, 223A W. Miami Ave., 941/486-8486, are side-by-side shops features antiques, gifts, and limited-edition collectibles. At **Richard's Vintage Accessories—The 20th Century Connection**, 217 W. Miami Ave., 941/485-7774, you'll find a small shop full of wonderful memorabilia, from deco to modern to nifty-fifties.

You'll hear a lot about sharks' teeth. That's because the sands of the beaches here—especially North Jetty Park on Albee Road—are cluttered with fossilized bits of bone and teeth. Wear flip-flops.
Details: *Take U.S. 41 south and cross the Intracoastal Waterway. Take Business U.S. 41 to Venice. W. Venice Ave. will intersect. Most shops open Mon–Sat 10–5; Sun 12–4. (4 hours)*

★ HISTORIC SPANISH POINT
337 N. Tamiami Tr., Osprey, 941/966-5214

Here's a one-stop history lesson just south of Sarasota in Osprey. Within this 30-acre site, you can see a preserved prehistoric community, complete with informative archaeological exhibits and a pioneer homestead. You'll see the turn-of-the-last-century home and gardens of one of Sarasota's favorite daughters, Mrs. Potter Palmer.
Details: *Mon–Sat 9–5, Sun noon–5. $5 adults, $3 children. (1–2 hours)*

FITNESS AND RECREATION

The Sarasota area and the Gulf Coast islands offer guests and visitors a great variety of outdoor activities. Golf has been Sarasota's game for over a hundred years. There are more than 60 golf courses in the Sarasota/Bradenton area. Sarasota's only municipal course is the Bobby Jones Golf Complex, 1000 Circus Blvd., 941/365-4653, with 45 holes of golfing fun and challenge. A finalist in the *Sarasota Herald Tribune* Readers Choice Awards, Forest Lakes Golf and Country Club, 2401 Beneva Rd., Sarasota, 941/922-1312, is recognized as one of Sarasota's best public golf courses. The par-71 course offers a traditional-style layout woven through water features and palm trees for a challenging, yet affordable, golf experience. In nearby Venice, Waterford Golf Club, 1454 Gleneagles Dr., 941/484-6621, uses its natural attributes—lakes, gnarled oaks, pine stands—to challenge golfers at this Ted McAntis–designed 27-hole course.

The water-sport possibilities here are seemingly endless. Choose your spot—the Gulf of Mexico, Sarasota Bay, Lemon Bay, the Myakka River, or the Intracoastal Waterway. Swimming, snorkeling, scuba diving, water skiing, sailing, windsurfing, and, of course, every type of fishing are all here. For boat and ski rentals, try Don & Mikes, 482 Blackburn Point Rd., Osprey, 941/966-1730. They have all kinds of ski boats, Jet Skis, pontoon boats, and more. You pay by the hour. How about some really relaxing water? Try Warm Mineral Springs Resort & Spa, 12200 San Servanto Ave., Warm Mineral Springs (about halfway between Sarasota and Fort Myers, take Exit 34 on I-75 to U.S. 41, then left for three miles), 941/426-1692. Swim in an 87-degree mineral-water lake. Tennis anyone? Hit the indoor courts at the Bath & Racquet Club, 2170 Robinhood St., Sarasota, 941/921-6675. There are scores of public parks, large and small. The Sarasota Parks and Recreation Department will give you a comprehensive map and list of services. Call them at 941/316-1172.

FOOD

Dining options here are many, and most places are Florida-casual. However, in Sarasota, probably because of the many arts-related events and venues, some can be quite formal. When there's any doubt, just call ahead to be sure. **Coasters**, 1500 Stickney Point Rd., 941/923-4848, is casual and fun with a boatyard ambiance. They offer lots of seafood, but also some outstanding steak and poultry choices. **Turtles on Little Sarasota Bay**, 8875 Midnight Pass Rd. (just opposite Turtle Beach), Siesta Key, 941/346-2207, has everything Floridians like—water view, early-bird specials, outdoor deck for waterfront dining, kids menus, and super Key West–style seafood served late.

FLORIDA'S ELUSIVE GREEN FLASH

Florida has many wonders, and the green flash is one of them. Not too many people have seen it, but maybe you'll be one of the lucky ones. The green flash is an atmospheric phenomenon that can occur when the upper lobe of the sun crosses the horizon—either at sunrise or sunset. (Scientists say it's the result of looking at a very low sun through the thickest part of the atmosphere.) Sometimes it's a flame or ray that shoots suddenly above the horizon. Occasionally the upper sliver of sun suddenly turns green. Even more rare is the flash that they say looks like a light bulb. Whatever it is, it comes and goes quickly. Blink, and you may miss it!

Another fun place is the **Fifty's Family Diner**, 3737 Bahia Vista St., 941/953-4637. There's a real 1950s feel here with all the sights and sounds of the good old days—real diner-style "home cooking" with great soups and breads. Hit the Farmers Market every Saturday, or admire the motorcycles on Monday Bike Night.

Be sure to have lunch at **Columbia**, 411 St. Armands Cr., 941/388-3987. Sit indoors or in the outdoor café and enjoy all the specialties of this original Tampa family-owned Cuban/American restaurant. From black beans and yellow rice to delicate flan, the food's a delight.

Captain Curt's Crab & Oyster Bar, 1200 Old Stickney Point Rd., Siesta Key, 941/349-3885, is a friendly no-nonsense seafood place where the locals like to order grilled grouper and baby-back ribs. There's a special menu for the kids and two full-service bars for the grown-ups. **Moore's Stone Crab Restaurant**, 800 Broadway, Longboat Key, 941/383-1748, is Manatee County's oldest family-owned and -operated restaurant. The fresh seafood and stone crabs they serve are from their own fleet of boats, and they have pretty good steaks, too. (Stone crab season is from Oct 15 to May 15.)

O'Leary's Deck Restaurant, 5 Bayfront Dr., Island Park, 941/953-7505, is downtown at the south end of Marina Jack's. Here's where to get a really big, old-fashioned, juicy burger or a quarter-pound hot dog. Wash it down with a cold beer and watch the action on the bay from O'Leary's 65-foot deck. **Rum Runners Tropical Grill & Bar**, 1266 Old Stickney Point Rd., Siesta Key, 941/346-7112, http://4sarasota.com/rumrunners, is a lively

SARASOTA REGION

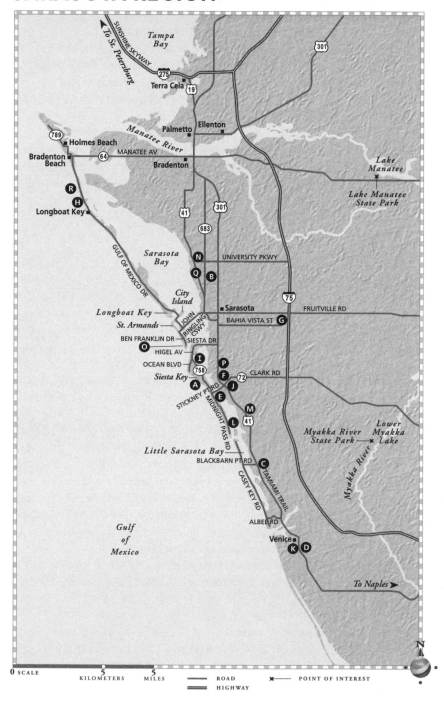

place with an eclectic sort of menu. The *Sarasota Herald Tribune* calls it "a deliciously adventurous menu." Lots of greenery, whirring overhead fans, and casual-chic décor make this place very hip.
Patisserie Cafe Continental, 5221 Ocean Blvd., Unit # 6 at Siesta Key Village, 941/346-3171, is a good place to know about if you're a little jet-lagged or just like breakfast any old time. They serve a full English breakfast all day long. Or try a freshly baked scone and a cup of cappuccino for a quick pick-me-up. Soups, salads, sandwiches, and pastries round out the menu.
Manhattan Bagel, 4065 S. Tamiami Tr. (U.S. 41), 941/927-9440, offers a wonderful variety of bagels complemented by an imaginative selection of cream cheeses. Open daily, they offer hefty hot breakfast sandwiches and New York–style deli food. **Marina Jack**, 2 Marina Plaza, 941/365-4232, offers you a hard choice—you can eat in the restaurant overlooking Sarasota Bay or, on Wednesday through Saturday, you can take a dinner cruise aboard *Marina Jack II*, an old-fashioned–style paddle-wheel boat with entertainment. Either way, you'll enjoy good, fresh Florida seafood.

Adjoining Holiday Inn Venice at 455 U.S. 41 Bypass N., Venice, 941/485-5411, is the **Golden Apple Dinner Theater**, offering stage plays and musicals along with a tasty buffet. **Sharky's on the Pier**, 1600 S. Harbor Dr., Venice, 941/488-1456, is a favorite with everybody. Don't bother to dress up. It's a casual eating spot with a million-dollar view of the Gulf. Fresh grilled catch-of-the-day is the specialty here. Enjoy dining next to the big picture windows inside or on the covered outdoor deck.

SIGHTS

Ⓐ Crescent Beach
Ⓑ G-Wiz Hands-on Museum
Ⓒ Historic Spanish Point
Ⓓ Venice

FOOD

Ⓔ Captain Curt's Crab & Oyster Bar
Ⓕ Coasters
Ⓖ Fifty's Family Diner

FOOD *(continued)*

Ⓓ Golden Apple Dinner Theater
Ⓗ Moore's Stone Crab Restaurant
Ⓘ Patisserie Cafe Continental
Ⓙ Rum Runners Tropical Grill & Bar
Ⓚ Sharky's on the Pier
Ⓛ Turtles on Little Sarasota Bay

LODGING

Ⓗ Arbors by the Sea
Ⓜ Best Western Midtown
Ⓝ Budget Inn of Sarasota
Ⓙ Calais Motel-Apartments
Ⓞ Half Moon Beach Club Resort
Ⓟ Hampton Inn
Ⓓ Holiday Inn Venice
Ⓠ Hyatt Sarasota
Ⓡ Wicker Inn

Note: Items with the same letter are located in the same area.

LODGING

Stay in town or enjoy a beachfront place on one of the barrier islands. Choose a big-name chain or a tidy B&B. There's certainly no shortage of accommodations in the area. The Sarasota Convention & Visitors Bureau will send you a very nice visitors guide with a pretty comprehensive listing of what's available. Holiday Inn has some attractive properties here. Try **Holiday Inn Sarasota/Siesta Key**, 6600 S. Tamiami Tr., Sarasota, 941/924-4900. It's newly renovated and offers data ports and voice mail. A pleasant touch is complimentary afternoon tea and cookies. **Holiday Inn Venice**, 455 U.S. 41 Bypass N., Venice, 941/485-5411, has a quiet location and is handy to the interesting Venice Historic District.

    Hampton Inn, 5995 Cattleridge Rd., 941/371-1900, is a new five-story hotel, not directly on the beach, but just minutes away from one of the best (Siesta Key Beach). Rooms are bright and attractive. You're close to beaches and malls here, and you can walk to several nearby restaurants. In Sarasota, **Budget Inn of Sarasota**, 8110 N. Tamiami Tr., 941/355-8861, is an oldie but a goodie, centrally located with attractive plantings and a good pool. The hotel is nothing fancy, but it's clean and convenient to beaches, shopping, restaurants, and attractions. Another budget spot is **Calais Motel-Apartments**, 1765 Stickney Point Rd., 941/921-5031, with one-bedroom efficiencies. (Watch for Calais's coupons in local publications. Sometimes rates are under $40.) There's a pool with sundeck and you're half a mile from the beach. **Hyatt Sarasota**, 1000 Blvd. of the Arts, 941/953-1234, not only has a water view from all the rooms, but the restaurant overlooks the marina and is convenient for boaters. A stone's throw from the Van Wezel Performing Arts Hall, you'll be in the midst of all the art action on this Cultural Coast. **Best Western Midtown**, 1425 S. Tamiami Tr., 941/955-9841, is handy to several restaurants, and if you've forgotten anything, you can walk to a good-sized shopping center. The rooms are clean and comfortable with a very tropical look. Beaches are only minutes away. **Half Moon Beach Club Resort**, 2050 Ben Franklin Dr., Lido Key, 800/358 3245, www.halfmoon-lidokey.com, is nicely located in a beach setting, yet minutes from the Sarasota cultural scene. It's expensive and very chic. On Longboat Key, the area's "Rolls Royce of Islands," you're away from everyday traffic and amidst some really charming accommodations. **Arbors by the Sea**, 5441 Gulf of Mexico Dr., Longboat Key, 941/383-8464, offers private beach cottages directly on the gulf. The one- or two-bedroom cottages are brightly decorated in Key West style, with picket fences, flower gardens, and private patios—strictly first class. Just down the street, the **Wicker Inn**, 5581 Gulf of Mexico Dr., Longboat Key, 941/383-5562, www.wickerinn-longboatkey.com, is a gracious Victorian resort on the Gulf.

One-, two-, and three-bedroom apartments are available, and there are wicker rocking chairs on the porch, vine-covered arbors, a gazebo, and a heated pool.

CAMPING

Primitive camping under the stars or state-of-the-art, creature-comfort parks—take your pick. There are camping options in privately operated parks, national chains, or state park sites. Venice Campground, 4085 E. Venice Ave., Venice, 941/488-0850, www.concentric.net/~vencamp/, is about 10 minutes away from the beach, situated in some nice old Florida piney woods landscape. They offer some waterfront sites, too. Sun-N-Fun RV Resort, 7125 Fruitville Rd., Sarasota, 941/371-2505, is handy to the Ringling home and not far from the beaches. Wooded sites and a small fishing lake are here, along with a big pool, spas, and even a fitness center. Myakka River State Park, upper Myakka Lake on Rt. 72, 941/361-6511, is one of the best of the state park camping areas. It's a huge 28,875-acre park, and you can arrange for wildlife tours through the surrounding wilderness with Myakka Wildlife Tours, 941/365-0100. (No pets are allowed in state park campgrounds, but you can take them leashed in the rest of the park.)

NIGHTLIFE

Live local rock groups and sometimes national artists show up at the Patio at the Columbia, 411 St. Armands Cr., 941/388-3987. And at Cha Cha Coconuts, 417 St. Armands Cr., 941-388-3300, there's live entertainment every night. In town, there's plenty of theater and concert action. There are more than 100 annual offerings on stage at the Frank Lloyd Wright–designed Van Wezel Performing Arts Hall, 777 N. Tamiami Tr., 800/826-9303. Check out what else is happening in the Friday *Ticket* section of the *Sarasota Herald Tribune*, or pick up a copy of *The Weekly*. The *Sarasota Herald Tribune* has a 24-hour "Artsline," 941/953-4636, ext. 6000, for information on the local cultural scene.

11
LEE ISLAND COAST

There are more than 100 islands of varying sizes and shapes strung out like scattered puzzle pieces along the coast of Florida's Lee County. (The county was named for Robert E. Lee, even though the general never visited the area.) The coastline here is especially beloved by shell-seekers, because of the more than 400 species of multicolored seashells to be found on area beaches, making this one of the best "shelling" areas in the whole world. The Lee Island Coast of Southwest Florida includes Sanibel, Captiva, Pine Island, Cape Coral, Boca Grande, Fort Myers, Fort Myers Beach, Bonita Springs and beaches, Useppa Island, Cabbage Key, and Lehigh Acres.

The subtropical communities that form the Lee Island Coast provide some favorite getaway spots for Floridians, as well as for visitors from all around the United States and abroad. There are several distinct areas here, each one with its own unique character. Probably the best known are Sanibel and Captiva Islands, connected to the mainland by a scenic three-mile causeway. Sanibel is noted worldwide for its shelling, and it was on Captiva that Anne Morrow Lindbergh wrote her best-selling memoir *A Gift from the Sea* (Pantheon, 1955). (Shelling is fine, too, in some of the less-populated areas, like Cayo Costa and North Captiva.)

There are some real old-timey fishing villages here and the most wonderful parks and gardens and nature centers. Shoppers will enjoy exploring the many stores, galleries, and boutiques. Great restaurants abound. But it's probably the outdoor activities that keep visitors coming back to this coast again and again. Besides the beautiful natural environment and the many miles of gorgeous beaches, active travelers are delighted to find plenty of golf, tennis, and water sports here.

A PERFECT DAY ON THE LEE ISLAND COAST

Start with some early-morning shelling on Sanibel Beach. Some really avid shell-seekers get up before dawn and search the shoreline wearing lighted miner's helmets. Wait until the sun comes up though, so you can appreciate the sea birds that populate these special islands, as well as the multicolored bounty of shells the tide has deposited along the beach. Select a few special ones as souvenirs of this day, then head for Windows on the Water and dig into the bounteous breakfast buffet. You're going to head over to neighboring Captiva Island via a blink-and-you'll-miss-it bridge at Blind Man's Pass. (On the way, stop at the Bailey-Matthews Shell Museum and learn about the shells you found.) Travel the five-miles-or-so length of the island, enjoying canopy roads and lush, junglelike vegetation.

Then spend a little time in downtown Captiva, stopping for a seafood lunch at The Green Flash Restaurant along Captiva Drive. This afternoon rent a bike and explore the famous J. N. "Ding" Darling National Wildlife Refuge for a close-up look at ospreys, herons, egrets, and other fascinating wildlife. When dinnertime rolls around, head for Captiva's Mucky Duck restaurant, where you'll order a seafood platter and eat every bite.

ORIENTATION

From Sarasota head for the Lee Island Coast islands via the scenic U.S. 41, also known here as Tamiami Trail. For a faster route, take I-75 south. Both intersect with SR 776, which leads you to Gasparilla Island and Boca Grande. Further south along U.S. 41 and I-75 is SR 80, which takes you to the three-mile causeway from the mainland to Sanibel. The toll for crossing is $3.

SIGHTSEEING HIGHLIGHTS

★★★★ **CAPTIVA, CAYO COSTA, GASPARILLA, AND SANIBEL SHELLING BEACHES**
Captiva, Cayo Costa, Gasparilla, and Sanibel Islands

LEE ISLAND COAST

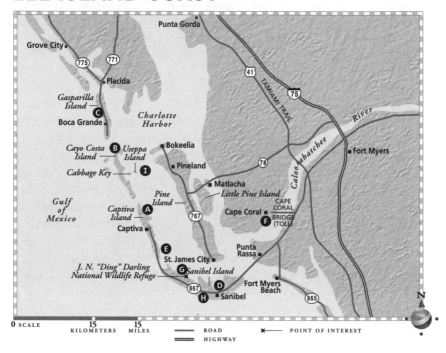

0 SCALE   15   15
        KILOMETERS   MILES   ━━━ ROAD   ✖━━ POINT OF INTEREST
                                       ═══ HIGHWAY

SHELLING BEACHES

Ⓐ Captiva Island
Ⓑ Cayo Costa Island
Ⓒ Gasparilla Island
Ⓓ Sanibel Island

SIGHTS

Ⓔ Bailey-Matthews Shell Museum
Ⓕ Children's Science Center

SIGHTS (continued)

Ⓖ J. N. "Ding" Darling National Wildlife Refuge
Ⓗ Sanibel Lighthouse Boardwalk
Ⓘ Useppa Island

These are perhaps the best places for shelling along the Lee Island Coast, although good specimens can certainly be found on most of the islands here. On **Gasparilla Island**, South Beach is where the shells are, along with a goodly showing of fossilized sharks' teeth. While at **Cayo Costa**, in-the-know shell-seekers check first around Johnson Shoals at the north end of the island. Be sure that the shells you take do not contain live creatures. If they do, return the shells gently to the water, and search for uninhabited ones.

Sanibel's top spot is at the southeast end of the island, near the old lighthouse. On Captiva, the best shelling is on the island's north-end beach. Best times for shelling are an hour before and an hour after the low tide. Always check out the "shell line." That's where the highest waves stop as they come up on the beach. Live shelling (collecting shells with living creatures still inside) on Sanibel has been banned by law since 1995.

Details: Cruise boats carry visitors to Cayo Costa and Gasparilla. (Gasparilla is also accessible by automobile, but you have to drive far into neighboring Charlotte County to get there. The boat takes only a few minutes.) A three-mile causeway ($3 toll) crosses from the mainland about 15 miles southwest of Fort Myers to the twin islands of Sanibel and Captiva. (Captiva is connected to Sanibel by a bridge.) For more information, contact the Lee Island Coast Visitor & Convention Bureau, 941/338-3500 or 800/237-6444, or visit www.LeeIslandCoast.com. (1 day)

★★★★ J. N. "DING" DARLING NATIONAL WILDLIFE REFUGE
1 Wildlife Dr. (off Sanibel-Captiva Rd.), Sanibel Island, 941/472-1100, www.iline.com/ddws/ding.htm

This big, sprawling, 6,000-acre wildlife refuge was named for Pulitzer Prize–winning cartoonist Jay Norwood Darling, who was a pioneer environmentalist back in the 1930s. There's a five-mile scenic drive (or bike ride) within the park that leads visitors through a lush tropical landscape. Hundreds of native birds live here, along with raccoons, otters, alligators, and other wild creatures. There are delightful footpaths and some winding canoe trails.

Details: Sat–Thu 7:30 a.m.–30 minutes before sunset. Visitor center open Nov–Apr Sat–Thu 9–5, May–Oct Sat–Thu 9–4. $5 to drive, $1 to bicycle or walk. (2–4 hours)

★★★ BAILEY-MATTHEWS SHELL MUSEUM
3075 Sanibel-Captiva Rd., Sanibel Island, 941/395-2233 or 888/679-6450, www.uwp.edu/academic/biology/bmsm/bm_shell.htm

It's actually the only shell museum in the United States and conchologists from all over the world come here to view some of Neptune's finest treasures. Each display shows examples of each type of shell in its natural environment, and exhibits explain the role of shells in both natural and human history. There's a children's room here, too, with a "touch tank" and an awesome Great Hall of Shells. The variety and beauty of the shells displayed, from the tiniest wentletrap to the mighty giant clam, amaze most visitors.

Details: *Tue–Sun 10–4. $5 adults, $3 children 8–16, free for children 7 and under. (1 hour)*

★★ USEPPA ISLAND
East of Cayo Costa Island, accessible only by boat or seaplane

Useppa is a "shell-mound island" created long by the Calusa Indians, who lived here as far back as 5000 B.C. It's a private island, but you're welcome to visit for lunch and sightseeing. Legend has it that the island was named for a Mexican princess named Joseffa, a favorite captive of Spanish pirate Jose Gaspar. There's an interesting old Calusa Indian excavation site here, and you can visit the **Useppa Museum**, 941/283-9600, whose signature exhibit is a forensic restoration of the "Useppa Man," taken from a skeleton unearthed here during a 1989 archaeological dig, and the "Useppa Woman," found during the restoration of the Collier Inn.

Details: *For boat transportation, call Captiva Cruises, South Seas Plantation Yacht Harbor, Captiva Island, 941/472-5300. Cruises run from 10:30–3:30 and take about an hour and 15 minutes each way. $27.50 adults, $15 children. For seaplane information, call Boca Grande Seaplane, 941/964-0234. Museum open Tue–Fri noon–2, Sat and Sun 1–2. $2.50 donation suggested. (2 hours for island visit)*

★ CHILDREN'S SCIENCE CENTER
2915 NE Pine Island Rd., Cape Coral, 941/997-0012, www.cyberstreet.com/csc

This center has some neat hands-on exhibits using electricity, optical illusions, and the like to entertain and educate. There's a live snake show, too. Telescope viewing offered February through April.

Details: *Mon–Fri 9:30–4:30, Sat and Sun noon–5. $4 adults, $2 children 3–16, free for children under 3. (1–2 hours)*

★ SANIBEL LIGHTHOUSE BOARDWALK
Southern tip of Sanibel Island, 941/472-6477

The 100-year-old lighthouse—a rarity—may be the county's most photographed structure. Add a photo or two to your own album and enjoy a stroll on the 400-foot boardwalk. There's a kiosk where seasonal information on native plants and wildlife is posted. **Details:** *No admission fee. Metered parking. (1 hour)*

FITNESS AND RECREATION

Each community on the Lee Island Coast has that special mystique peculiar to islands. There's a laid-back, typically tropical feel to each of the little cities and towns represented here, along with spectacular natural beauty. Tranquil beaches are washed daily by surf gently rolling in from the Gulf, bringing with it some of the most beautiful seashells found anywhere. Even if you've never been particularly interested in shells, it's almost a sure thing that while you're here you'll acquire that bent-over shell-seekers' posture known locally as the "Sanibel Stoop." Dedicated shell-hunters will take one of Mike Fuery's Tours, Captiva Island, 941/472-1015. Mike is extremely knowledgeable about shells and also can take you on a deep-sea fishing trip, a relaxing boat ride, or a nature tour. You'll need reservations.

Hikers and bikers love to explore the tree-canopied trails. Canoeing and kayaking are favorite pursuits, and deep-sea fishing, sailing, and watercraft-

RIVER KAYAKING

Lee Island Coast Convention and Visitors Bureau

LEE ISLAND COAST

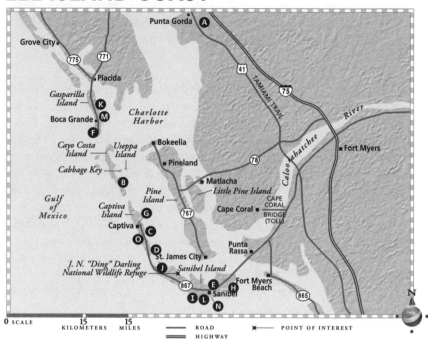

FOOD

- **A** Aqui Esta Diner and Family Restaurant
- **B** Cabbage Key Restaurant and Lounge
- **C** Chadwick's
- **D** The Green Flash Restaurant

FOOD (continued)

- **E** The Greenhouse Grill
- **F** The Loose Caboose
- **G** The Mucky Duck
- **H** Uncle Henry's
- **E** Windows on the Water

LODGING

- **H** Beachview Cottages
- **I** The Blue Dolphin
- **J** The Castaways
- **K** Gasparilla Inn and Cottages
- **L** Island Inn
- **M** Palm Island Resort
- **N** Sandy Bend Resorts
- **O** 'Tween Waters Inn

Note: Items with the same letter are located in the same area.

riding take full advantage of the "water, water, everywhere" geography. At Tarpon Bay Recreational Area, 900 Tarpon Bay Rd. (inside J. N. "Ding" Darling National Wildlife Refuge), 941/472-8900, a knowledgeable naturalist guide accompanies you on an open-air tram tour of the refuge, pointing out and describing the wildlife living here. They also have naturalist-guided kayak/canoe tours. Either way, you'll have the chance to view some of Florida's fascinating wild creatures, including some endangered species. Kayak tours of Pine Island Sound and the Buck Key area are available here, too. All guided tours require reservations. Call 941/472-8900 for times and availability. People who like nature love Florida's newest state park, Lovers Key State Recreation Area, between Bonita Beach and Fort Myers Beach, 941/463-4588. It provides a remarkable combination of recreational and educational experiences. Picnic, hike, swim, and explore canals, tidal pools, and mangrove-lined lagoons. Look up once in a while; hawks and eagles may be watching you.

If you're traveling with kids, a visit to Sun Splash Family Waterpark, 400 Santa Barbara Blvd., Cape Coral, 941/ 574-0557, is probably a must. Check out the really fast tube slide aptly named Cape Fear. Another family amusement center that rescues kids from inevitable travel boredom is Mike Greenwell's Family Fun Park, also in Cape Coral at 35 NE Pine Island Rd., 941/574-4386. There are nice old-fashioned bumper cars, go-cart tracks, and remote-control boats, along with a high-tech game arcade. Babcock Wilderness Adventures, 8000 SR 31, Punta Gorda, 800/500-5583, will take you for an hour-and-a half swamp-buggy ride through the woods and waters of Telegraph Cypress Swamp. You may see bison, alligators, panthers, and exotic birds. (You have to make reservations for this one. Call ahead.)

There are so many golf courses here that golfers will discover that they can literally play 18 holes a day, seven days a week, and not play the same hole twice in two months. South Seas Plantation Golf Course on Captiva, 941/472-5111, www.southseas.com, may be the prettiest. A bit more challenging is Sanibel's Dunes Golf & Tennis Club, 941/472-3355. On the mainland side of the Lee Islands is Punta Gorda, where serious golfers recommend Burnt Store Marina and Country Club, 5000 Burnt Store Rd., Punta Gorda, 941/639-4151.

FOOD

Seafood reigns, of course, and why not? A recent survey indicates that visitors come to the Lee Island Coast primarily for the food. Each of the islands and mainland areas has a wealth of eating places, most of them on the casual side and virtually all of them offering seafood specialties. On Sanibel, **The**

Greenhouse Grill, 2407 Periwinkle Way, 941/472-6882, has an updated diner décor and a wonderful way with seafood. They welcome kids. It's not very big though, so you may have to wait. Try to get reservations. At **Windows on the Water**, 1451 Middle Gulf Dr., 941/395-6014, you get a great view and some interesting "Floribbean" cooking. (It's Florida seafood with Caribbean spices.)

Captiva has lots of eateries. **Chadwick's**, at the entrance to South Seas Plantation Resort & Yacht Harbor, 941/472-7575, features fresh seafood caught locally. Folks who like to eat healthy—even when on vacation—will appreciate the menu offerings here. **The Mucky Duck**, on Andy Rosse Ln., Captiva, 941/472-3434, www.muckyduck.com, is a busy spot. It looks like an English pub right out of a Martha Grimes mystery novel. Try the barbecued shrimp; it's very special. Another Captiva favorite is **The Green Flash Restaurant**, 15183 Captiva Dr., 941/472-3337. Boasting island ambiance and tales of "Green Flash" sightings, this restaurant offers good seafood for lunch or dinner. Pasta is a specialty and Sunday brunch is an island event enjoyed by locals and visitors alike. It's a good idea to phone ahead for reservations for brunch or dinners.

Sometimes you'll find shells that have been bleached by the sun's rays from long days on the sand. Wetting a seemingly bleached shell will sometimes reveal hidden color. If the shell looks better when it's wet, you can permanently restore the color by just wiping it with a little baby oil.

Boca Grande is worth a visit, if only to eat at **The Loose Caboose**, 433 W. Fourth St., Boca Grande, 941/964-0440. It was once the town's railroad station, but it now specializes in delicious huge sandwiches and lovely homemade ice cream among other treats. Another Boca Grande favorite is **Uncle Henry's**, 5800 Gasparilla Rd., 941/964-2300. (It's in the courtyard.) Have you had enough seafood already? Order a steak.

Everyone who has time to do it takes a boat ride to **Cabbage Key Restaurant and Lounge**, on Cabbage Key, 941/283-2278, for a dockside lunch. A tourist trap for sure, but what a charming one. (Cruise there via Captiva Cruises, 941/472-5300.) Jimmy Buffet's original "Cheeseburger in Paradise" was served here. Cabbage Key is famous for key lime pie, too. **Aqui Esta Diner and Family Restaurant**, 3105 S. Tamiami Tr., Punta Gorda, 941/639-6667, is a favorite with locals and you'll be welcome, too. American, Greek, and Italian dishes are on the big menu. Punta Gorda is on the mainland side of the Lee Islands, where the Old Tamiami Trail winds along the coast.

LODGING

Tourism has become such an important part of island life, that lodging places have sprung up all over the place. Some are fancy seaside resorts, some are older mom-and-pop motels, some are quaint waterfront cottages, and some are trendy B&Bs. They each seem to have something special to offer guests. With more than 20,000 hotel, motel, and resort units available, you're pretty sure to find one that suits your needs. There are plenty of national chains represented, but if you prefer an independent place, look for the "Superior Small Lodging" sign.

On Sanibel, **Beachview Cottages**, 3325 W. Gulf Dr., 941/472-1202, www.beachviewcottages.com, puts you right on the beach so that you can get a really early start on shelling. The **Island Inn** on Sanibel, 311 W. Gulf Dr., 941/472-1561, is another waterfront spot with tennis courts on the premises and a golf course nearby. Décor is old-time island—not fancy but fun. **The Castaways**, 6460 Sanibel-Captiva Rd., 941/472-1252, www.thecastaways.com, isn't fancy either, but boaters like the attached marina. Pets and kids are welcome, and there's a restaurant for meals and snacks.

Sandy Bend Resorts, 3057 W. Gulf Dr., Sanibel, 941/472-1190, is convenient and roomy. Screened porches face the good shelling beach. **The Blue Dolphin**, 4227 W. Gulf Dr., Sanibel, 941/472-1600, is another beachfront spot with a private dock marina. You can rent a bike here for exploring the rest of the island. On Captiva, **'Tween Waters Inn**, 15951 Captiva Dr., 941/472-5161, www.tween-waters.com, has all kinds of accommodations—cottages, efficiencies, hotel rooms facing the Gulf or the bay—and a restaurant and entertainment lounge as well. Bike and boat rentals are available here, too.

Palm Island Resort, Placida Rd., Cape Haze, 941/697-4800, can only be reached by boat. A ferry will take you on a 12-minute ride across the Intracoastal Waterway. A golf cart picks you up and delivers you to your villa overlooking a pristine beach. Bikes, canoes, surf kayaks, windsurf-boards, and more are available to rent. The Rum Bay Restaurant is open for lunch and dinner. **Gasparilla Inn and Cottages**, Palm Ave., Gasparilla Island, 941/964-2201, is elegant, historic, and expensive. The rich and famous still stay there, as they did a century ago, so be sure to make your reservation well in advance.

12
FORT MYERS

Fort Myers is an old city. It was a military outpost during the Seminole Indian War of the 1830s. The city gained prominence when Thomas Edison came to the area in 1884 looking for a suitable filament for his incandescent lamp invention. He saw plenty of bamboo growing along the banks of the Caloosahatchee River and thought it might be the right stuff. So he bought a sizable chunk of Fort Myers real estate (for $2,750) and built a winter home and laboratory on the site. Before too long, some of Edison's influential friends took a liking to the place. Henry Ford bought the property right next door, and Harvey Firestone became a frequent visitor.

Fort Myers is sometimes called "the City of Palms" because of the 1,800 palm trees—some of which were planted by Edison himself—that line both sides of elegant McGregor Boulevard. The city's riverfront area boasts some of Florida's finest seafood restaurants, and the downtown area sparkles with a variety of theaters and nightspots. Plenty of golf courses, tennis courts, parks, marinas, and spas keep physical activity levels high, while museums, theaters, galleries, and shops provide less strenuous fun. Seekers after nature will enjoy hiking in Manatee Park, where they can observe the endangered West Indian manatee it its natural environment.

Carry sunscreen with you everywhere, bearing in mind that Fort Myers is the most tropical in climate of any city in the United States with the exception of Key West.

A PERFECT DAY IN FORT MYERS

Start your day in the Fort Myers Historic District on Cleveland Avenue. There's a 24-hour restaurant at the Holiday Inn, so start as early as you like. Then go around the corner to McGregor Boulevard. Here's a street that looks exactly like a Florida street is *supposed* to look like! For 15 sun-dappled miles, orderly rows of stately royal palm trees cast shadows onto the broad gently curving road. (This was only a cattle trail when Edison bought his property. He imported trees from Cuba, and began the beautification project by setting out the first two miles of palms himself.) You'll be first in line to visit the Edison-Ford complex, paying close attention as the guide shows you around the houses, gardens, and laboratory. A few hours pass quickly here. If the Red Sox are in town for spring training, walk the three blocks over to City of Palms Stadium and see what's going on. Then head for the McGregor Boulevard Antiques District. Have a healthy lunch at the Garden Greens Salad Bar on nearby Hendry Street. Then you're off to Manatee Park. Walk along the boardwalk and out to the viewing platform and hope for a sighting of an endangered manatee here in a noncaptive natural environment. Head back to the hotel for a swim and a rest. Then go up to the rooftop at Peter's La Cuisine to wait for the sun to set on this perfect day.

ORIENTATION

You can drive into Fort Myers via I-75 or U.S. 41, and you'll cross the wide Caloosahatchee River on the way. McGregor Boulevard, lined on each side with stately palms, runs alongside the Caloosahatchee and is also called SR 867. You can take this route from Sanibel and Captiva islands to reach Fort Myers. At the Caloosahatchee River Bridge, SR 867 becomes SR 80 and heads west. SR 867 will take you toward Cape Coral and intersects with SR 865, the road to Fort Myers Beach. (Just to confuse things, SR 865 is also known variously as Hickory Boulevard, Estero Boulevard, and San Carlos Boulevard.) Some of the major airlines offer service to Southwest Florida Regional Airport. Several other small commuter airlines also offer regional service.

SIGHTSEEING HIGHLIGHTS

★★★★ BURROUGHS HOUSE
2505 First St., Fort Myers, 941/332-6125
It's always fun to prowl around in somebody else's house, making comments about the owner's taste in furniture and the like—even if

FORT MYERS

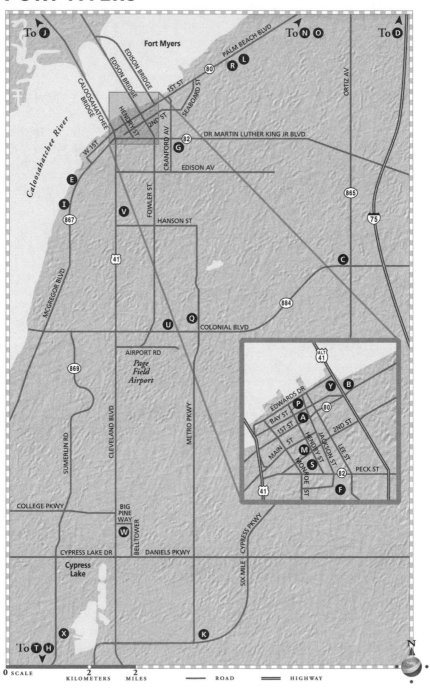

To **J**

Fort Myers

To **N O**

To **D**

PALM BEACH BLVD

80

R **L**

EDISON BRIDGE

EDISON BRIDGE

15T ST

SEABOARD ST

ORTIZ AV

CALOOSAHATCHEE BRIDGE

HENDRY ST

2ND ST

CRANFORD AV

82

DR MARTIN LUTHER KING JR BLVD

G

W 15T

Caloosahatchee River

EDISON AV

E

FOWLER ST

I

867

V

HANSON ST

865

41

75

MCGREGOR BLVD

C

884

U **Q**

COLONIAL BLVD

AIRPORT RD

Page Field Airport

869

CLEVELAND BLVD

METRO PKWY

SUMERLIN RD

ALT 41

EDWARDS DR

Y **B**

P

BAY ST

80

1ST ST

A

2ND ST

MAIN ST

HENDRY ST

JACKSON ST

LEE ST

M

S

MONROE ST

82

PECK ST

41

F

COLLEGE PKWY

BIG PINE WAY

W

BELLTOWER

CYPRESS LAKE DR

DANIELS PKWY

CYPRESS PKWY

Cypress Lake

SIX MILE

X

K

To **T** **H**

N

0 SCALE   2 KILOMETERS   2 MILES   —— ROAD   ══ HIGHWAY

the owner lived there a hundred years ago. This Georgian Revival three-story home was the property of a wealthy businessman, Jettie Burroughs, and his wife, Mona, and it's furnished with original family pieces. Costumed guides pretend to be characters from Fort Myers history.

Details: *Tue–Fri 11–3 (hours may be different during peak season). $3 adults, $1 children. (1 hour)*

★★★★ **EDISON-FORD ESTATE COMPLEX**
2350 Mcgregor Blvd., Fort Myers, 941/334-3614,
www.edison-ford-estate.com
This is a must-see part of any visit to Fort Myers. Edison designed the large rambling Victorian, with its broad porches and graceful French doors, and had it built up in Fairfield, Maine—pre-fab fashion. It was shipped to Florida aboard four schooners. In addition to his success as an inventor, Edison was also a first-rate botanist. The estate features a five-acre garden full of exotic foliage, giant trees, and brilliant flowers. Probably the most important structures here, though, are Edison's office and laboratory. Visitors often comment on the relatively primitive laboratory equipment with which the great

---

SIGHTS
- Ⓐ Arcade Theater
- Ⓑ Burroughs House
- Ⓒ Calusa Nature Center and Planetariaum
- Ⓓ ECHO (Educational Concerns for Hunger Organization)
- Ⓔ *Edison Electric Launch*
- Ⓔ Edison-Ford Estate Complex
- Ⓔ Edison Park
- Ⓕ Fort Myers Historical Museum
- Ⓖ Imaginarium: Hands On Museum and Aquarium
- Ⓗ Koreshan State Historical Site

SIGHTS (continued)
- Ⓘ Mcgregor Boulevard Antiques District
- Ⓙ The Shell Factory
- Ⓚ Sun Harvest Citrus

FOOD
- Ⓛ Casa de Guerrera
- Ⓜ Garden Greens Salad Bar
- Ⓝ The Hut Restaurant
- Ⓞ Perkins Family Restaurant
- Ⓟ Peter's La Cuisine
- Ⓠ Seminole Gulf Railway
- Ⓡ Shooters Waterfront Cafe
- Ⓢ The Veranda

LODGING
- Ⓣ Best Western Pink Shell Beach Resort
- Ⓤ Budgetel Inn
- Ⓥ Holiday Inn Historic District
- Ⓡ Holiday Inn Sunspree Resort
- Ⓦ Homewood Suites Hotel
- Ⓧ Radisson Inn Fort Myers
- Ⓨ Sheraton Harbor Place Hotel

Note: Items with the same letter are located in the same area.

---

man's remarkable experiments were carried out. The museum houses a large collection of his inventions and many personal effects, including his automobile.

Henry Ford and Thomas Edison became good friends when they met at the Detroit Edison Illumination Company. In 1916 Ford bought the property next door to Edison's Fort Myers winter home, and the friends became neighbors. The Ford house, called "Mangoes," is furnished in typical 1920s fashion, with deco touches and nouveau flair. Wait till you see what's in the garage—three Tin Lizzies, all in operating condition.

Details: Admission is by guided tour only. Tours begin every 30 minutes Mon–Sat 9—3:30, Sun noon–3:30; closed Thanksgiving and Christmas. Admission includes homes, gardens, museum, and laboratory. Wear comfortable shoes. You'll walk a lot. $10 adults, $5 children. (2–4 hours)

★★★★ FORT MYERS HISTORICAL MUSEUM
2300 Peck St., Fort Myers, 941/332-5955

This is a really interesting museum, one of those neat places with a little of this and a little of that. The building itself is great. It's the old Atlantic Coastline Railroad depot. Displays cover area history from 800 B.C. on. One of the best things is a 1930 private railroad car. There's even an old World War II P-39 bomber that crashed into Estero Bay during the war. History buffs will like the museum store with its good selection of books and photos on important events and people in Florida's history.

Details: Open Tue–Sat 9–4. $4 adults, $2 children. The museum is handicapped accessible. Exhibits are labeled in Braille for the visually impaired. (1–2 hours)

★★★ IMAGINARIUM: HANDS ON MUSEUM AND AQUARIUM
2000 Cranford Ave., Fort Myers, 941/337-3332

This is an interactive learning center that focuses on the local geographic area. There's a wetlands section, a realistic Florida thunderstorm (not *that* realistic—you don't get wet), and a hurricane experience. Kids will enjoy meeting Eelvis the Eel, one of the aquarium stars. The Imaginarium also has a maze to get lost in and a crash car you can drive.

Details: Tue–Sat 10–5. Admission is $6 for adults, $3 for children. (1–2 hours)

★★★ KORESHAN STATE HISTORICAL SITE
8661 Corkscrew Rd., Estero, 941/992-2184
This is one of the more unusual features of long, sandy, and, unfortunately, over-developed Estero Island. The historic area encompasses the remains of a most unusual pioneer settlement. A religious visionary named Cyrus Teed moved here from Chicago with his followers in 1894. They called their religion "Koreshan Unity" and held the unusual view that the earth was a hollow sphere that contained all life, planets, sun, moon, and stars inside. Teed's aim was to build a New Jerusalem here. With their high ceilings and sharply pitched roofs, the buildings represented a practical approach to subtropical heat and humidity. Eleven buildings and their Victorian furnishings still remain for you to explore at this interesting architectural site.

Details: *Park open daily 8 a.m.–sunset; historic site open daily 8–5. Ranger tours offered Sat and Sun at 1. $3.25 per car, $1 for hikers or bicyclist, tours $1 adults, 50 cents children. (2 hours)*

★★ CALUSA NATURE CENTER AND PLANETARIUM
3450 Ortiz Ave., Fort Myers, 941/275-3435
This center offers a realistic look at the natural history of southwest Florida. There's an outdoor tour of 105 acres of subtropical environment. You'll walk along a rustic boardwalk that leads you through an Indian village and an Audubon aviary. Snake and alligator demonstrations happen a couple of times a day, and you can get a guided tour of the place. The planetarium has laser light show.

Details: *Mon–Sat 9–5, Sun 11–5. $4 adults, $2.50 children. Admission to nature center $4 adults, $2.50 children. Admission to planetarium shows $3 adults, $2 children. Laser light shows $5 person. (1–3 hours)*

★★ *EDISON ELECTRIC LAUNCH*
Fort Myers Yacht Basin, 941/334-3614
This is a faithful replica of Thomas Edison's own passenger boat, *The Reliance*. You'll cruise along the Caloosahatchee River as the captain tells tales of the days when the Edisons entertained guests this very same way. The Electric Launch departs from the Fort Myers Yacht Basin, and a van will take you from the Edison-Ford Estate Complex to the marina.

Details: *Van leaves the estate every 30 minutes Mon–Fri 9:10–3:10. Cruise lasts 15 minutes. $3 per person. (30 minutes)*

★★ EDISON PARK
Bounded by McGregor Blvd., Llewellyn Dr., Marlin and Menlo Rds. (U.S. 41), Fort Myers, 941/338-3500

Much of the city, particularly in areas close to the banks of the Caloosahatchee River, is regarded as "historic," and outstanding sites are plainly marked with signs. The best known of these are the Edison and Ford houses on McGregor Boulevard. But after you leave the complex, walk over to the Edison Park subdivision just south of the ticket office. There's a statue of a scantily clad Greek maiden at the entrance. She was originally quite nude, but Mrs. Edison complained about that, so a special marble-epoxy veil was applied to clothe the cement nymph.

Take a walk on Llewellyn Drive and admire the 16 cast-iron Arcadian-style street lamps installed in 1926. The private homes here are representative of the Spanish- and Mediterranean-style architecture in vogue here in the 1920s and 1930s. If you have time, wander along Marlin and Menlo Roads. Menlo will take you back to the entrance as you walk beneath a lovely green canopy formed by ancient oak trees.

Details: For information, contact Greater Fort Myers Chamber of Commerce, 941/332-3624, www.fortmyers.org. (1 hour)

★★ MCGREGOR BOULEVARD ANTIQUES DISTRICT
12600–12800 block of McGregor Blvd., Fort Myers

When you're trying to fit some antiquing in your vacation schedule, it's always a pleasure to find an antiques district—a gathering of shops

MCGREGOR BOULEVARD
McGregor Boulevard was once a simple cow path. In 1907 Thomas Edison offered to "have royal palms planted on both sides of the road." Indeed, Edison himself planted some of the palm trees that he had imported from Cuba. At first the stately trees only lined the road for two miles, but today they extend from Fort Myers to Fort Myers Beach—15 miles. It's from this stretch of road that Fort Myers earned its nickname, "the City of Palms."

within walking distance of one another. Fairly recently, the McGregor Boulevard/College Parkway area has become such a district.

Look for the red awning that marks **Judy's Antiques**, 12710 McGregor Blvd., 941/481-9600. This shop has doubled in space and now boasts a 2,000-square-foot display area, featuring antiques, furniture, and jewelry. At **Valerie Sanders**, 12680 McGregor Blvd., 941/433-3229, you'll find yourself among memorabilia from the '50s, '60s, and '70s. **McGregor Antique Mall**, 12720 McGregor Blvd., 941/433-0200, brings several dealers together, who are offering a good selection of old toys, Fiesta Ware, pottery, and antiques.

Details: Most shops open Mon–Sat 10–5; some open Sun. It's best to call ahead and verify times. (1–3 hours)

★★ SUN HARVEST CITRUS
14810 Metro Pkwy., Fort Myers, 941/768-2686

It's just a working citrus-packing house, but if you've never seen the process, it can be most interesting. You'll see how Indian River citrus is cleaned, sized, and packaged. Then you'll see how the juice is extracted and you get to sample a half-dozen different juice blends. There's a playground for the kids, too.

Details: Open year-round, Mon–Sat 8 a.m.–9 p.m., Sun 10–6. No admission charge. (30 minutes)

★ ARCADE THEATER
First St. between Hendry and Jackson Sts., Fort Myers, 941/332-4488

If you're in the McGregor Boulevard neighborhood scouting out good antique buys, take a peek at the landmark Arcade Theater. Built in 1908 as a vaudeville playhouse, it has been carefully restored, and now offers plays, vintage movies, and special children's programs.

Details: Hendry St. is at the southern end of the Caloosahatchee Bridge. (30 minutes)

★ ECHO (EDUCATIONAL CONCERNS FOR HUNGER ORGANIZATION)
17430 Durrance Rd., North Fort Myers, 941/543-3246

ECHO is a Christian ministry involved in trying to combat world hunger. At this unique facility you'll see one of the largest collections of tropical food plants in Florida, pet the sheep without wool, and maybe nibble on moringa tree leaves. See how ECHO combines animals, plants, and recycled materials for practical ideas for growing food all over the world.

Details: *One free tour only on Tue, Fri, and Sat 10 a.m. Please be on time; it's a working farm and they offer just the one tour. The Edible Landscape Nursery and the Bookshop are open Mon–Sat 9–noon. Durrance Road is off SR 78, one mile east of I-75, Exit 26. (1 hour)*

★ **THE SHELL FACTORY**
2787 N. Tamiami Tr., North Fort Myers, 941/995-2141,
www.shellfactory.com
When does a retail business become a tourist attraction? The Shell Factory is a good example of one that has done so. It's been here for 60 years, and it's billed as the "world's largest collection of rare shells, corals, sponges, and fossils from the seven seas." It probably is—with more than 5,000,000 shells in inventory. Besides shells and shell-related merchandise, you can ride on the bumper boats, play in the video arcade, visit the alligator cove, and watch a light show. There are all kinds of entertainment—and it's free.

Details: *Open every day, including holidays. Admission and parking are free. (1–2 hours)*

FITNESS AND RECREATION

Fort Myers has long been a baseball town, and people here are pretty wild about the home teams. The Boston Red Sox and the Minnesota Twins each have spring training here. Workouts begin in mid-February and exhibition games are in March. The Sox play at City of Palms Park on Edison Avenue, and the Twins are at Lee County Sports Complex on Six Mile Cypress Road.

Kids of all ages like Kartworld, 1915 Colonial Blvd., 941/936-3233, where there are nearly 100 pinball and video games, a miniature golf course with mountains and tunnels, and a race track with three different kinds of carts.

Fort Myers has lots to offer visiting golfers. Gateway Golf Club, 11360 Championship Dr., 941/561-1010, is a 72-hole championship course. It was designed by Tom Fazio and features the trademark Fazio combination of both pot bunkers and grass bunkers. It's possible to combine the golf game with the beach experience at Bay Beach Golf Club, 7401 Estero Blvd., Fort Myers Beach. They welcome the public and are happy to rent you a cart. If you don't plan to leave until you've "caught a big one," check out all the fishing options you'll find at Adventures in Paradise, 14341 Port Comfort Road, 941/472-8443, www.portsanibelmarina.com. They have charter boats and party boats,

---

FERRY TO KEY WEST

So, you may say, how can I make a trip all the way to Key West, if I'm up here in Fort Myers? The answer is Buquebus. That's pronounced BOO-kee-bus, and it's a high-speed ferry service. Buquebus is one of the world's leading fast-ferry operators, and they have vessels operating in South America, Spain, and Scandinavia. Fort Myers is their first U.S. operation. Buquebus makes two round-trips a day aboard the *Thomas Edison*, carrying passengers and cars between Fort Myers and Key West. Each trip takes three hours. Travelers will move at a leisurely pace along the Caloosahatchee River, because of speed and no-wake zones, so there's time to enjoy the scenery from the deck or big windows. But once you hit the Gulf of Mexico—zoom. You'll zip along while enjoying light snacks, sandwiches, or a full meal. There's a full-service bar and a luxurious VIP lounge aboard, too. Entertainment includes feature films as well as informational videos on the Lee Island Coast and Key West. The vessel carries 300 passengers in both coach and first class.

Enjoy a great day in fascinating Key West. Shop, sightsee, and then hop back aboard and—zoom—you're back in Fort Myers. One-way fares are around $55 for coach and $65–$70 for first-class accommodations. The 10,000-foot state-of-the-art terminal is at the foot of Hendry Street in Fort Myers' attractive downtown waterfront section. Call 941/461-0999 to make reservations or to ask for more information.

so you can ride with a captain or, if you like, rent a boat and be your own captain. (They do regular boat tours, too, if you don't want to fish.)

Visitors can travel through a 2,200-acre wetland ecosystem on a mile-long boardwalk trail at Six Mile Cypress Slough Preserve, Six Mile Cypress Pkwy. (Exit 21 off I-75), 941/432-2004. See subtropical ferns and bromeliads and watch the wading birds while you walk or jog. At Manatee Park on SR 80, 941/432-2004, visitors can rent a canoe and observe endangered manatees in their own habitat during the winter (November through March). At Lakes Park, 7330 Gladiolus Dr., 941/432-2000, travelers enjoy swimming, nature trails, and bike and boat rentals. One of the highlights here is the "Fragrance

Garden." It was created especially for visually impaired people, but everyone enjoys it!

FOOD

If you're one of those folks who puts "eating in restaurants" at the top of the things-to-do-on-vacation list, Fort Myers is a good choice. Seafood is incredibly fresh because you're so close to the source. Shrimp seems to be a specialty here, so order them as often as possible. You won't be disappointed. **The Veranda**, 2122 Second St., 941/332-2065, is set in a pair of renovated, circa-1900, Georgian Revival homes. The décor is charmingly Southern. You can even eat out on the brick-paved courtyard if the weather is fine. At **Peter's La Cuisine**, 2224 Bay St., 941/332-2228, local people come to celebrate big occasions. It's dressy, as Florida places go, and on the expensive side. Health-conscious folks love **Garden Greens Salad Bar**, 1512 Hendry St., 941/479-7788. This big, sumptuous, express salad bar has homemade soups, pasta, and desserts, as well as every salad ingredient you can think of. For a different kind of dining experience, you may enjoy the **Seminole Gulf Railway**, located at Colonial Station (Exit 22 off I-75), 941/275-6060, www.semgulf.com, where you'll be served a five-course meal aboard an old-fashioned dining car. If an all-you-can-eat seafood buffet sounds tasty, try **The Hut Restaurant**, 5100 Buckingham Rd., 941/694-4178, on Wednesday nights. They put out a handsome Sunday brunch, too, and there are different specials going on the rest of the week as well. **Casa de Guerrera**, 2225 First St., 941/332-4674, specializes in chicken and steak fajitas and chimichangas. It's all done up in authentic Mexican style with a casual sombrero-and-serape décor. There are several **Perkins Family Restaurants:** 12300 S. Cleveland Ave., 941/936-1150; 4921 Palm Beach Blvd., 941/694-4499; and 12629 N. Cleveland Ave., 941/656-1999. It's one of Florida's favorite chains for family dining. They have a good take-out bakery, too. **Shooters Waterfront Cafe**, 2220 W. First St., 941/334-2727, is located alongside the Holiday Inn Sunspree Resort, but it seems that everyone in town, including hotel guests, has found this lively spot. There's a big menu for all three meals, and the Sunday brunch (10 a.m. to 2 p.m.) is awesome.

LODGING

Fort Myers is a big, spread-out city, and you have lots of choices when it comes to lodging. Will you choose a deco-styled palace in the historic district or sleek modern high-rise on the waterfront? A spacious all-suite hotel or a cozy B&B? There are several Holiday Inns here—some in town, some on the beach or riverfront. On the one hand, **Holiday Inn Historic District**, 2431 Cleveland Ave., 941/332-3232, is bright with tropical color and deco details. It's near the Edison-Ford Complex.

On the other hand, **Holiday Inn Sunspree Resort**, 2220 W. First St., 941/334-3434, is a riverfront resort in the heart of downtown. They include boat docking among their many services. There's a special playroom for the kids, a game room for bigger kids, and an exercise room. Shooter's Waterfront Cafe is the on-site restaurant. The **Homewood Suites Hotel**, 5255 Big Pines Way, 941/275-6000, is a new hotel with a homey atmosphere and fully equipped kitchens. It's close to upscale shops and not far from the airport. The **Sheraton Harbor Place Hotel**, 2500 Edwards Dr., 941/337-0300, is a big, beautiful place with a superb downtown location. **Radisson Inn Fort Myers**, 20091 Summerlin Rd. SW, 941/466-3797, has a soft Southwestern décor, and rooms are spacious and light. Lots of the rooms have balconies, most overlooking the attractive courtyard with its gracefully shaped pool.

If you're going shopping at the McGregor Boulevard Antique District, think about wearing a fanny pack. Many dealers will ask you to stow your large backpacks and purses in specially provided lockers while you browse. Don't get them wrong—it's not that they don't trust you. But the shops are often crowded with people and items, and big bags mean big breakage. Skip the hassle by carrying your wallet in a fanny pack or small purse.

Budgetel Inn, 2717 Colonial Blvd., 941/275-3500, www.budgetel.com, offers special senior rates and room-delivered continental breakfasts. The **Best Western Pink Shell Beach Resort**, 275 Estero Blvd., Fort Myers Beach, 941/463-6181, is a little way out of town, but if the beach is what you had in mind anyway, it's worth the trip. They offer several kinds of accommodations from motel rooms to beach cottages and Gulf-front villas. There are three heated swimming pools and two lighted tennis courts. There's a marina here, and golf courses aren't far off.

CAMPING

Government figures tell us there are 3,500 sites available in Fort Myers and the neighboring islands. RVers and campers have counted this region as a favorite destination for years. Roads are wide and rig-friendly, and so many campsites have beach access and water views, it's no wonder this region is such a popular spot. Quite a few have boat-launching facilities and, with all this water around, most are within easy distance of swimming or fishing spots. Some folks prefer wooded sites, and there are plenty of those available, too.

Fort Myers Beach RV Resort, 16299 San Carlos Blvd., Fort Myers, 941/466-7171, is a big, popular park with heated pool, spa, and a well-stocked store. Take part in the planned activities, or do your own thing. You'll be three and a half miles from the beach and five miles from Sanibel Island. Lazy J Adventures, 1263 Golden Lake Dr., 941/275-7227, is close to I-75 and perfect for day trips. You're a short drive from Lake Okeechobee and the Everglades attractions. On nearby Fort Myers Beach, San Carlos RV Park, 18701 San Carlos Blvd., 941/466-3133, is within walking distance of charter fishing boats and several restaurants. There are waterfront sites with hookups available, and they have some mobile home rentals available. There are boat docks, too.

Red Coconut RV Resort, 3001 Estero Blvd., Fort Myers Beach, 941/463-7200, has a pleasant beachfront location and all the expected amenities. If you like the RV lifestyle but don't have one of your own, there are rental trailers available. Koreshan State Historical Site, 3850 Corkscrew Blvd., Estero, 941/992-0311, isn't fancy, but it's in a really interesting area and, as part of the state park system, is reasonably priced and well maintained. Fort Myers/Pine Island KOA, 5120 Stringfellow Rd., Pine Island (near St. James City), 941/283-2415, is another waterfront park. It's on a clean and beautiful bog, and in season they offer guests boat trips, shelling expeditions, and some free bus trips.

NIGHTLIFE

Nightlife is one area in Fort Myers that overlaps into restaurants. Even if you don't stay for dinner, go to the Sky Bar on the rooftop at Peter's La Cuisine (see "Food" listings). It's a great place to watch the sunset while listening to some fine blues! If you like a little mayhem while you dine, check out the Murder Mystery Train at Seminole Gulf Railway. The train departs Wednesday to Saturday at 5:30 p.m. and promises a night to die for! Also, there's live music most evenings at Shooters Waterfront Cafe.

13
NAPLES

Naples is a study in contrasts. Stroll trendy Fifth Avenue, with its upscale boutiques, gleaming white storefronts, dazzling window displays, and beautiful
people. Then drive just five miles out of town and you're at the Rookery Bay
National Estuarine Research Reserve, where sprawling mangrove trees shelter
a wonderful variety of rare birds and marine life. Gorgeous homes and posh
condominiums give this sparkling town a look of tidy opulence, and some say
that the number of golf courses per capita is the highest in the world. Naples
boasts miles of sun-drenched white beach, all of which have been fiercely protected from overdevelopment and are easily accessible to visitors. Just east of
all this civilization lies the wilderness of the Big Cypress National Preserve,
and a bit more to the southeast is the western gateway to the "river of
grass"—the vast and mysterious Everglades National Park.

ORIENTATION
Most folks get to Naples via the Tamiami Trail, U.S. 41. (Once that highway
reaches Naples it becomes Fifth Avenue, then it turns into the Tamiami Trail
again, but it's all the same road.) I-75 runs parallel and is faster, but perhaps not
so interesting a ride. The closest airport is Naples Municipal Airport, handling
daily flights via American Eagle Airline to and from Tampa, Orlando, and
Miami, along with a few major airline flights.

NAPLES

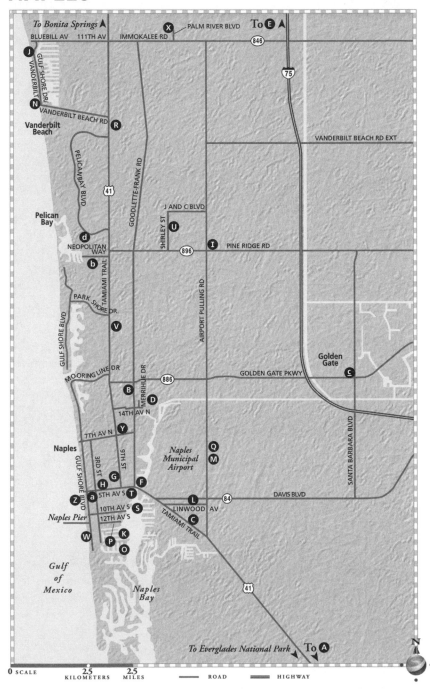

A PERFECT DAY IN NAPLES

Start with a hearty breakfast at Merriman's in the fascinating "Tin City" area. Look out the big windows and watch the fishing fleet on its way out to the Gulf as you enjoy fat fluffy waffles topped with fruit. Then explore the rest of this area, known as the Old Marine Market Place. Then take a short walk over to the depot and enjoy a narrated ride aboard a bright blue open-air trolley. When you get back to your starting point, dash over to the hotel, pick up swimsuits, sunscreen, and picnic lunch, and you're off to the gorgeous white sands of Bonita Springs Public Beach. Swim and sun and just relax. That's one of the special things about Naples—that lovely feeling that you don't have to do *anything* unless you feel like it. This evening put on a light-colored outfit to show off your tan. Head for Olde Naples Seaport and take a dinner cruise aboard one of those handsome big cruise boats.

SIGHTSEEING HIGHLIGHTS

★★★★ BRIGGS NATURE CENTER
401 Shell Rd., 941/775-8569

This nature center is in the Rookery Bay National Estuarine Research

---

SIGHTS

- **Ⓐ** Briggs Nature Center
- **Ⓑ** Caribbean Gardens
- **Ⓒ** Collier County Museum
- **Ⓓ** Conservancy of Southwest Florida
- **Ⓔ** Corkscrew Swamp Sanctuary
- **Ⓕ** Naples Depot Civic and Cultural Center
- **Ⓖ** Naples Trolley Tour
- **Ⓗ** Old Marine Market Place
- **Ⓘ** Teddy Bear Museum of Naples

FOOD

- **Ⓙ** The Chickee at the Vanderbilt Inn on the Gulf
- **Ⓚ** Chris' Whistle Stop Steak House
- **Ⓛ** The English Pub Restaurant
- **Ⓜ** Frascatti's Italian Restaurant and Deli
- **Ⓝ** Lighthouse Restaurant
- **Ⓞ** Merriman's at Tin City
- **Ⓟ** Michelangelo
- **Ⓠ** Michelbob's Championship Ribs
- **Ⓡ** Naples Cheesecake Co.
- **Ⓢ** *Naples Princess* and *Naples Royal Princess* Cruise Ships

FOOD (continued)

- **Ⓣ** Riverwalk Fish and Ale House
- **Ⓤ** Stevie Tomato's Sports Page Bar and Grill

LODGING

- **Ⓥ** Courtyard by Marriott
- **Ⓦ** Edgewater Beach Hotel
- **Ⓧ** Fairways Resort
- **Ⓨ** Howard Johnson Motor Inn
- **Ⓩ** Naples Beach Hotel & Golf Club
- **ⓐ** The Olde Naples Inn & Suites
- **ⓑ** Park Shore Resort
- **ⓒ** Quality Inn and Suites Golf Resort
- **ⓓ** The Registry Resort

Reserve between Naples and Marco Island. This is the place to join a canoe ride among the mangroves, regularly scheduled nature excursions during which you'll learn so much about our fragile ecosystem that you'll never forget it. Bird-watchers get excited about this area, too. You may see wood storks here, and they're a rarity. There's a very pleasant elevated boardwalk for you, if you'd rather not canoe. It extends for half a mile into a tropical hardwood hammock. Watch for baby alligators, but don't worry, they're safely behind glass. There's the Butterfly Garden and an informative interpretive center.

Details: *Jan–Mar Mon–Sat 9–4:30, Sun 1–4:30; closed Sun rest of year; closed Sat and Sun in summer. Free admission to center. Boardwalk $3 adults, $1 children. Canoe and boat fees vary. (1–3 hours)*

★★★★ CARIBBEAN GARDENS
1590 Goodlette Rd., 941/262-5409
Here's a good, Old Florida attraction. The gardens were originally laid out back in 1919. (Yes, when you were a kid this was called Jungle Larry's. It's the same place, updated with new animal shows, boat cruises, and wildlife exhibits.) There's a self-guided trail winding through the junglelike 52-acre preserve where you can see exotic birds and friendly animals. You will see no cages here. The wild birds and animals live together and wander around wherever they like. There's a petting farm where kids can get acquainted with all sorts of good-natured domesticated animals, and places for you to picnic. A 30-minute boat ride will take you to an island where primates live. Handsome plantings and floral displays add color and fragrance to the adventure.

Details: *Daily 9:30–5:30; closed major holidays. $14 adults, $9 children. (4–5 hours)*

★★★★ CONSERVANCY OF SOUTHWEST FLORIDA
1450 Merrihue Dr., 941/262-0304
This is a most remarkable educational center where visitors can see, at one stop, an aviary, a wildlife rehabilitation clinic, a nature discovery center, and even a narrated boat tour of a real mangrove forest and lagoon. You can observe recuperating wildlife on special monitor screens. You'll get to know a little about some of the creatures you've read about and may have seen since you've been in Florida. Meet a loggerhead turtle, snakes, and other elusive creatures. Southwest Florida's unique subtropical ecosystems are highlighted

with hands-on exhibits, video presentations, and some special programs that change from time to time. A knowledgeable guide leads you on a 45-minute boat ride through the mangrove forest and lagoon, or, if you prefer, you can rent a kayak or canoe and explore on your own.

Details: Jan–Mar Mon–Sat 9–4:30, Sun 1–4:30; closed Sun rest of year; closed Sat and Sun in summer. Grounds fee $5 adults, $1 children. (1–3 hours)

★★★★ CORKSCREW SWAMP SANCTUARY
375 Sanctuary Rd., 941/675-3771

This is the Florida that used to exist. It's virtually untouched by humans and is under the watchful protection of the National Audubon Society. North America's largest remaining stand of virgin bald cypress lies within the sanctuary's 11,000 acres—and some of them rise to 130 feet with girths of up to 25 feet. Some of the trees here are over 700 years old. Notice the plants: ferns, bromeliads, lilies, and wild orchids. A big colony of wood storks calls this sanctuary home from November through April. You'll probably see lots of other birds, too. Watch for herons, egrets, and woodpeckers. Alligators, turtles, and chameleons are plentiful. Deer, otter, and bear are definite possibilities. If you see an alligator on the boardwalk, he has the right of way. Please don't collect or disturb plants, and don't disturb or feed the animals.

Details: Dec–Apr daily 7–5; rest of year 8–5. $6.50 adults, $3 children. (2 hours)

★★★★ OLD MARINE MARKET PLACE
U.S. 41 E. at Goodlette Rd., 941/262-4200.

Back in the heyday of fishing, this section of town was filled with old tin fishermen's shacks, which led to its nickname of Tin City. Renewed interest in this historic and fabled district, along with some entrepreneurial know-how, sparked the development of Old Marine Market Place. The district includes about 40 shops, restaurants, and charter-boating establishments, all promising an exciting day's adventures. At **Caribe Jewels**, 941/262-2215, there's an astonishing selection of costume jewelry—literally thousands of rings, necklaces, earrings, bracelets, and pins. Open Monday to Saturday 10 to 9; Sunday 10 to 5. **The Osprey**, 941/263-4015, has some neat resort wear for children and adults. Wildlife T-shirts are available here, as

THE NAPLES PIER

Visit Florida

are Florida's own Jimmy Buffet Ts and Guy Harvey originals. Open Monday to Saturday 10 to 9; Sunday noon to 5.

Details: *Other shop hours vary. (4–8 hours)*

★★★ TEDDY BEAR MUSEUM OF NAPLES
2511 Pine Ridge Rd., 941/598-2711,
www.teddymuseum.com
This is such a cool place. Imagine more than 3,000 teddy bears all in one spot. Some are huge, some just tiny, all are lovable. Displays and exhibits change regularly, so you may not see the same stuffed animals on every visit. There's a library stocked with books about (what else?) bears. The youngest travelers will enjoy going inside the House of the Three Bears.

Details: *1 mile from Exit 16 on I-75. Wed–Sat 10–5, Sun 1–5; also open Mon 10–5 Dec–Apr. $6 adults, $4 children. (1 hour)*

★★ COLLIER COUNTY MUSEUM
3301 Tamiami Tr. E., 941/774-8476
History buffs will enjoy learning about the history of this frontier county. The museum highlights interesting people and events from

the Calusa Indian period right up to the present. You'll see a steam-powered logging locomotive and a re-created Seminole Indian village. **Details:** *Mon–Fri 9–5; closed holidays. Free. (I hour)*

★★ **NAPLES DEPOT CIVIC AND CULTURAL CENTER**
1051 Fifth Ave. S., 941/262-1776
This is an old railroad depot built in 1927. When passenger service was discontinued and the building became run-down, it became a Jaycees project. The refurbished depot is now recognized as a historical site, recorded on the National Register of Historical Places and is a gallery for changing art exhibits. A caboose stands beside the depot, and a collection of old railroad memorabilia is displayed inside.
Details: *Depot open Mon–Fri 10–4. Free. (30 minutes)*

★★ **NAPLES TROLLEY TOUR**
Tenth St. S. and Sixth Ave. S., 941/262-7300
Take a ride on one of Naples's famous trolleys and enjoy a narrated tour of the area. Learn historical facts (and possibly some humorous fiction) from well-trained guides. There are several trolleys, and you'll see them here and there around town. One pass allows you to board and reboard at as many trolley stops as you like. The trolley goes as far north as Vanderbilt Inn and as far south as Third Street South.
Details: *Mon–Sat 8:30–5:30, Sun 10:30–5:30. $11 adults, $5 children (includes all-day boarding pass). (1–8 hours)*

FITNESS AND RECREATION

Naples offers a broad spectrum of nature activities, including fishing, birding, boating, sailing, shelling, and beachcombing for sharks' teeth, along with visiting the various nature centers. But there's certainly plenty of other activity to fill vacation days and nights. Delnor-Wiggins State Recreation Area, 111th Ave. (west end), North Naples, 941/597-6196, is a spic-and-span park with miles of beach, as well as grills, picnic tables, and lots of parking. Fishing is good here. (Try Wiggins Pass.) There's a small fee for out-of-state beach goers. Another good public beach is Bonita Springs Public Beach, Bonita Beach Rd. on the southern end of Bonita Beach, 941/353-0404. There are picnic tables for your use and nearby refreshment concessions, and the parking is free. There's a family fun center called King Richards, 6780 N. Airport Rd., 941/598-1666, in a big castle-shaped building where kids, moms, and dads can scoot around in go-carts and bumper boats, and enjoy miniature golf and many video games. You only pay by the game or buy family tickets. There's no admission charge.

You can take a Dolphin Watching Cruise from Tin City aboard *Double Sunshine*, 941/263-4949. There are over 30 golf courses in the Naples area. Although most are for private membership only, several are open to the public. Golfers will enjoy playing the Robert Trent Jones course at Lely Flamingo Island Club, 8004 Lely Resort Blvd., 941/793-2223. You'll need to phone ahead to reserve tee times. The public park system is fine and some parks offer lighted tennis courts and lighted racquetball, volleyball, and basketball facilities.

FOOD

It stands to reason that an upscale community like this one would have plenty of great restaurants. It's true. But they're not all really pricey. **Merriman's at Tin City**, 1200 Fifth Ave. S., 941/261-1811, has award-winning seafood and steaks at reasonable prices in a charming turn-of-the-last-century décor. Naples's favorite pizza is served at **Stevie Tomato's Sports Page Bar and Grill**, 5310 Shirley St., 941/566-7060. Big TV screens, pool tables, and darts accompany Chicago-style pizza. Not far from Tin City on Goodlette Road is **Chris' Whistle Stop Steak House**, 200 Goodlette Rd. S., 941/263-8440. This out-in-the-country atmosphere goes well with steaks, prime ribs, and seafood. **Frascatti's Italian Restaurant and Deli**, 1258 N. Airport Rd., 941/643-5709, has a complete Italian menu as well as an attached Italian deli for take-out. (It's located within River Reach Plaza—a strip mall on N. Airport Rd.) **Michelangelo**, 755 12th Ave. S., 941/643-6177, serves Italian food, too, in a more sophisticated atmosphere. (Try Fazzoletti Michelangelo—crepes stuffed with crab and lobster in cognac sauce.) For casual waterfront dining on an outdoor deck, try **Lighthouse Restaurant**, 9180 Gulf Shore Dr., 941/597-2551.

For dining on a cruise, try *Naples Princess* and *Naples Royal Princess Cruise Ships*, Olde Naples Seaport, 1001 Tenth Avenue S., 941/649-2275. Big, roomy cruise ships offer daily brunch, lunch, and dinner cruises. Menus are somewhat limited, but good. The Gulf air will give you an appetite, and the scenery in this area is delightful—sea birds galore, beautiful waterfront homes to peek at, and sailboats and such on the horizon. The Olde Naples Seaport, where the cruises originate, is fun to visit—lots of art galleries, antiques shops, boutiques, and even an aquarium.

Try **The Chickee at the Vanderbilt Inn on the Gulf**, 11000 Gulf Shore Dr. N., 941/597-3151. ("Chickee" is a Seminole Indian word that refers to the palm-frond–thatched roof shelters that the long-ago Seminoles devised for use in the Everglades.) This chickee is, of course, an elegant one! The atmosphere is casual, though, and there are even some palm-thatched roofs in evidence. The Chickee serves lunch and dinner complemented by happy music and exotic island drinks. **The English Pub Restaurant**, 2408 Linwood Ave., 941/774-2408, offers traditional English dishes and real British draught beers. Not just a theme restaurant, it really is an English pub. (Hard to find, it's behind the 7-Eleven on U.S. 41 E.) **Riverwalk Fish and Ale House**, 1200 Fifth Ave. S., 941/263-2734, is at the Tin City Shopping Center (Naples on U.S. 41 E at Goodlette Rd.). It's casual and rustic, as are all the Tin City venues, with an open view of the docks and harbor activity and simple good seafood and steaks for dinner, and burgers, salads, and sandwiches for lunch. **Michelbob's Championship Ribs**, 371 Airport Rd., 941/643-RIBS, long a favorite for their prize-winning ribs, is worth seeking out. The décor is strictly '50s. Eclectic memorabilia from those good old days line the walls. It's a fun place for the whole family and there's a special menu for the kids. It's not really a restaurant, but if you want some nibbling to take back to the motel room, check out the **Naples Cheesecake Co.**, at 8050 N. Trail Blvd., 941/598-9070, www.naplescheesecake.com. The cheesecakes are the real thing, in traditional and exotic flavors.

LODGING

There are accommodations in Naples to suit every pocketbook. Top-notch suite hotel **Edgewater Beach Hotel**, 1901 Gulf Shore Blvd., 941/403-2000, has balconied suites, many with beach views. The **Howard Johnson Motor Inn**, 221 Ninth St. S., 941/262-6181, www.hojo.com, is in Olde Naples, close to great shops, and its architecture is interesting. Prices are moderate. **Quality Inn and Suites Golf Resort**, 4100 Golden Gate Pkwy., 941/455-1010, puts you close to golf action. **Fairways Resort**, 103 Palm River Blvd., 941/597-8181, is located in the golfing community of Palm River Estates, about a mile east of U.S. 41 on SR 846. It's quiet and friendly and your room opens onto a tranquil courtyard. It's close to golf, of course, but also not far from beaches, restaurants, and shopping. **The Olde Naples Inn & Suites**, 801 Third St. S., 941/262-5194, is an older facility, on the quaint side. The inn has efficiencies and apartments as well as motel rooms, and everybody gets a refrigerator. It's well located, just a couple of blocks from the beach. The **Naples Beach Hotel & Golf Club**, 851 Gulf Shore Blvd N., 941/261-2222, is a fine family-owned resort featuring six architecturally distinct buildings. Rooms feature art and photos by local artists. Beach and golf are both here. Fresh orchids from the hotel's own greenhouse adorn guest areas.

There's a **Courtyard by Marriott**, 3250 U.S. 41 N., 941/434-8700, just about a half mile from the beach. This is a quiet spot, yet it's close to shopping and restaurants. The buffet breakfast is a nice touch. You'll love the **Park Shore Resort**, 600 Neapolitan Way, 941/263-2222, if shopping is one of your vacation activities. It's right behind Neapolitan Shopping Plaza and lots of upscale shops. It's a pretty place with some water-view suites. They'll shuttle you to the beach and back. **The Registry Resort**, 475 Seagate Dr., 941/597-3232, is surrounded by beautiful Pelican Bay and offers luxurious rooms, championship golf courses, tennis courts, health club, spa, and a couple of really good restaurants. There's even an old-fashioned ice-cream parlor. (And you're right next door to one of the best beaches in the world, as designated by "Dr. Beach" Stephen Leatherman. It's the rather inelegantly named Clam Pass Park.)

CAMPING
The Collier-Seminole State Park Campground, 941/394-3397, is located within the Collier-Seminole State Park. There are 150 campsites, about half of them with hook-ups. Naples-Marco Island KOA, 1700 Barefoot Williams Rd., 941/774-5455, has shaded grassy sites along with air-conditioned camping cabins to rent. A boat ramp has access to the Gulf, and you can rent a canoe. Port of the Islands RV Resort, 12425 Union Rd., 941/642-5343, is on the Tamiami Trail about 22 miles southeast of Naples, with 99 grassy sites on a canal that leads to the gulf. There's a skeet/trap range, nature trails, and nearby resort restaurant.

NIGHTLIFE
For all its well-bred charm, Naples can still kick up its elegant heels after dark. Check out the Backstage Tap and Grill, 5335 Tamiami Tr., 941/598-1300, for live entertainment on weekends. Club Zanzibar at the lovely Registry Resort, 475 Seagate Drive, 941/514-3777, throws a dance party on Friday and Saturday nights with a D.J. on hand to keep the beat going. At the Lizard Cafe, 1780 Commerce Drive, alternative-rock bands perform nightly. Theme nights are also a feature here. Latin and South Beach sounds prevail at Tommy Bahama's, 1220 Third Street S., 941/643-3889.

APPENDIX

Consider this appendix your travel tool box. Use it along with the material in the Planning Your Trip chapter to craft the trip you want. Here are the tools you'll find inside:

1. **Planning Map.** Make copies of this map and plot various trip possibilities. Once you've decided on your route, you can write it on the original map and refer to it as you're traveling.

2. **Mileage Chart.** This chart shows the driving distances (in miles) between various destinations throughout the area. Use it in conjunction with the Planning Map.

3. **Special Interest Tours.** If you'd like to plan a trip around a certain theme—such as nature, sports, or art—one of these tours may work for you.

4. **Calendar of Events.** Here you'll find a month-by-month listing of major area events.

5. **Resources.** This guide lists various regional chambers of commerce and visitors bureaus.

PLANNING MAP: Florida Gulf Coast

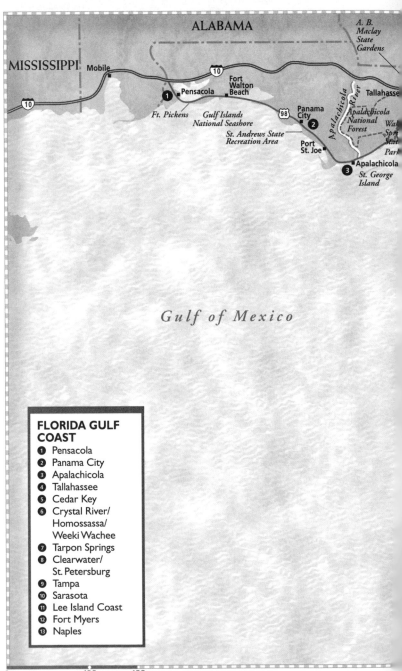

ALABAMA

MISSISSIPPI Mobile

A. B. Maclay State Gardens

Fort Walton Beach

Pensacola

Tallahassee

Ft. Pickens Gulf Islands National Seashore

Panama City

Apalachicola National Forest

St. Andrews State Recreation Area

Port St. Joe

Apalachicola

St. George Island

Gulf of Mexico

FLORIDA GULF COAST

1 Pensacola
2 Panama City
3 Apalachicola
4 Tallahassee
5 Cedar Key
6 Crystal River/ Homossassa/ Weeki Wachee
7 Tarpon Springs
8 Clearwater/ St. Petersburg
9 Tampa
10 Sarasota
11 Lee Island Coast
12 Fort Myers
13 Naples

0 SCALE   100 KILOMETERS   100 MILES

━━ ROAD
═══ HIGHWAY

--- AREA/PARK BOUNDA
✕— POINT OF INTEREST

GEORGIA

Jacksonville

Atlantic Ocean

Suwannee
Cedar Key
Yankee Town
Homosassa Springs Crystal River
State Wildlife Homosassa
Preserve

Weeki Wachee Spring

Orlando

Tarpon Springs
Caladesi Island Tampa
State Park Clearwater

FLORIDA

St. Petersburg

Ringling Museums
Sarasota

Lake Okeechobee

Gasparilla Island

Boca Grande
Captiva Island Captiva
Pine Island Sanibel
Sanibel Island

Fort Myers *Corkscrew Swamp*

Ft. Lauderdale

Naples
Marco
Miami

Everglades City

Everglades National Park

Biscayne National Park

N

	Apalachicola	Cedar Key	Crystal River	Fort Myers	Homosassa	Naples	Panama City	Pensacola	St. Petersburg	Sanibel Island	Sarasota	Tallahassee	Tampa
Cedar Key	211												
Crystal River	267	56											
Fort Myers	436	255	199										
Homosassa	274	63	7	206									
Naples	471	290	234	35	87								
Panama City	63	274	330	499	413	552							
Pensacola	139	350	406	575	212	628	76						
St. Petersburg	331	150	94	105	212	140	394	470					
Sanibel Island	446	299	219	20	132	55	519	595	169				
Sarasota	376	195	139	72	171	107	439	515	45	92			
Tallahassee	84	183	164	398	87	433	119	195	253	412	326		
Tampa	331	150	94	129	53	164	394	470	24	149	57	275	
Tarpon Springs	297	116	60	139	53	297	361	437	34	182	78	224	34

SPECIAL INTEREST TOURS

With *Florida Gulf Coast Travel•Smart* you can plan a trip of any length—a one-day excursion, a getaway weekend, or a three-week vacation—around any special interest. To get you started, the following pages contain six tours geared toward a variety of interests. For more information, refer to the chapters listed—chapter names are bolded and chapter numbers appear inside black bullets. You can follow a suggested itinerary in its entirety, or shorten, lengthen, or combine parts of each, depending on starting and ending points.

Discuss alternative routes and schedules with your travel companions—it's a great way to have fun, even before you leave home. And remember: don't hesitate to change your itinerary once you're on the road. Careful study and planning ahead of time will help you make informed decisions as you go, but spontaneity is the extra ingredient that will make your trip memorable.

FAMILY FUN TOUR

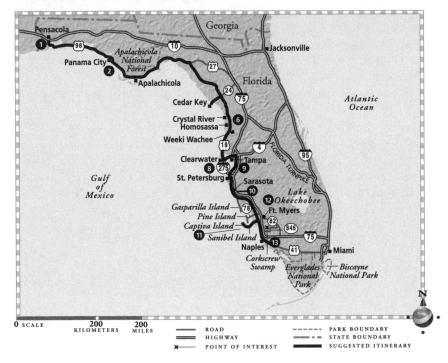

Our coast is always fun for families—both the families who live here and those who just come to visit. Indoor and outdoor family adventures await you all.

❶ **Pensacola** (National Museum of Naval Aviation, The ZOO)

❷ **The Emerald Coast** (Miracle Strip Amusement Park, Morgan's)

❻ **Crystal River/Homosassa/Weeki Wachee** (Mermaid Show, Buccaneer Bay, Homosassa Springs State Wildlife Park, River Tours)

❽ **Clearwater/St. Petersburg** (Great Explorations Museum, Suncoast Seabird Sanctuary, Captain Memo's Pirate Ship, Pirate's Cove Adventure Golf)

❾ **Tampa** (Adventure Island, Busch Gardens, Lowry Park Zoo)

❿ **Sarasota** (Museum of the Circus, Sarasota Jungle Gardens)

⓫ **Lee Island Coast** (Children's Science Center, Sun Splash Family Waterpark)

⓬ **Fort Myers** (Imaginarium, *Edison Electric Launch*, Seminole Gulf Railway)

⓭ **Naples** (Corkscrew Swamp Sanctuary, Teddy Bear Museum)

Time needed: 2 weeks

HISTORY LOVERS' TOUR

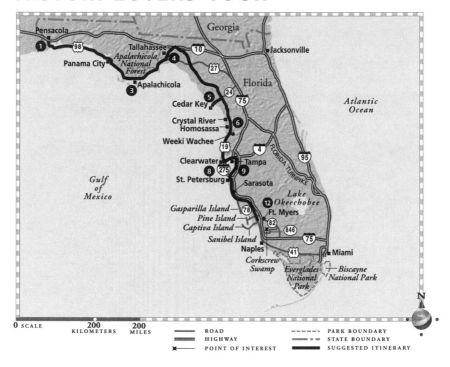

Florida's history is rich and varied—from prehistoric Florida (yes, we have dinosaur bones!) to Indian civilizations.

❶ Pensacola (National Museum of Naval History, Civil War Soldiers Museum)
❸ Apalachicola (*Governor Stone* Gulf Coast Schooner, John Gorrie State Museum)
❹ Tallahassee (San Luis Archaeological Site, Museum of Florida History)
❺ Cedar Key (Cedar Key Historical Society Museum)
❻ Crystal River, Homosassa, and Weeki Wachee (Crystal River State Archaelogical Site, Yulee Sugar Mill Ruins State Historic Site)
❽ Clearwater/St. Petersburg (Museum of Fine Arts, Tampa Bay Holocaust Memorial Museum and Educational Center)
❾ Tampa (Ybor City National Landmark District, Henry B. Plant Museum)
⑫ Fort Myers (Edison-Ford Complex, Fort Myers Historical Museum)

Time needed: 2 weeks

BEACHCOMBERS' TOUR

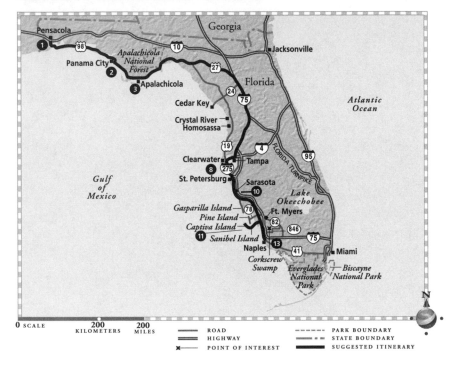

Florida's beaches regularly place among the best in the United States, and you can visit 10 of them on your Gulf Coast tour! Of course, there are hundreds of other beaches besides these!

❶ Pensacola (Perdido Key State Recreation Area)
❷ The Emerald Coast (St. Andrews State Recreation Area, Grayton Beach State Recreation Area)
❸ Apalachicola (St. George Island State Park)
❽ Clearwater/St. Petersburg (Caladesi Island, Fort De Soto Park, Sand Key)
❿ Sarasota (Crescent Beach)
⓫ Lee Island Coast (Captiva Island)
⓭ Naples (Clam Pass Park)

Time needed: 2 weeks

GARDEN TOUR

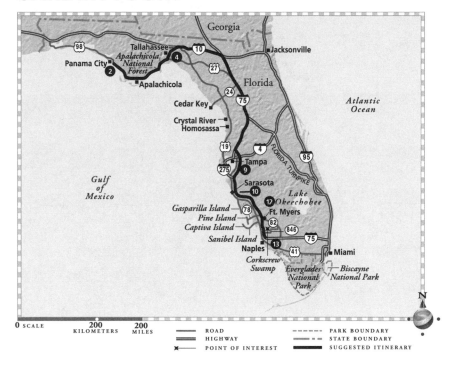

With a climate like ours, it's no wonder that we have wonderful gardens! A good many of them are carefully maintained for the enjoyment of the public. These are just a few of the colorful garden sites you'll enjoy along the Gulf Coast.

❷ **The Emerald Coast** (Eden State Gardens, Monet Monet)
❹ **Tallahassee** (Maclay State Gardens)
❾ **Tampa** (Bok Tower Gardens)
❿ **Sarasota** (Sarasota Jungle Gardens, Marie Selby Botanical Gardens)
⓬ **Fort Myers** (Edison Botanical Gardens)
⓭ **Naples** (Caribbean Gardens)

Time needed: 1 week

ARTS AND CULTURE TOUR

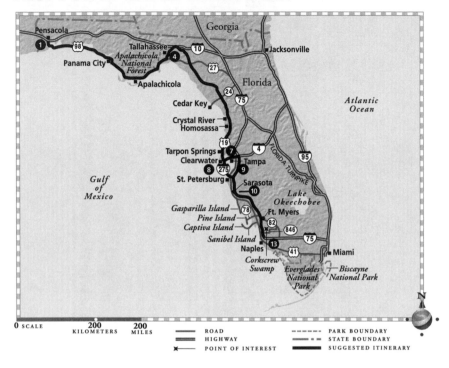

Florida's arts and culture scene reflects the influences of many nations and cultures. Some museums house remarkable collections of classical art, while others specialize in the very best contemporary offerings.

❶ **Pensacola** (Pensacola Historical Museum, Pensacola Museum of Art)

❹ **Tallahassee** (Alfred B. Maclay State Gardens, San Luis Archaeological Site)

❼ **Tarpon Springs** (George Inness Jr. Paintings, Historic District, St. Nicholas Greek Orthodox Cathedral)

❽ **Clearwater/St. Petersburg** (American Stage Company, Museum of Fine Arts, Salvador Dalí Museum, Florida International Museum)

❾ **Tampa** (Henry B. Plant Museum, Ybor City State Museum, Tampa Theater)

❿ **Sarasota** (Asolo Theater, John and Mable Ringling Museum of Art, St. Armands Key Galleries)

⓭ **Naples** (Collier County Museum, Trolley Tours, galleries)

Time needed: 2 weeks

NATURE LOVERS' TOUR

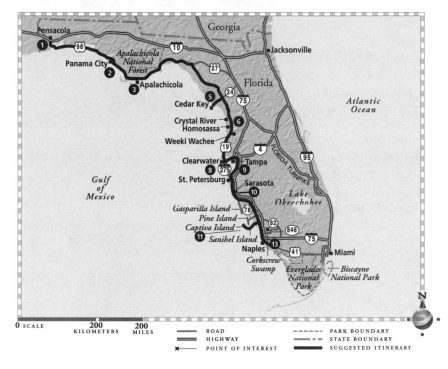

Nature lovers never tire of the wonders of this coastline with its fragile ecosystem and fascinating population of wildlife. Photographers, bring lots of film.

❶ **Pensacola** (Blackwater River State Forest, Gulf Islands National Seashore)
❷ **The Emerald Coast** (Gulf World Marine Park, Grayton Beach)
❸ **Apalachicola** (Apalachicola National Forest, St. Vincent Wildlife Refuge)
❺ **Cedar Key** (Cedar Keys National Wildlife Refuge)
❻ **Crystal River, Homosassa, and Weeki Wachee** (Homosassa Springs State Wildlife Park, Chassahowitzka National Wildlife Refuge)
❽ **Clearwater/St. Petersburg** (Suncoast Seabird Sanctuary)
❾ **Tampa** (Busch Gardens, Florida Aquarium, Lowry Park Zoo)
❿ **Sarasota** (Myakka River State Park, Pelican Man Bird Sanctuary)
⓫ **Lee Island Coast** (J. N. "Ding" Darling National Wildlife Refuge)
⓭ **Naples** (Big Cypress National Preserve, Corkscrew Swamp Sanctuary)

Time needed: 2 weeks

January

Annual Florida Brewers Guild Beer Festival, The Emerald Coast, 850/654-9771
Brewers from around Florida ask visitors to help decide which beer is best.

Festival of the Epiphany, Tarpon Springs, 727/937-3540
Greek Orthodox Church's celebration of Christ's baptism—procession, Greek food, and diving for the cross at Spring Bayou.

Hernando de Soto Winter Encampment, Tallahassee, 850/922-6007
Living history portrayal of 1539 winter encampment featuring interpreters of Spanish and Apalachee Indian cultures.

Outback Bowl, Tampa, 813/874-BOWL
Annual football game at Raymond James Stadium matches third-place teams from the Southeastern Conference and the Big Ten Conference.

Snowfest, Pensacola, 850/434-1234
A make-believe winterfest with snow in Florida!

February

Edison Festival of Light, Fort Myers, 914/332-7600
Annual tribute to inventor Thomas Edison, with parade and parties.

Florida State Fair, Tampa, 813/621-7821
The big daddy of Florida fairs, featuring livestock, agriculture, art, crafts, rides, food, and big-name entertainers.

Gasparilla Pirate Invasion, Tampa, 813/353-8070
A pirate invasion with fully rigged pirate ship takes over downtown with music, food, entertainment, a big parade, and even a marathon.

Mardi Gras Celebration at Sandestin, The Emerald Coast, 850/267-8135
Parade, street party, golf tournament, formal Krewe Ball.

Plant City Strawberry Festival, Tampa, 813/752-9191
Entertainment by country music's top stars and lots of strawberry shortcake.

March

Dunedin Highland Games and Festival, Clearwater/St. Petersburg, 727/736-5066
Scottish band competitions, highlands dancing, piping, drumming, and athletic events.

Festival of the States, Clearwater/St. Petersburg, 727/898-3654
The South's largest civic celebration. Bands from throughout the United States compete. Three major parades, concerts, sporting events.
Jazz & Blues Festival, Tallahassee, 850/376-1636
Nonstop jazz, blues, and gospel, showcasing local musicians.
Sanibel Annual Shell Fair and Show, Lee Island Coast, 941/472-2155
Devoted to rare shells, marine exhibits, and shell crafts.

April
Annual Mainsail Art Festival, Clearwater/St. Petersburg, 727/464-7200
Spotlight on the arts with a big, outdoor, juried show.
Annual Wine Festival, The Emerald Coast, 850/267-8092
Voted "Best Festival in the Southeast." Wine seminars, samples of hundreds of wines, and live music.
Sarasota Jazz Festival, Sarasota, 941/957-1877
Local and national artists flock to Sarasota for this big musical event.
Swamp Buggy Races, Naples, 941/262-6376
Fun and excitement as the big buggies race for prizes.

May
Annual Spring Tour of Historic Homes, Apalachicola, 850/653-9419
Visit Apalachicola's lovely Victorian homes.
Billy Bowlegs Festival, The Emerald Coast, 850/244-8191
Fort Walton Beach celebrates a pirate who ruled the area long ago.
Pensacola Lobster Fest, Pensacola, 850/434-1234
Annual festival and feast honors the tasty crustacean.
Southern Shakespeare Festival, Tallahassee, 850/671-0742
Renaissance festival featuring elaborate costumes, mimes, games, food, and Shakespeare in the Park.

June
Fiesta of Five Flags, Pensacola, 850/434-1234
Art shows, parade, contests, reenactments in Historic District.
International Hemingway Festival, Lee Island Coast, 941/338-3500
Sanibel and Captiva make Father's Day "Papa's Day" with literary workshops, contests, and a fishing tournament.
Kids' Week, Clearwater/St. Petersburg, 727/461-0011
Clearwater Beach celebrates kids with magic shows, marine programs, plays, beach activities, and a fishing tournament.

Sarasota Music Festival, Sarasota, 941/957-1877
Music sounds all over the city, indoors and out.
Taste of Pinellas, Clearwater/St. Petersburg, 727/898-7451
Area restaurants set up shop at St. Pete's Straub Park, offering tasty samples along with music.

July
Annual Caribbean Calypso Carnival, Clearwater/St. Petersburg, 727/821-6164
St. Petersburg features a weekend of steel drums, food, and pageantry.
Fourth of July Celebration, The Emerald Coast, 850/233-5070
Big celebration at the beach draws thousands every year.
Port of the Islands Annual Shark Tournament, Naples, 941/394-3101
Anglers compete for prizes in annual tourney.
Pensacola International Billfish Tournament, Pensacola, 904/444-7696
Anglers from around the world compete to bring in the elusive sailfish, marlin, or swordfish.
Summer Swamp Stomp, Tallahassee, 850/413-9200
Old Florida celebration of food and music.

August
Annual Indian Summer Food Festival, The Emerald Coast, 850/434-1234
Tribute to the fare of the sea.
Caribbean Carnival, Tallahassee, 850/878-2198
Reggae, calypso, and soca at this West Indian weekend with a parade, food, and dawn celebration.

September
Native American Heritage Festival, Tallahassee, 850/575-8684
Traditional Indian games, canoe sculpting, and more at Tallahassee Museum of History and Natural Sciences.

October
Annual Orchids of the World Symposium, Naples, 942/597-3232
Seminars, hands-on workshops, orchid show, and banquet at Naples Beach Hotel.
Guavaween at Ybor City, Tampa, 813/248-3712
Halloween celebration begins with the "Mama Guava Stumble" parade.

John's Pass Seafood Festival, Clearwater/St. Petersburg, 727/464-7200
Thousands come to Madeira Beach to taste seafood, see arts and crafts, and listen to music.
North Florida Fair, Tallahassee, 850/878-3247
Largest event in north Florida and south Georgia—11-day fair with agricultural shows, big-name music stars, rides, and more.
Taste of Florida, Tampa, 813/259-7376
Restaurants serve specialties at outdoor park. Music and activities for all.

November
Beethoven Festival, Sarasota, 941/488-1010
The Venice Symphony sponsors special events.
Bradley's Historic Country Store Fun Day, Tallahassee, 850/893-1647
Country celebration, Model-A car rides, sugar making, and cane grinding.
Fort Myers Beach Sand Sculpting Festival, Lee Island Coast, 941/338-3500
Prizes and fun as amateur and professional sand sculptors do their thing.
Mailou Art Festival, Tampa, 813/272-2466
Leading African American artists celebrate with workshops, exhibits, entertainment, and an outdoor juried show at the Museum of African-American Art.
Ruskin Seafood and Arts Festival, Tampa, 813/645-3808
Seafood, arts, crafts, and entertainment on the shores of Tampa Bay.
Selby Gardens Fall Plant Fair, Sarasota, 941/366-5731
Famous garden offers rare plants for sale.

December
Christmas Boat Parades, Fort Myers, 941/454-7500
Boats routed through the Intracoastal Waterway, decked out in an array of lights and decorations.
Christmas Boat Parades, Clearwater/St. Petersburg, 727/893-7494
Lighted boats travel along the Intracoastal Waterway and through beach communities.
Victorian Christmas Stroll, Tampa, 813/254-1891
Candlelight tours of decorated Victorian historic homes.
Ybor City Christmas Crafts Festival, Tampa, 813/274-8518
Gifts and decorations all over Ybor. Buy them or get ideas.

RESOURCES

Apalachicola Bay Chamber of Commerce, 99 Market St., Ste. 100, Apalachicola, FL 32320-1776; 850/653-9419

Beaches of South Walton, Tourist Development Council, P.O. Box 1248, Santa Rosa Beach, FL 32459; 850/267-1216 or 800/822-6877

Cedar Key Area Chamber of Commerce, P.O. Box 610, Cedar Key, FL 32625; 352/543-5600

Emerald Coast Convention & Visitors Bureau, Destin/Fort Walton Beach, 1540 Hwy. 98 E., Fort Walton Beach, FL 32548; 850/651-7131 or 800/322-3319; www.destin-fwb.com

Fort Myers Conference & Convention Council, P.O. Box 9322, Fort Myers, FL 33902; 941/332-7600 or 800/294-9516; www.fmharborside.com

Greater Fort Walton Beach Chamber of Commerce, P.O. Box 640, Fort Walton Beach, FL 32549; 850/244-8191

Homosassa Springs Area Chamber of Commerce, P.O. Box 709, Homosassa Springs, FL 34447-0709; 352/628-2666

Lee Island Coast Convention & Visitors Bureau, 2180 W. First St., Ste. 100, Fort Myers, FL 33901; 800/237-6444 or 941/338-3500; www.leeislandcoast.com

Naples Area Tourism Bureau, 3620 Tamiami Tr. N., Naples, FL 34103l; 800/605-7878 or 941/262-6376; www.naples.com

Panama City Beach Convention & Visitors Bureau, 12015 Front Beach Rd., Panama City Beach, FL 32407; 800/PCBEACH or 850/233-5070; www.panamacitybeachfl.com

Pensacola Convention & Visitors Center, 1401 E. Gregory St., Pensacola, FL 32501; 800/874-1234 or 850/434-1234; www.visitpensacola.com

St. Petersburg/Clearwater Area Convention & Visitors Bureau, 14450 46th St. N., Ste. 108, Clearwater, FL 33762; 800/345-6710 or 727/464-7200; www.stpete-clearwater.com

Sanibel–Captiva Islands Chamber of Commerce, 1159 Causeway Rd., Sanibel, FL 33957; 941/472-1080

Sarasota Convention & Visitors Bureau, 655 Tamiami Tr., Sarasota, FL 34236; 800/522-9799 or 941/957-1877; www.cvb.sarasota.fl.us

Seaside Community Development, P.O. Box 4730, Seaside, FL 32459; 850/231-1320

Tallahassee Area Convention & Visitors Bureau, 200 W. College Ave., Tallahassee, FL 32302; 800/628-2866 or 850/413-9200; www.co.leon.fl.us/visitor/index.htm

Tampa/Hillsborough Convention and Visitors Association, 400 N. Tampa St., Ste. 1010, Tampa, FL 33602; 813/223-1111

Tarpon Springs Chamber of Commerce, 11 E. Orange St., Tarpon Springs, FL 34689; 727/937-6109

Weeki Wachee, 6131 Commercial Way, Spring Hill, FL 34606; 352/596-2062

Ybor City Chamber of Commerce, 1800 E. Ninth Ave., Tampa, FL 33605; 813/248-3712

INDEX

Map Index

Guidebooks that really guide

City•Smart™ Guidebooks
Pick one for your favorite city: *Albuquerque, Anchorage, Austin, Calgary, Charlotte, Chicago, Cincinnati, Cleveland, Denver, Indianapolis, Kansas City, Memphis, Milwaukee, Minneapolis/St. Paul, Nashville, Pittsburgh, Portland, Richmond, Salt Lake City, San Antonio, San Francisco, St. Louis, Tampa/St. Petersburg, Tucson.* US $12.95 to 15.95

Retirement & Relocation Guidebooks
The World's Top Retirement Havens, Live Well in Honduras, Live Well in Ireland, Live Well in Mexico. US $15.95 to $16.95

Travel•Smart® Guidebooks
Trip planners with select recommendations to *Alaska, American Southwest, Arizona, Carolinas, Colorado, Deep South, Eastern Canada, Florida, Florida Gulf Coast, Hawaii, Illinois/Indiana, Kentucky/Tennessee, Maryland/Delaware, Michigan, Minnesota/Wisconsin, Montana/Wyoming/Idaho, New England, New Mexico, New York State, Northern California, Ohio, Pacific Northwest, Pennsylvania/New Jersey, South Florida and the Keys, Southern California, Texas, Utah, Virginias, Western Canada.* US $14.95 to $17.95

Rick Steves' Guides
See *Europe Through the Back Door* and take along guides to *France, Belgium & the Netherlands; Germany, Austria & Switzerland; Great Britain & Ireland; Italy; Scandinavia; Spain & Portugal; London; Paris;* or *Best of Europe.* US $12.95 to $21.95

Adventures in Nature
Plan your next adventure in *Alaska, Belize, Caribbean, Costa Rica, Guatemala, Hawaii, Honduras, Mexico.* US $17.95 to $18.95

Into the Heart of Jerusalem
A traveler's guide to visits, celebrations, and sojourns. US $17.95

The People's Guide to Mexico
This is so much more than a guidebook—it's a trip to Mexico in and of itself, complete with the flavor of the country and its sights, sounds, and people. US $22.95

 JOHN MUIR PUBLICATIONS
P.O. Box 613 ◆ Santa Fe, NM 87504

Available at your favorite bookstore.
For a catalog or to place an order call 800-888-7504.

ABOUT THE AUTHOR

Carol J. Perry loves living in her adopted state of Florida. A resident since the early '70s, she never tires of traveling the highways and side roads of the Sunshine State, sharing travel information and tips with readers of both national and regional magazines and newspapers. Perry also writes fiction and nonfiction for young people, and several of her novels are set in Florida.

She is a member of the Florida Freelance Writers Association and the Florida Outdoor Writers Association, and is a member and past president of the Bay Area Professional Writers Guild.

Perry and her husband Dan and grandsons Stephen and Kevin live in Seminole, Florida.